Volume VII

Chivalry and the Medieval Past

ISSN 2043-8230

Series Editors
Karl Fugelso
Chris Jones

Medievalism aims to provide a forum for monographs and collections devoted to the burgeoning and highly dynamic multidisciplinary field of medievalism studies: that is, work investigating the influence and appearance of 'the medieval' in the society and culture of later ages. Titles within the series investigate the post-medieval construction and manifestations of the Middle Ages – attitudes towards, and uses and meanings of, 'the medieval' – in all fields of culture, from politics and international relations, literature, history, architecture, and ceremonial ritual to film and the visual arts. It welcomes a wide range of topics, from historiographical subjects to revivalism, with the emphasis always firmly on what the idea of 'the medieval' has variously meant and continues to mean; it is founded on the belief that scholars interested in the Middle Ages can and should communicate their research both beyond and within the academic community of medievalists, and on the continuing relevance and presence of 'the medieval' in the contemporary world.

New proposals are welcomed. They may be sent directly to the editors or the publishers at the addresses given below.

Professor Karl Fugelso
Art Department
Towson University
3103 Center for the Arts
8000 York Road
Towson, MD 21252-0001
USA
kfugelso@towson.edu

Professor Chris Jones
School of English
University of St Andrews
St Andrews
Fife KY16 9AL
UK
csj2@st-andrews.ac.uk

Boydell & Brewer Ltd
PO Box 9
Woodbridge
Suffolk IP12 3DF
UK

Previous volumes in this series are printed at the back of this book

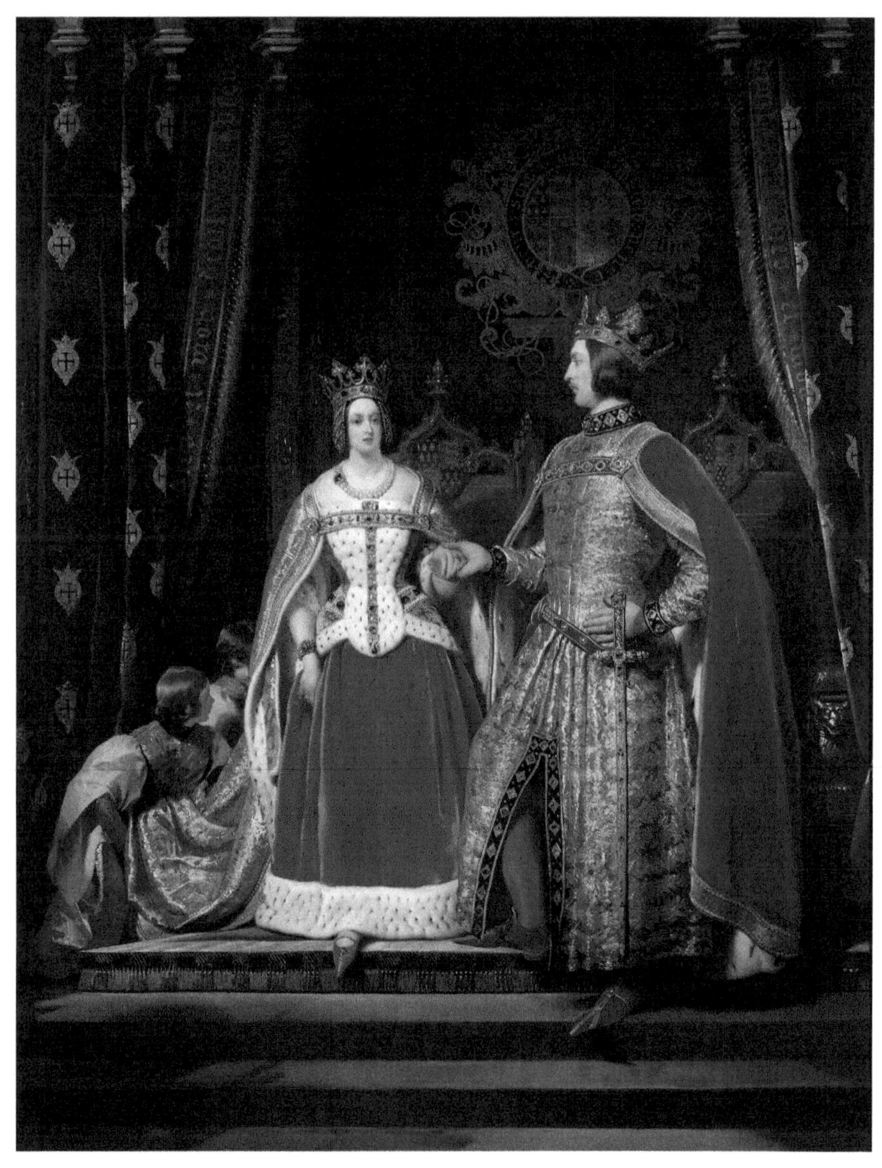

Sir Edwin Landseer, Queen Victoria and Prince Albert at the *Bal Costumé* of 12 May 1842 (1842–46). RCIN 404540. Royal Collection Trust / © Her Majesty Queen Elizabeth II 2015.

Chivalry and the Medieval Past

Edited by
Katie Stevenson *and* Barbara Gribling

THE BOYDELL PRESS

First published 2016
Paperback edition 2021

The Boydell Press, Woodbridge

ISBN 978 1 84383 923 1 hardback
ISBN 978 1 78327 642 4 paperback

The Boydell Press is an imprint of Boydell & Brewer Ltd
PO Box 9, Woodbridge, Suffolk IP12 3DF, UK
and of Boydell & Brewer Inc.
668 Mt Hope Avenue, Rochester, NY 14620-2731, USA
website: www.boydellandbrewer.com

A CIP catalogue record for this book is available
from the British Library

This publication is printed on acid-free paper

Printed and bound in Great Britain by
TJ Books Limited, Padstow, Cornwall

Contents

Illustrations

The editors, contributors and publishers are grateful to all the institutions and persons listed for permission to reproduce the materials in which they hold copyright. Every effort has been made to trace the copyright holders; apologies are offered for any omission, and the publishers will be pleased to add any necessary acknowledgement in subsequent editions.

Contributors

David Allan is Reader in Scottish History at the University of St Andrews.

Stefan Goebel is Reader in Modern British History at the University of Kent at Canterbury.

Barbara Gribling is a CoFund Junior Research Fellow in History at Durham University.

Steven C. Hughes is Professor of History and department chair at Loyola University Maryland.

Peter N. Lindfield is a Postdoctoral Research Fellow at the University of Stirling on the AHRC-funded project *Writing Britain's Ruins 1700–1850: The Architectural Imagination*.

Antti Matikkala is a Principal Investigator at the University of Helsinki.

Rosemary Mitchell is Associate Principal Lecturer in History, Reader in Victorian Studies, and Director of the Leeds Centre for Victorian Studies at Leeds Trinity University.

Paul Pickering is Professor in the Centre for Heritage and Museum Studies and Dean of the College of Arts and Social Sciences at the Australian National University, Canberra.

Katie Stevenson is Director of the Institute of Scottish Historical Research and Senior Lecturer in Late Mediaeval History at the University of St Andrews.

Introduction: Chivalry and the Medieval Past*

Katie Stevenson and Barbara Gribling

In late spring 1842 Queen Victoria and her consort Prince Albert hosted a medieval-themed costume ball. For inspiration they looked to the fourteenth century and chose to dress as Edward III, the most illustrious king of the 'Age of Chivalry', and his wife, Philippa of Hainault. Edwin Landseer's contemporary portrait commission is displayed on the cover of this book. Newspapers chronicling the event remarked on its chivalric splendour and paid particular attention to the costumes of the queen and prince and to the way in which they had recreated a medieval throne room from 'authentic' historical sources.[1] Scholars have made much of Victoria's decision to hold a ball with a medieval theme in the early years of her reign.[2] The careful and 'accurate' recreation of Edward III's court – which the Victorians considered to be the high point of chivalry – has been seen as reflecting Victoria's own desire to depict her reign as a new golden age. Edward III was widely credited with major military achievements (and particularly for success in his wars in France), as well as restoring royal authority, enacting vital legislation and legal reforms, and overseeing major evolution in centralised government and bureaucracy (of which parliament was regarded as a particularly fine achievement). With the re-enacted medieval jousting of the Eglinton tournament of 1839 still in recent memory and the ever-growing popularity of Sir Walter Scott's novels, many of

* The editors wish to thank the Carnegie Trust for the Universities of Scotland and acknowledge the generous grant it awarded to us for the publication of illustrations in this volume.

1 *The Times*, 13 May 1842; *Morning Chronicle*, 13 May 1842; *Examiner*, 14 May 1842; *Bristol Mercury*, 14 May 1842; *Illustrated London News*, 14 May 1842; *North Wales Chronicle*, 17 May 1842. According to *The Times*: 'The throne was removed, and another erected, copied from an authentic source, of the time of Edward III. It was lined (as well as the whole alcove on which the throne was placed) with purple velvet, having worked on it in gold the Crown of England, the cross of St George, and emblazoned shields with the arms of England and France.'

2 Mark Girouard, *The Return to Camelot: Chivalry and the English Gentleman* (New Haven and London, 1981), pp. 112–14; Joanna Banham and Jennifer Harris, eds, *William Morris and the Middle Ages: A Collection of Essays, Together with a Catalogue of Works Exhibited at the Whitworth Art Gallery, 28 September – 8 December 1984* (Manchester, 1984), pp. 74–5; Clare Broome Saunders, *Women Writers and Nineteenth-Century Medievalism* (New York, 2009), p. 106.

which took inspiration from the Middle Ages, the costume ball was the expression of a burgeoning Victorian medievalism. It offered an idealised and sanitised vision of the medieval past, but one which was refitted for a contemporary elite audience.

Victoria and Albert's *bal costumé* demonstrated the tension between a desire for accuracy and a desire to present an imagined vision of the Middle Ages by offering one royal reinterpretation of the Age of Chivalry. The event also raises a number of questions about the appropriation of the medieval past that are central to this book. Throughout this volume we probe issues of audience, understanding, meaning and misappropriation. Most importantly, we seek to understand the ways in which historical material was modified to recreate different visions of the medieval past, and ask what that can tell us not only about contemporary concerns, but also about the malleability of the ideals and values of chivalry. Chivalry is an enlightening category in the study of medievalism, as it has a clearly identifiable and particular association with the period understood as the Middle Ages and it is an ethos which, while still integral to the military, masculine and elite cultures of each century since, has changed in meaning in different contexts.

Chivalry is one of the most elusive ethical and cultural codes to define; it is ever-changing, adapted in the hands of medieval knights, Renaissance princes, early modern antiquarians, Enlightenment scholars, modern civic authorities, authors, historians and re-enactors. The premise of this book, and the argument that our contributors lay out here, is that chivalry was always looking back to the past, even in the Middle Ages, when a mythical past was created to explain chivalry to knights at court and beyond. Chivalry's trajectory is remarkable: in the Middle Ages it was a military ethic that regulated the behaviour and values of the knightly elite; it was transformed via Renaissance *civitas* and Victorian gentlemanly citizenship and imperial responsibility, arriving in a post-feminist present where women lead global tournament re-enactment organisations via Facebook. As one of the premier scholars of medieval chivalry, Richard Kaeuper, has remarked, in contemporary society it is impossible to look back into the medieval past without looking through Victorian stained glass.[3] So profound was the revival of interest in chivalry and its repurposing for nineteenth-century British interests that our cultural inheritance and understanding of what chivalry is – and was – are considerably compromised. But stripped of the sentimental romanticism encouraged by the Gothic revival of the late eighteenth and nineteenth centuries, it can be defined in its medieval context as the cultural ethos of the medieval military elites.

The term 'chivalry' comes from Old French *chevalerie*, itself a derivative of Latin *caballerius* or 'horseman', and implies a focus on the deeds and mores of the military elites as represented by the figure of the mounted knight. If the chivalric ethos originated on the battlefield, its relevance to wider medieval society must nevertheless be recognised: the knightly rank was that from which all medieval secular leaders were drawn, so each had a stake in the ethos governing the 'order of knighthood' to which

[3] Richard W. Kaeuper, *Chivalry and Violence in Medieval Europe* (Oxford, 1999), p. 2: 'For the great danger in the study of chivalry is to view this important phenomenon through the rose-tinted lenses of romanticism, to read chivalry in terms of what we want it to be rather than what it was.'

they all (at least in theory) subscribed. The centrality of the ideals of chivalry to medieval social order meant that it remained a subject of keen interest and debate. It was regularly reshaped or customised and inevitably developed multiple shades of meaning for different groups, even during its medieval 'heyday'.[4]

From as early as the late Middle Ages, commentators looked back to the 'medieval past' and sought illumination and understanding of their contemporary values through recasting chivalry for their own times. In 1412, for instance, John Lydgate penned the *Troy Book*, commissioned by Prince Henry of England (later an esteemed military hero in his own right, Henry V), in which Lydgate remarked that Henry wished to recall the 'old chevalrie' of ancient times. In the late Middle Ages, the epics of the Classical period were recast as chivalric tales for contemporary knightly audiences, with three heroes of particular serviceability – Hector of Troy, Alexander the Great and Julius Caesar. By the early fourteenth century these ancient worthies joined with three heroes of the Old Testament, Joshua, David and Judas Maccabeus, and three of the most esteemed Christian kings, Arthur, Charlemagne and Godfrey de Bouillon, to form the Nine Worthies. This group quickly became an established chivalric cult and shorthand for a continuous chivalric inheritance that stretched back to pre-Christian times and that linked directly to contemporary European kings through a lineage-by-association.[5] Yet scholars of a previous generation – particularly Johan Huizinga and Raymond Kilgour – argued that this coincided with the terminal phase of the Middle Ages and, specifically, the death of chivalry.[6] This view has unhelpfully diverted scholars away from considering that chivalry was already being reinterpreted as a 'medieval' legacy in the latter part of what we now identify as the Middle Ages. The rise of new expressions of subscription to the cult of chivalry, such as the invention of the Nine Worthies, the exponential increase across Europe of orders of chivalry, the substantial production of copies and creation of entirely new literature and chivalric biographies, and the increased use of chivalry to influence politics and express power in the fourteenth, fifteenth and sixteenth centuries had, at its heart, a vision of the medieval past in which the best qualities of that imagined past were emphasised in order to be channelled into the present and future. This is a significant contributing factor in why scholars have long struggled with the seemingly simple question of 'what is chivalry?' There is no clear answer and, as this volume seeks to demonstrate, this should not be the question at all. Instead, we should understand that chivalry was *always* perceived

[4] For more on medieval chivalry see, in the first instance, Maurice Keen, *Chivalry* (London, 1984); Kaeuper, *Chivalry and Violence*; Richard Barber, *The Reign of Chivalry* (Woodbridge, 2005); Katie Stevenson, *Chivalry and Knighthood in Scotland, 1424–1513* (Woodbridge, 2006); Craig Taylor, *Chivalry and the Ideals of Knighthood in France during the Hundred Years War* (Cambridge, 2013); Maurice Keen, *The Origins of the English Gentleman: Heraldry, Chivalry, and Gentility in Medieval England, c. 1300-c.1400* (Stroud, 2002); Richard Barber, *The Knight and Chivalry* (Woodbridge, 1995).

[5] See Keen, *Chivalry*, pp. 102–24; Horst Schroeder, *Der Topos der Nine Worthies in Literarur and Bildender Kunst* (Göttingen, 1971).

[6] Johan Huizinga, *The Autumn of the Middle Ages*, trans. Rodney J. Payton and Ulrich Mannitzsch (Chicago, 1996); Raymond Lincoln Kilgour, *The Decline of Chivalry as Shown in the French Literature of the Late Middle Ages* (Cambridge, MA, 1937).

to be from a 'medieval past'. It had always been a construct and thus was always constructed. What is important are the values it lauded or condemned, and the ways in which these were put into the service of the state, community and society.

This collection of essays explores the relationship between chivalry and ideas of the medieval past. More specifically, chivalry is used as a lens through which ideas of history, national narratives, politics, and social customs and values can be explored. At present, most studies of medievalism are literary in their focus. This is understandable, given the vast literary source base which is inspired by the Middle Ages: from Sir Walter Scott to George R. R. Martin, chivalry has been central to literary visions of the medieval world.[7] Studies which have been more historical in methodology have tended to concentrate on a limited chronology, principally the nineteenth century, and a restricted geographical area, usually Britain, France and Germany. This collection both revisits this material and places it in a broader geographical and chronological context. To the credit of our contributors, included herein are assessments of Italy, Sweden, Australia and the United States, as well as Scotland, England and Germany. These essays together identify new ways of *seeing* the medieval past through material and visual culture, including display, ornament, furniture and re-enactments, while new approaches to this past are suggested here by extending chronological, geographical and disciplinary boundaries. Our goal is to provide a crucial plank in the dialogue between those exploring the medieval, early modern and modern periods; those examining history, history of art and material culture; and those investigating local, national and global medievalism. Our contributors lay out the case for the significance of the cultural manifestations and products of reimagined and reinterpreted medieval chivalry across time, which challenges current ideas about the uses of the medieval past.

Wider studies on the uses of the past in literature, art and history do, of course, explore chivalry, but this is usually done by focusing on the Victorian Gothic revival. Most notably, Mark Girouard's pioneering 1981 book, *Chivalry and the English Gentleman*, probed the Victorian fascination with the chivalric ethos and the many revivals of the chivalric code.[8] While Girouard argued that chivalry ended with the Great War, this line of argument is now being challenged; indeed, this collection illustrates a renewed, revitalised and reinterpreted interest in chivalry into the present day through film, re-enactment and tourism. Scholars of nineteenth-century medievalism have been principally concerned with the way in which their subjects used the Middle Ages to offer a commentary on their own times. Alice Chandler, for instance, placed her important discussion of the revival of chivalry amidst the backdrop of industrialisation, arguing that nineteenth-century authors

7 For a selection of works on literature and medievalism see: Michael Alexander, *Medievalism: The Middle Ages in Modern England* (New Haven and London, 2007); Alice Chandler, *A Dream of Order: The Medieval Ideal in Nineteenth-Century English Literature* (Lincoln, 1970); Kristine Louise Haugen, 'Chivalry and Romance in the Eighteenth Century: Richard Hurd and Disenchantment of "The Faerie Queene"', *Medievalism and the Quest for the 'Real' Middle Ages*, ed. Clare Simmons (London, 2001), pp. 45–60; Inga Bryden, *Reinventing King Arthur: The Arthurian Legends in Victorian Culture* (Aldershot, 2005).

8 Girouard, *The Return to Camelot.*

presented the Middle Ages as a place of order, harmony and faith, in contrast to their own modern society.[9] Charles Dellheim's *The Face of the Past* moved the field forward by considering architecture, delving into the Victorian desire to create new Gothic structures, as well as to preserve medieval castles, churches and cathedrals through the development of local and national societies.[10]

While this work on Victorian medievalism has offered innovative ways of understanding the nineteenth-century interpretation and appropriation of the medieval past, new studies on the uses of this past – including those in this volume – are beginning to demonstrate that chivalry was a vital component of understanding medieval inheritance over time. In this way, this volume articulates our distinctive contribution and we have consciously extended the range of periods under discussion. By taking a longer view, this book builds on the single-period studies that have thus far dominated the field. Historians of the late Middle Ages, for example, have examined the use of Arthurian legends by both Edward I and Edward III of England, while scholars of chivalric orders of knighthood have charted the use in the early modern period of their (real or imagined) medieval origins.[11] Michèle Cohen has explored chivalry and its inherent connection to masculinity, which she argues shifted from eighteenth-century polite forms affiliated with an elite and feminised mode of manliness to a more 'inclusive' chivalric masculinity that valued bravery and honour in the early nineteenth century.[12]

Significantly, the proffering here departs from other works on chivalry in that it consciously attempts to consider source materials beyond the literary.[13] Discussions of chivalric literature and its influence have, of course, opened up new ways of seeing the Middle Ages, such as how the Lancelot-Guinevere story shaped attitudes towards sex and gender in the Victorian period, or the influence of Sir Walter Scott's novels in bringing chivalry to new audiences in the early nineteenth century. However, this collection offers a fuller, more nuanced picture of the uses of medieval ideas and values by stressing a greater array of evidence. Material culture and performance, for instance, enable us to rethink what is (and was thought to be) chivalric, from the trade in Gothic items in the eighteenth century, to the social

9 Chandler, *A Dream of Order.*

10 Charles Dellheim, *The Face of the Past: The Preservation of the Medieval Inheritance in Victorian England* (Cambridge, 1982).

11 Juliet Vale, *Edward III and Chivalry: Chivalric Society and its Context 1270–1350* (Woodbridge, 1982), pp. 14–24, 42–75; Richard K. Morris, 'The Architecture of Arthurian Enthusiasm: Castle Symbolism in the Reigns of Edward I and His Successors', *Armies, Chivalry and Warfare in Medieval Britain and France, Proceedings of the 1995 Harlaxton Symposium*, ed. Matthew Strickland (Stamford, 1998), pp. 63–81; R. S. Loomis, 'Edward I, Arthurian Enthusiast', *Speculum* 28 (1958), pp. 114–27; W. M. Ormrod, 'For Arthur and St George: Edward III, Windsor Castle and the Order of the Garter', *St George's Chapel Windsor in the Fourteenth Century*, ed. Nigel Saul (Woodbridge, 2005), esp. pp. 22–3; Antti Matikkala, *The Orders of Knighthood and the Formation of the British Honours System, 1660–1760* (Woodbridge, 2008); Katie Stevenson, 'The Unicorn, St Andrew and the Thistle: Was there an Order of Chivalry in Late Medieval Scotland?', *Scottish Historical Review* 83 (2004), pp. 3–22.

12 Michèle Cohen, '"Manners" Make the Man: Politeness, Chivalry, and the Construction of Masculinity, 1750–1830', *Journal of British Studies* 44 (2005), pp. 312–29.

13 Alexander, *Medievalism*, pp. 24–49; Chandler, *A Dream of Order*, pp. 38–9, 195.

conventions of duelling culture in the nineteenth century, and to the motivation to join a society for creative anachronism today.

A central theme of these essays is the changes both in audiences for chivalry and in those who promoted it, from the medieval to the modern period. The narrative usually espoused in scholarly studies suggests a smooth transition from an elite medieval chivalry to a more inclusive contemporary one. According to this view, medieval chivalry catered to a much more restricted audience. This is not to suggest that tournaments, chivalric feats of arms and so forth were not visible to a range of social groups, but rather that discussion of chivalry, and indeed the capacity to be chivalric, was the purview of the medieval aristocracy. In the sixteenth and seventeenth centuries, chivalry was rejuvenated to be more of a code of conduct for the civic gentleman than an ethical code for warriors, and yet it remained part of a larger aristocratic concern with courtly behaviour.[14] By the nineteenth century the audience for chivalry had expanded even further. The reprinting of medieval texts, the publication of chivalric tales in magazines and novels, and the opportunity to view chivalric escapades on stage opened up chivalry and made it relevant and meaningful to a far more diverse audience. Building on developments in the early modern period, the chivalry of the nineteenth century was appealing for its usability in shaping contemporary mores and in providing useful models for citizenship. In more recent times, chivalry has undergone something of a democratisation and has come firmly into public use and consumption. No longer is the audience exclusively aristocratic, or even 'elite' more broadly; now, trades apprentices from inner-city suburbia can invest in crafting a vision of themselves as chivalric medieval heroes. Twentieth – and twenty-first-century films, video games, performances and re-enactments have served to widen participation and engagement with ideas of the Middle Ages, and here chivalry is an important lens through which modern understandings of ethical social conduct and gender relations are negotiated. Indeed, through its manifestly enormous range of reinventions and meanings, chivalry continues to capture the imagination and shape understandings of the medieval past.

David Allan opens this volume by considering the overlooked published histories by the Scottish Enlightenment figure Gilbert Stuart. Stuart treated the Middle Ages, and chivalry and chivalric culture specifically, whilst engaging with wider Enlightenment trends in the writing of history, which included the importance of the medieval legal heritage and an awareness of an increased contemporary readership that included women. Allan argues that Stuart's medieval revisionism was fuelled by personal animosity towards William Robertson, the highly accomplished historian and principal of the University of Edinburgh. In Stuart's view, Robertson's biggest shortcomings in his account of medieval history were his ignorance of legal scholarship and his lack of jurisprudential knowledge. Stuart's revisionism questioned Robertson's characterisation of the Middle Ages as regressive and violent, barbaric and uncivilised, and claimed that contemporary understanding of the medieval past

[14] Norbert Elias, *The Civilizing Process: The History of Manners* (Cambridge, 1994). See also *Chivalry in the Renaissance*, ed. Sydney Anglo (Woodbridge, 1990); Alex Davis, *Chivalry and Romance in the English Renaissance* (Cambridge, 2003).

had substantial limitations. Indeed, Allan persuasively argues that Stuart's positive treatment of feudalism and the virtues of chivalry was set in marked contradistinction to the remarkably dim assessment of Robertson. Allan explores Stuart's understanding of the legal foundations of feudalism and the cohesive bonds of medieval society, including honour and dependence, directly linking the origins of feudal landholding with those of chivalry. Stuart's work reveals much about his contemporary world, for eighteenth-century Scottish society was underpinned by medieval legal structures that enabled landholders to enjoy substantial privileges of wider concern after the Treaty of Union in 1707, such as the law of entail and, in particular, the ability of Scottish lairds to raise private armies, a potential military threat to the nascent British state. Stuart, however, looked back at the military obligations of the medieval past and saw these as a stabilising force in political and social order.

Antti Matikkala shifts the focus to Scandinavia with his exploration of the creation of a medieval past for the Swedish orders of knighthood in the mid eighteenth century. Matikkala establishes that from the 1680s there was a pan-European burgeoning of fabricated and newly created 'ancient orders'. While the phenomenon was not exclusive to Sweden, this study nevertheless reveals much about the way in which a medieval antiquity could provide authority and legitimacy to a new political group. Moreover, Matikkala suggests that using a medieval past enabled contemporaries to explore aspects of religion and politics which were no longer acceptable in mainstream circles. By concentrating on antiquarian scholarship, Matikkala highlights the profound importance that antiquarians had in the shaping of history in the early modern period and provides insights into the ways in which this in turn shaped nineteenth-century recastings of chivalry. The seventeenth-century antiquarian explanation for the origin of the Swedish chivalric orders often gave these falsified medieval pasts, but Matikkala sees this as indicative of the liberal use and abuse of 'history' in the early modern period. At this time historical veracity was understood differently, and antiquarians and historians were often guilty of misunderstanding and inventing sources to prove their arguments. Indeed, as Matikkala demonstrates, despite antiquarian insistence, none of the Swedish orders were medieval in origin. Yet the claim to medieval foundations was central to their importance and value in seventeenth-century society. Matikkala finds that the fabricated medieval origins of the Swedish orders was entirely understandable in their context, demonstrating the ways in which medieval chivalric culture was used to wrestle with contemporary ideas. In doing so, he raises important questions about the nature of truth in history and the veracity of the past.

Looking at the same period, Peter Lindfield assesses the revival of Gothic styles in Georgian architecture and interior design. He argues that this revival demonstrated a palpable interest in the motifs and language of medieval chivalry, despite the rise of Classicism as the dominant mode in this same period. Indeed, points of tension are identified between proponents of Classicism and those who favoured the Gothic, for ideological and cultural reasons as well as aesthetic ones. Using eighteenth-century furniture and furnishings, Lindfield considers the extent to which chivalric overtones were incorporated into fashionable consumption as a unique way of accessing complex messages. His principal interest is in commissioned furniture, and the ways in which chairs, tables and other carefully designed pieces revealed an interest in medieval chivalric values. Exploring figures such as Sir Christopher Wren, Lindfield argues that while Classical architecture was considered to be sophisticated and modern, this overshadowed a vibrant discussion about the value of Gothic for much of the eighteenth century. The 'old', 'native' Gothic styles were important to maintain continuity with the medieval past and to signify antiquity and gravitas; so, as Lindfield demonstrates, a preference for Gothic came to indicate and confirm that one's taste was inherited from an ancient, noble and chivalric lineage. Lindfield suggests that the interweaving of Gothic architecture and British history served to provide an established narrative of the nation's past. Lindfield further sees the employment of the barbaric medieval past in negotiating eighteenth-century values: Gothic architecture was inherently bound up with ideas of the Goths, and this could be construed negatively for Classicists or held up to demonstrate freedom from tyranny and over-mighty monarchy. For some, the Goths could be framed as the fountainhead of liberty. Indeed, when Daniel Defoe remarked that he was concerned that, on the eve of the Treaty of Union, the Scots were in danger of returning to a 'Gothic constitution of government', which he characterised as violent, turbulent and unstable, he advised distance from these regressive aspects of the Middle Ages and suggested instead that only the positive, useful elements of the medieval past be deployed in contemporary society. Interwoven with these ideas were the values and ideals of medieval chivalry. Many criticised chivalry as unenlightened, whereas others, such as Richard Hurd, identified Gothic with an imagined medieval world of honour, civility and politeness. Lindfield establishes that chivalry's usability in Gothic Revivalism related to the establishment of the Perpendicular Gothic in the fourteenth century, with a direct coeval correlation to the rise in chivalric institutions and what came to be called the 'golden age' of chivalry.

Rosemary Mitchell retains the focus on architecture and the built environment, and considers the way in which chivalry might be used in urban contexts to express civic values in the nineteenth-century industrial age. She seeks to demonstrate how chivalric ideas and imagery could be appropriated by Victorian urban elites to legitimise and historicise their public lives and achievements. Taking two case studies to explore some of these themes – one of the Manchester-based Scottish engineer, James Nasmyth, and the other, the Manchester Albert Memorial – Mitchell argues that chivalry was used as a language through which to debate civic values. Nasmyth provides an excellent case study of a 'knight of industry', who appropriated chivalric ideals into his commercial management and enterprises. Nasmyth's autobiography offers an insight into self-made men's attempts to shape a burgeoning middle-class identity, resting heavily on the chivalric antics of his (perhaps) imagined medieval forebears and continuously referring to his ancestry in the deployment of heraldry and other iconography. Mitchell argues that Nasmyth reveals the tensions that existed in the new industrial men, who 'wanted to see themselves as the agents of historical continuity as well as change' (p. 101–2). During his business trips Nasmyth not only visited the sites of industrial and engineering works, but also those of historic buildings and cathedrals in the vicinity. His preference was for the narrative that modernisation had emerged organically from the medieval world, that the medieval knight had evolved seamlessly into the modern man of commerce, and for keeping the positive dimensions of the chivalric past and shedding the negative qualities no longer of service to industrial society. Nasmyth's retirement from business and purchase of Hammerfield (a mock Tudor manor house near the site of the medieval manor house of Penshurst, the sixteenth-century family home of Sir Philip Sidney, who was for many Victorians an established model of chivalry) signified some of the ways in which Nasmyth grappled with negotiating the past and the present. In Hammerfield, Nasmyth was enamoured of both his juxtaposition to the physical remains of the medieval past and the easy access to the thriving metropolis of London by the modern transport of the railway. In the second part of her essay, Mitchell considers the chivalric dialogue between the memory of Prince Albert and the Mancunian people. While Mitchell identifies an uneasy appropriation of chivalry in the Manchester Albert Memorial itself, it is only when it is considered in its context – and specifically its juxtaposition with the façade of the Town Hall – that its full significance can be understood. This façade, Mitchell argues, is a 'triumphant appropriation of the medieval and chivalric to modern and civic commercial purposes' (p. 109). However, when the site is viewed holistically, a contradictory relationship between medieval and modern chivalry emerges. Mitchell suggests that Manchester Town Hall articulates a modern civic and commercial chivalry, which sits in contrast and challenges the uncomplicated medieval chivalric values presented in the Albert Memorial.

Remaining in nineteenth-century Britain, Barbara Gribling provides a rather different view of the recasting of chivalry. She argues that a negative interpretation was given to the values of medieval chivalry in reaction to the Romantic and Tory visions that had been disseminated, especially in literature aimed at young boys, such as magazines and adventure novels. Gribling argues that criticisms of medieval chivalric values were used to express wider discussions about the nature of democracy and the progress of the people – ideas that clearly distinguished Victorian Britain from the medieval past. At the heart of the use of chivalry was the desire for proper and fitting role models to help shape ideas of good citizenship and British manhood and masculinity. Thus, in Gribling's view, chivalry became a 'site of reflection' to understand the continuities and changes between the medieval past and the Victorian present. Gribling traces a trajectory from the eighteenth-century Whig narrative of the Middle Ages as intellectually and socially regressive and oppressed, through the early nineteenth-century revival of chivalry as a model of commendable virtue for British boys and men, and then on to the competing visions of the medieval past that served politically-charged interpretations from the 1830s onwards. Tensions arose, for instance, as Whigs criticised the ideals of Young England, which they claimed was elitist aristocratism, with the aim of re-establishing medieval models and promoting antiquated feudal and chivalric – and also Catholic – codes in what should be and was a new age of reform. Gribling has identified a further shift by the 1870s that led to increased criticism of chivalry and the medieval past more generally – the result of new historical scholarship that rejected Romanticism and of a political radicalism that foregrounded social inequality. Gribling identifies these ideas, emerging especially in the mass-market historical readers for children and in popular history texts, which suggested that the medieval values of chivalry had become problematic to contemporary society. Gribling considers, for example, the late-nineteenth-century works by the non-conformist liberal historian Samuel Rawson Gardiner, who believed chivalry to be inherently barbaric and who used biographies of medieval knights to demonstrate that chivalric heroism harmed 'the people'. A decade earlier, in *A Short History of the English People*, the liberal historian J. R. Green had consciously and conspicuously sidelined the chivalric and heroic exploits of the late Middle Ages, labelling these as 'the personal adventures of kings and nobles', and instead foregrounded the constitutional, intellectual and social advances of medieval England, and, crucially, the role of the people in the development of the nation. The view emerged that chivalry was restrictive because it encouraged social hierarchy, was far too profligate both in terms of financial extravagance and in the loss of life in war, and, most seriously, distracted kings and the nobility from the unquestionably more important business of governing. Gribling concludes that, despite these views, throughout the nineteenth century chivalry was still used to educate boys about good citizenship, codified in 1908 by Robert Baden-Powell's *Scouting for Boys*, which took entrenched ideas of imperial boyhood and linked them with rugged character building.

Steven Hughes also considers the nineteenth century, but his focus is on post-unification Italy, where chivalry was put to effective use in public life and in the formation of new cultural identities. Hughes takes as his point of access the highly popular *Italian Code of Chivalry* by Iacopo Gelli, which immediately served as the standard authority and reference work in civic, intellectual, military and legal contexts from its first publication in 1886. For Italians, Gelli's work spoke to them in a period of intense 'duellomania' that saw the new country of Italy negotiating its national identity, by providing a model for new citizenship and encouraging bonds of masculinity. Vehement and outspoken criticism of the frequent and widespread practices of duelling communicated the tensions of the times, expressing incomprehension that a nation and people that had been restored to the path of progress and civilisation through unification could express this with the furious, 'barbaric', medieval custom of duelling. As Hughes demonstrates, the new national elites who so encouraged duelling had a monopoly over chivalric honour, which in turn reinforced social divides and the disenfranchisement of the lower orders. Hughes explores the bookplates and covers of editions related to the works of Gelli and others, to determine the range of messages that were being presented to Italians and the central function that evocations of anachronistic medieval chivalry had in presenting a moral code for the new, modern Italy. Hughes considers the relationship between duelling and the emergence of fencing in the Renaissance, suggesting that the connection between medieval chivalry and nineteenth-century duelling was a deliberate misappropriation that bypassed the significant step in the sixteenth century of the development of fencing, with its special weapons, techniques and famed Italian fencing masters. Thus nineteenth-century Italian nationalism took more from the cultural and social values of the medieval past than it did from the more recent Renaissance scientific tracts on the proper defence of one's honour. Hughes argues that this was also to reject the Renaissance as a period of relevance during the Risorgimento, as the Italian Wars were directly associated with Italy's loss of independence to foreign powers. The chivalric duel was thus a means of reasserting Italy's military, cultural and national valour as it progressed beyond unification.

In a quite different context, Stefan Goebel also considers national identity, but this time in its links to memory and commemoration in Germany. Goebel explores the coincidence of two historically significant battles that were sited in near proximity, both acquiring the name of the Battle of Tannenberg (1410 and 1914). These were decisive battles in their own historical contexts, and there was significant loss of life and destruction in both 1410 and 1914. Goebel argues that the success on the Eastern Front at Tannenberg in 1914 was consciously prioritised for remembrance within a framework of the military defeat of the Great War, fusing together layers of memory to manipulate existential memory of death in war with a cultural memory of the distant, medieval past, to obliterate recent history and to 'medievalise' the memory of the Great War. Medievalism as a tool for understanding the present, Goebel observes, had been particularly useful in the decades before the Great War, when the desire to return to an imagined past was a way of channelling dissatisfaction with the condition of contemporary society. But, as Goebel argues, the Great War transformed the use of the medieval past, from what had been in the era of industrialisation a mechanism to consider and understand national identity, to what became during the years of the Great War 'a discourse of remembrance in an age of industrialised slaughter' (p. 170). This extended to the rebuilding of destroyed medieval castles of the Teutonic Order, defeated at Tannenberg in 1410 and never to recover, in honour of the revered military commanders of the First World War. Goebel sees the Hindenburg shrine at Marienburg Castle as the centrepiece of triumphal monumentality in this commemorative recasting of the medieval past, although it did not achieve official Reich memorial status until after the Nazis' accession to power.[15] The original plan, which had sited centrally a mass grave of twenty unknown soldiers fallen at the battle in 1914, was interfered with by Hitler himself; he demanded the removal of the mass grave to refocus attention and create space for a crypt in which the bodies of the victorious Tannenberg commander and former *Reichspräsident* Paul von Hindenburg and his wife were entombed in 1935. The memorial was thus relaunched as a mausoleum of the hero of the battle, and the unknown dead – once the focal point of the commemoration – were subsumed into the cult of military leadership. As espoused by the values of medieval chivalry, elite heroism was favoured at the expense of the modern idea of the equality of sacrifice in war. Moreover, Marienburg, and its destruction by Polish and Lithuanians victorious against the Teutonic Order, could be used to defend German interests and to warn of the perceived Polish danger in the east.

Finally, we turn to modern and contemporary re-enactments of chivalry. Opening with a discussion of Sir Walter Scott's hero Ivanhoe and the cultural impact of *Ivanhoe* in the British world that extended as far as Australia, Paul Pickering reconsiders Scott's role in initiating the medieval revival that 'gripped the Anglophone world' (p. 189). When Scott's contemporaries satirised his collection

[15] For more on heroism and the afterlives of heroes, see Geoffrey Cubitt and Allen Warren, eds, *Heroic Reputations and Exemplary Lives* (Manchester, 2000).

of 'rusty pikes, shields, helmets, swords, and tattered banners' (p. 189) they identified Scott's uncritical vision of the medieval past as a perfect age in which society was in its best state. Of particular interest here is the role of Scott in inspiring the medieval chivalric re-enactment in 1839, the Eglinton tournament, which Pickering classes as the first secular, civilian and unofficial re-enactment, a crucial distinction that saw a marked change in the purpose and development of re-enactments. The discussion of the enthusiasm for re-enactment, satirical responses and criticisms of elitism from political radicals paves the way for the essay's main focus – an exploration of modern re-enactment, 'one of the fastest growing forms of public history' (p. 192). Pickering suggests that the practice of re-enactment can be viewed through various categories, including entertainment, commercialism, realism and affect, and acknowledges that re-enactors can be placed into subgroups along 'an authenticity axis' (p. 192). Nevertheless, Pickering identifies common ground across all groups of medieval re-enactors, specifically with respect to their visions and appreciations of chivalry and their understandings of the medieval past. The Society for Creative Anachronism, for instance, explicitly connects itself in a direct line to Eglinton; thus, modern re-enactors are seeking the medieval in a nineteenth-century medievalism, which is in itself a reinterpretation of the medieval past. Pickering takes to task the trend in education (which has even found its way into the academy) of immersive and experiential learning, which has witnessed a move towards some historians donning period costume in the name of 'exploring the proposition that we can learn about the past by doing it' (p. 196). Indeed, the re-enactors at the far end of the 'authenticity spectrum' operate with the view that they produce knowledge.[16] Pickering critiques the commercialised nature of modern medievalism, arguing that the transformation of heritage sites such as Warwick Castle into living-history enterprises of large-scale anachronism is *reductio ad absurdum*. But, as Pickering argues, both in the early nineteenth century and today, re-enactment and a desire to recreate the Middle Ages in the present was escapism of the sort that could and can temporarily transform lives away from the mundane and into a world where real constraints no longer limit personal freedoms and choices. For re-enactors, much as for those inhabiting the world of digital games, the opportunity to assume new personae enables an alternative experience to the realities of their real social and cultural positions. Worth within these groups is measured differently from the real world, but it is a worth based on the imagined values of the Middle Ages. For Scott and those participating in the Eglinton tournament, the escape to the Middle Ages was appealing precisely because it represented 'an age of lost values' (p. 203).

In articulating this sentiment, Pickering encapsulates the principal thread running through all of the essays in this volume – that the medieval past was imagined to be a time of values that could be and should be of use, but are often lost, in the present. Thus chivalry, with its codes of military honour and community obligation, and with a heavy dose of Christian (and specifically Catholic) ethics, was eminently pliable in presenting a vision of the medieval past for new contexts.

[16] See Iain McCalman and Paul A. Pickering, eds, *Historical Reenactment: From Realism to the Affective Turn* (Basingstoke, 2010).

But what of the uneasy tension with modern values that are incompatible with the medieval past – for instance, social equality, gender equality, religious tolerance and non-violent dispute resolution? As Pickering demonstrates, wrenching values from the past into the modern world necessarily brings with it a selection and an editing of the past, which calls into question those very claims of veracity put forward by re-enactors and reinterpreters of that past.

There are several thematic strands running throughout that further illuminate the various uses of chivalry. One such strand considers the negative dimensions of chivalry. These emerged in opposition to or coexisted with positive forms, illustrating the complex and contested nature of chivalry. For example, David Allan's essay exposes a strain of romantic eighteenth-century chivalry in the works of Gilbert Stuart that counters the dominant Enlightenment view of the chivalric past. Barbara Gribling's piece points to a late Victorian liberal and radical focus on chivalry's dark side that challenged 'normal' depictions of chivalry as the ideal ethos for men and boys. Similarly, Stefan Goebel's contribution illustrates some of the disturbing ways in which chivalry was employed in the period after the Great War. Here, our contributors seek to counterbalance the dominant mode of understanding chivalry as a positive force for social (and military) good.

Nationalism is a prominent theme; many of our authors show how chivalry was used as a way to help form national identity and to promote social cohesion in national contexts. For example, Steven Hughes' analysis of Italian duelling culture and Antti Matikkala's discussion of Swedish chivalric orders demonstrate the ways in which chivalry provided a shared, albeit invented, medieval heritage that could be repurposed to express ideas of national character and nationhood. Goebel shows how, in post-1918 Germany, the Middle Ages became part of a 'discourse of remembrance' in which military and chivalric values were put to use in the service of national territorial ambitions. In contrast, Paul Pickering's essay illustrates the transition and tensions between these earlier nationalist reinventions and later global ones, where promoters sought to appeal to new markets and new groups through re-enactments and gaming culture.

Religion also features heavily in the discussion in this volume. The Middle Ages were inherently Catholic, and bound up in the values of medieval chivalry were explicitly Catholic values. In the post-Reformation world, tensions between different Christian persuasions were also revealed in attitudes and re-evaluations of chivalry. Antti Matikkala, for instance, explores some of the issues in giving Catholic antiquity to Swedish chivalric orders in a post-Reformation context, suggesting that for some orders the point of rooting their past in the Middle Ages was to give licence to an inherent Catholicism, which was conflated with 'the medieval'. Matikkala points out that some critiqued this conflation explicitly, such as Gregorio Leti, an Italian Calvinist, who considered it self-evident that the orders of chivalry had been 'instituted for the defence of the Catholic religion' (p. 46) and that the Swedish orders had been established 'for this purpose against the doctrine of Luther' (p. 46). Like Matikkala, Peter Lindfield has identified something of a conflation of the meanings of medievalism and Catholicism, and he herein explores the problems that the inherent Catholicism of the Middle Ages caused in informing cultural fashions;

Lindfield concludes that medieval ruins stood as a moral reminder to those who sought to rebuild the past. Yet, in his exploration of Horace Walpole's Strawberry Hill, Catholicism and medievalism combined in architecture and interior decor to present Walpole's vision of his ancestry and nobility, and of medieval chivalry.

A final strand embedded in many of the essays is the relationship between chivalry and commerce. Lindfield, for instance, identifies a vibrant eighteenth-century trade in Gothic furniture among fashionable elites and socially aspirational merchants; here the language of chivalry was purchased and deployed to denote social status. Rosemary Mitchell explores the tensions inherent in Victorian uses of chivalry in commercial and civic architecture, where the Manchester Albert Memorial with its romantic values stood in stark contrast to the medieval and commercial Manchester Town Hall with its more complicated negotiations of the chivalric past. Pickering too exposes the global market for chivalry-themed products and events, and its place in contemporary mass culture. Together these strands point to the complex nature of chivalry's legacy and emerge here as an agenda for the future combined study of chivalry and medievalism.

1

'An Institution Quite Misunderstood': Chivalry and Sentimentalism in the Late Scottish Enlightenment

David Allan

THE SCOTTISH ENLIGHTENMENT is now commonly acknowledged as a pivotal moment in the emergence of modern historiography. Part of a broader phase of cultural and intellectual brilliance in Scotland associated with path-breaking philosophers of mind like David Hume and Thomas Reid and innovative social theorists like Adam Smith and Adam Ferguson, its historical scholarship not only produced some best-selling studies of the past – Hume's own deeply philosophical *History of England* (1754–62) and his friend William Robertson's probing narrative works *The History of Scotland* (1759) and *The History of the Reign of the Emperor Charles V* (1769) being perhaps the pre-eminent examples – but also established new ways of thinking and writing about past human existence that proved widely and enduringly influential.[1] This essay will focus on one almost entirely overlooked historical work from late in the period, Gilbert Stuart's *View of Society in Europe, in Its Progress from Rudeness to Refinement* (1778). An exploration of medieval society and manners, at its heart is a distinctive and extraordinarily rich treatment of the history of chivalry. As we shall see, this was to a considerable extent the result of Stuart's extreme antipathy towards other leading Scottish scholars and, in particular, to the dominating presence of Robertson. But the idiosyncratic analysis that resulted was not merely aggressively polemical within the narrow confines of Scotland's incestuous scholarly community. The focus on chivalric culture also allowed Stuart to engage with some of the wider trends which, by the late 1770s, were reshaping and successfully popularising historical writing. These included a topical interest in Scotland's medieval legal heritage, an awareness of a growing female readership, an intensifying sentimentalism associated with the rise of the novel as a major literary

[1] David Allan, 'Scottish Historical Writing of the Enlightenment', *The Oxford History of Historical Writing*, ed. Daniel Woolf, Edoardo Tortarolo, José Rabasa and Masayuki Sato (Oxford, 2012), iii, pp. 497–517; David Allan, 'Identity and Innovation: Historiography in The Scottish Enlightenment', *The Historiography of the Enlightenment*, ed. Sophie Bourgault and Robert Sparling (Leiden, 2013), pp. 307–41.

form, and an emerging fascination – ultimately critical to both historical writing and imaginative literature in the coming decades – with the peculiar virtues of the Germanic progenitors of eighteenth-century English-speaking society.

The *View of Society* is the most intriguing product of a relatively short career that was marked not only by prodigious authorial output and literary versatility, but also by the lengthening shadow cast by deep embitterment and unfulfilled ambition. Those frustrations were closely linked to a most unusual childhood and upbringing. From the outset Stuart had been steeped in academic culture. The favoured son of the professor of humanity at the University of Edinburgh, he was born in the college buildings in 1743. He was also raised there, was a teenaged assistant in the college library, where he exploited special borrowing privileges to absorb a vast range of literature, and then spent twice the normal period – a full eight years – as an undergraduate.[2] This background clearly raised his academic expectations (and those of his father) to towering heights, making Stuart's subsequent failures as an applicant for the Edinburgh professorship of public law, first in 1768 and again in 1777, a shattering blow.[3] But what rendered these disappointments so transformational for Stuart's historical writing was the fact that, at least in his own mind, the slight, absolutely devastating on the second occasion, was the fault of William Robertson, not just Scotland's greatest living historian but also the principal of the University, to whom Stuart had previously displayed considerable youthful deference.

As it happens, Robertson's decision was defensible on relevant criteria. Stuart's peppery disposition, intellectual eccentricities and worrying fondness for alcohol were no secret: even in an age when to be a 'two-bottle man' (meaning the daily consumption of two bottles of port) was considered not unreasonable, his 'habitual dissipation' was already attracting adverse comment.[4] By contrast, the successful candidate at the second time of asking, Allan Maconochie – although admittedly a relation of Robertson – had a much more emollient temperament and, as an established Edinburgh advocate with experience of the English bar, was probably better qualified. Nonetheless, Stuart became convinced by the end of 1777 that sheer malicious spite on Robertson's part was the only possible explanation for a very public humiliation. Accordingly, throughout the remainder of his active literary career until his early death in 1786, hastened by the ever-present drink, Stuart exploited every available opportunity to undermine not just the professional reputation but also the scholarly achievements of the man whom he held personally responsible.

Severely injured pride, then, formed a key part of the background to the strongly revisionist account of medieval Europe that Stuart composed in the immediate aftermath of the decisive final rebuff at Edinburgh. In particular, rebutting Robertson's interpretation of the same subject understandably became central to Stuart's defiant

[2] William Zachs, *Without Regard to Good Manners: A Biography of Gilbert Stuart, 1743–1786* (Edinburgh, 1992), pp. 1–9.

[3] Gilbert Stuart, *A View of Society in Europe, in Its Progress from Rudeness to Refinement* (Edinburgh and London, 1778), pp. 33–4, 105–8.

[4] Ibid., p. 107. An obituarist concurred, calling him 'a martyr to intemperance': *Gentleman's Magazine* 59 (1786), p. 716.

attempt to assert his own scholarly credentials. This objective was even hinted at in the Advertisement with which the work opens, with Stuart relating that he had read all of the recent writing on medieval Europe and found it comprehensively wanting: 'From the most able historians of our own and foreign nations, who might naturally be expected to be intelligent guides for the paths I have chosen,' he claimed – with Robertson's *Charles V* clearly foremost in mind – 'I could derive no advantage.'[5] Nor did Stuart confine himself to coded attacks.[6] In the middle of Book Two he again attacked 'the courtly and agreeable introduction to the History of Charles the Fifth', the expansive prefatory essay which Robertson had called, coining a title which Stuart's own work now echoed, 'A View of the Progress of Society in Europe from the Subversion of the Roman Empire to the Beginning of the Sixteenth Century'.

Here Stuart's critique focused specifically on what he suggested was Robertson's habit of ignoring some of the most important and determinative features of feudal social relations:

> It is remarkable, that, amidst a wide variety of other omissions, there is not even the slightest consideration of knight-service, and the knight's fee. Yet these circumstances were of the most powerful operation, both with respect to government and manners. I make not this remark to detract from the diligence of an author whose laboriousness is acknowledged, and whose total abstinence from all ideas and inventions of his own, permitted him to carry an undivided attention to other men's thoughts and speculations; but that, resting on these peculiarities, I may draw from them this general and humiliating, yet, I hope, not unuseful conclusion, that the study and knowledge of the dark ages are still in their infancy.[7]

Stuart here not only insinuated that Robertson was an unoriginal and largely derivative scholar who had overlooked some difficult legal issues, whose historical significance he had simply not grasped, but he also argued that Robertson had in many cases failed to interpret the evidence competently or even fairly, because of a fundamental prejudice against medieval society. This accusation of ineptitude allied to bias informed many other put-downs by Stuart. In Book One, for example, it lay behind the allegations that Robertson had unjustly maligned the barbarian peoples who over-ran the Roman world by asserting that they were capable only of

5 Stuart, *A View of Society in Europe*, p. vii.

6 Richard B. Sher, '*Charles V* and the Book Trade: An Episode in Enlightenment Print Culture', *William Robertson and the Expansion of Empire*, ed. Stewart J. Brown (Cambridge, 1997), pp. 164–95.

7 Stuart, *A View of Society in Europe*, pp. 377–8. Writing to his publisher John Murray shortly before publication, Stuart privately amplified his accusation that the lengthy medieval preamble to *Charles V* suffered from chronic technical shortcomings, particularly – and significantly, given that the final breach had just occurred over the Principal's choice of a new professor of public law – arising out of what he considered to be Robertson's complete ignorance of legal scholarship. Stuart explained that this was why the *View of Society* was going to 'treat of all the topics on which Dr. Robertson has *touched* in his illustrations to his first volume. I say *touched*; for he has not examined them with attention, and has little knowledge of Jurisprudence': Zachs, *Without Regard to Good Manners*, p. 101.

'destructive violence' and 'havock', and also that he had misrepresented the nobility of Norman England by seeming 'to imagine' that they had lost their capacity for waging private war.[8] Robertson's repeated suggestions that the backward medieval monarchies of Europe had been incapable of enjoying civilised interactions with each other were also dismissed at the end of Book One and, in another of Stuart's characteristically cutting asides, said 'not to be relied upon in all their force, but to be understood with much reserve and many limitations'.[9]

It is thus difficult not to read Stuart's much more favourable depiction of feudalism, with its insistent harping on the virtues of chivalry, as in substantial part a determined attempt to over-paint the generally unattractive picture of medieval society sketched by Robertson. In fact, this strongly personal motivation makes much sense of several aspects of Stuart's account, especially where it is at its most strikingly idiosyncratic. In particular, the central argument rests upon a highly unorthodox chronology; one which daringly relocates the flourishing of feudal tenures and social organisation to the sub-Roman period instead of in the Norman era, and which also moves the golden age of chivalric culture back to no later than the ninth and tenth centuries, rather than the thirteenth and fourteenth. Stuart was aided in this reordering of events by a stylistic oddity, presumably deliberate, which involved offering almost nothing by way of precise dating. Indeed the *View of Society* only very occasionally mentions individual years, while an account of more than a millennium of history, running to 433 pages in the first edition, somehow contrived to use the key orienting words 'century' or 'centuries' on just six occasions (one of these unavoidable because it was inside a direct quotation from Hume). By contrast *Charles V*, which possesses a much more overt chronological framework, reached the same total in just seventeen pages, and even Robertson's *Scotland*, though largely focused on the sixteenth century alone, had used them as many times in the first five. Yet even as this literary quirk would necessarily have important consequences for anyone reading the *View of Society* (because it clearly served to soften the wrenching jolt that Stuart was administering to the conventional narrative, preventing the sheer magnitude of his historical revisionism from playing constantly on the reader's mind), he still could not resist at one point rendering its implications troublingly stark, declaring in relation to the technical foundation of the feudal system that the fief 'was known in every country of Europe in the commencement of the tenth century'.[10]

As well as in its underlying chronology, the essential character of feudal society and the place of chivalry within it also appeared entirely different in Stuart's hands, precisely because a clear contrast with Robertson's account was absolutely essential. Much as in Hume's *History of England*, with its systematic critique of the 'vast fabric of feudal subordination', feudalism in *Charles V* had appeared unambiguously repellent, its consequences for the human condition wretched.[11] As a result, chivalric culture, to which Robertson devoted just a couple of pages, was viewed positively,

8 Stuart, *A View of Society in Europe*, pp. 199, 261.
9 Ibid., p. 303.
10 Stuart, *A View of Society in Europe*, p. 96.
11 David Hume, *The History of England*, 2 vols (London, 1762), i, p. 401.

but, crucially, as also evolving only in the period during and especially after the crusades, and thus as a late and largely inadequate response to a series of grave moral problems which could be laid squarely at the door of feudalism:

> The feudal state was a state of perpetual war, rapine, and anarchy; during which the weak and unarmed were exposed every moment to insults or injuries. The power of the sovereign was too limited to prevent these wrongs; and the administration of justice too feeble to redress them. There was scarce any protection against violence and oppression, but what the valour and generosity of private persons afforded. The same spirit of enterprize which had prompted so many gentlemen to take arms in defence of the oppressed pilgrims in Palestine, incited others to declare themselves the patrons and avengers of injured innocence at home. When the final reduction of the Holy Land under the dominion of Infidels put an end to these foreign expeditions, the latter was the only employment left for the activity and courage of adventurers.[12]

Robertson's version of chivalry's historical function – a palliative eventually applied to soothe the pain generated by the very nature of feudal tenures in the later Middle Ages – was what Stuart seems to have been determined to contradict. And he tried to do so not only by the bold device of moving the growth of chivalry forward by several centuries, but also by insisting that it was in fact a normal part of medieval life.

In Stuart's view the legal foundations of feudalism, by which a lord conferred property and protection upon his vassals in return for service, had clearly become established during the early Middle Ages. As a consequence those times had also been characterised by the sort of social harmony that is only possible when mutual dependence binds men together, nurturing respect, a sense of honour and genuine amity:

> While the greatness and simplicity of those manners, which the conquerors of Rome brought with them from their woods, continued to animate their posterity, the feudal association was noble in its principles, and useful in its practice. The solicitudes, and the mercenary spirit which rise up with

[12] William Robertson, *The History of the Reign of the Emperor Charles V*, 3 vols (London, 1767), i, pp. 69–70. If Robertson was relatively laconic on chivalry – though what he wrote of this response to feudalism's inherent evils was necessarily favourable – it is intriguing to note that Hume actually penned the Scottish Enlightenment's only known coherent standalone discussion of the topic, in what he called 'An Historical Essay on Chivalry and Modern Honour'. Unfortunately it is extremely unlikely that Stuart, no friend of either man, had read it; indeed, it is unlikely that he even knew of its existence, since it was an unpublished juvenile effort (perhaps the future philosopher's very first experiment with the fashionable essay format), probably written when Hume was an Edinburgh undergraduate around 1725–26. A fragment survives amongst the Hume papers at the Royal Society of Edinburgh and this has stimulated two modern analyses: E. C. Mossner, 'David Hume's "An Historical Essay on Chivalry and Modern Honour"', *Modern Philology* 45 (1947), pp. 54–60; Donald T. Siebert, 'Chivalry and Romance in the Age of Hume', *Eighteenth-Century Life* 21 (1997), pp. 62–79.

> commerce, were unknown, and the fullest scope was given to nature and the passions. The actions and conduct of men were directed by sentiment and affection. In the ardour of private confederacies, the general feelings of generosity were augmented. The emotions of the heart increased their force by confinement. And the lord and the vassal were linked to each other in the closest connection.[13]

The benefits of this development for wider Anglo-Saxon society in particular were quite clear, according to Stuart. It had created strong social bonds grounded in obligations which had then been a positive pleasure for men to fulfil:

> When the superior and the vassal were friends, and their connection was warm and generous, the feudal incidents were acts of cordiality and affection. When they were enemies, and their connection was preserved, not by the commerce of the passions and the heart, but merely by the tie of land, the feudal incidents were acts of oppression and severity. During the Anglo-Saxon times, the affectionate state of the feudal association prevailed. During the times of Duke William, and his immediate successors, their hostile condition was experienced. Hence the mildness and happiness of our Saxon ancestors; hence the complaints, and grievances of our Norman progenitors.[14]

This analysis also had the further advantage of explaining why so many other historians, and Robertson most of all, had failed to recognise feudalism's essential benevolence, for it was confusing the later perversion for the real thing, and overlooking the much more constructive pure form that had existed in earlier times, which had led to a serious misunderstanding of its true character. Once this was acknowledged, of course, it was easier to see how the cohesive society created by the development of feudal tenures in the early Middle Ages had also been dignified with the widespread acceptance of knightly values, since the latter naturally reflected and reinforced the kinds of obligation between lords and vassals that feudalism in its classic original form had both encouraged and required.

Indeed, chivalric culture, with its emphasis upon honour and duty, flowed automatically from this socio-legal framework. As Stuart argued, directly linking the origins of feudal landholding with the birth of knightly codes of conduct:

> Fiefs and chivalry were mutually to act upon one another. The feudal association was to direct and foster chivalry; and, from chivalry, it was to receive a support or lustre. They were plants which were destined to take root about the same period, and to sympathise in their growth, and in their decline.[15]

Chivalric activities were, in short, the product of the characteristic social organisation and distinctive virtues of the vigorous and noble people who had successfully overthrown Roman civilisation and created the barbarian kingdoms:

13 Stuart, *A View of Society in Europe*, pp. 70–1.
14 Ibid., p. 99.
15 Ibid., p. 37.

> Out of the impulse of their passions, the institutions of chivalry were gradually to form themselves. The passion for arms, the spirit of gallantry, and of devotion, which so many writers pronounce to be the genuine offspring of these wild affectations, were in fact their source; and it happened, by a natural consequence, that, for a time, the ceremonies and the usages produced by them, encouraged their importance, and added to their strength. The steps which marked their progress, served to foster their spirit; and, to the manner of ages, which we too often despise as rude and ignoble, not to political reflection or legislative wisdom, is that system to be ascribed, which was to act so long and so powerfully in society, and to produce infinite advantage and infinite calamity.[16]

Again underlining the fundamentally polemical intentions of the interpretation, this strongly positive depiction of the feudal system was concluded with yet another direct side-swipe at Robertson for allegedly judging medieval society from a wholly anachronistic perspective: 'It is to those only who apply to rude societies the ideas of a cultivated æra,' chided Stuart, 'that the institutions of chivalry seem the production of an enlightened policy. They remember not the inexperience of dark ages, and the attachment of nations to their ancient usages.'[17]

It would be quite wrong, however, to regard the origins and nature of feudalism in Stuart's eyes as nothing more than an opportunistic vehicle for the pursuit of an unseemly scholarly vendetta. Nor were the wider cultural implications of feudal tenures of purely antiquarian interest at the time the *View of Society* was being written. For Stuart actually lived in a country whose defining characteristics, especially when contrasted with those found in contemporary England (a comparison habitual among educated Scots in the first century following the Treaty of Union), were often held to revolve around the surviving relics of its feudal past. That this aspect of Scotland's distinctiveness was seriously problematic had also been strongly suggested as recently as the Jacobite Rebellion of 1745–46, when the traditional legal privileges enjoyed by Scottish landowners – the right to try their tenants in most criminal cases and to force them to provide military service under the form of tenure known as ward-holding – had allegedly been a material factor in allowing disaffected nobles and lairds to raise substantial private armies in support of Charles Edward Stuart's cause. Although most Scottish opinion had insisted that this was a misinterpretation, and that the real problem lay not in the peculiarities of Scots law in general but rather in the specific social and moral inadequacies of the Gaelic-speaking communities of the Highlands, English ministers had easily won the argument at Westminster over the political sociology of rebellion. In effect, they had insisted that in important respects eighteenth-century Scottish society continued to be underpinned by essentially medieval legal structures, and that therefore only a programme of enforced modernisation, directed from outside the country, could hope finally to eradicate these dangerous anachronisms and so

16 Ibid., p. 54.
17 Ibid., pp. 54–5.

prevent elements within its reactionary feudal elite from posing any future military threat to the British state. As a result, London had imposed what it took to be the appropriate legislative solution on Scotland as a whole. In 1746 parliament passed the Tenures Abolition Act, sweeping away ward-holding at a stroke. The following year the Heritable Jurisdictions Act was also passed over bitter opposition from most of Scotland's landowners, who complained loudly but impotently that this not only removed their own lucrative rights to collect fines in their own courts but also breached the terms of the Union, which had explicitly provided for the continuance of Scottish legal custom.

This is why it should be no surprise to find that the specifically military ramifications of the law of feudal tenure brooked so large in the *View of Society*. In the second chapter of Book Two, entitled simply 'Of the Military Power of a Feudal Kingdom', the aspects of feudal landholding that gave rise to knight service as the basis of armed force in medieval society were worked through in detail, though once again Stuart seems to have wanted to show that this development had definitely not been an inevitable recipe for political instability and regular rebellion. On the contrary, because the military duties arising out of feudal tenure fitted perfectly within the recognition of mutual reliance and the embracing of chivalric values, its natural tendency was in fact to promote good government and civil harmony. In a remarkable passage, Stuart even suggested that knight service had preserved political freedom in the early Middle Ages precisely because it had constrained the ambitions of the monarch by distributing power more evenly among the landed elite. This was, he proposed:

> a system, of which it was the admirable consequence, that those who were the proprietors of the land of a kingdom, were to defend it. They were the most interested in its welfare and tranquillity; and, while they were naturally disposed to act with union and firmness, against a foreign enemy, they were induced not less strongly to guard against domestic tyranny. Their interest and happiness, their pleasure and convenience, urged them equally to oppose invasions from abroad, intestine commotions, and the stretches of prerogative. A strength, so natural, and which could never be exhausted; a strength, in which the prince was to have less authority than the nobles, and in which the power of both was checked by the numerous class of inferior proprietors; a strength, which had directly in view the preservation of civil liberty, seems, on a slight observation, the perfection of military discipline.[18]

Again, chivalry was integral to this picture of properly-functioning feudalism, an inescapable feature of knight service in its classic form. The later decline of both chivalry and a vassal's military obligations necessarily also occurred in tandem:

> All the splendour and advantages of the antient chivalry could not uphold the feudal militia. The dubbed knight, or the knight of honour, was to fall with the mere military tenant, or the knight of tenure. Chivalry was to decay as well

[18] Ibid., p. 110.

> as knight-service. When they ceased to give a mutual aid and support, they were soon to operate in a contrary direction, and to promote the decline of each other.[19]

Stuart's warm sentiments on the military aspects of feudalism obviously spoke directly to the anxieties of contemporaries, not least in England, about the supposed dangers of customary forms of tenure which, even in the mid-1740s, appeared to have enabled Scottish proprietors to mobilise armed forces on their own account. Rather than inherently threatening rebellion, he implied, these tenures looked back to a distant past in which the obligation to provide military assistance for one's feudal superior had actually maintained rather than threatened the political order.

Importantly, however, as Stuart's pointed use of the term 'feudal militia' indicates, these same comments also served to reinforce the arguments of his fellow Scots, who by the 1770s had been campaigning for more than twenty years to be allowed by parliament to form a gentry militia to defend the Scottish coastline against potential French invasion.[20] London's obstinate refusal, largely based on the fear (fanned by the experience of the Jacobite rebellions of 1715 and 1745–46) that armed civilians in Scotland necessarily constituted a threat to peace and stability, caused much annoyance among loyal Scottish supporters of the British state, who could not help but notice that the English landed classes, whose reliability was obviously not in question, had long been permitted to raise their own defensive force. Stuart's distinctly evocative picture of the freedom-loving and intensely patriotic feudal armies raised and commanded by landed proprietors thus seems to have served as a positive historical prototype for the sort of militia that he and his friends among the Lowland social elite believed still needed to be re-created in modern Scotland.

The military dimension to feudal tenures was not the only topical contemporary question arising out of medieval property law that Stuart perceived a need to address. Other aspects of an essentially feudal regime for landholding and its putative consequences for life in modern Scotland also remained of great concern in the years immediately before the *View of Society* appeared. A particular controversy concerned the implications of entail – or 'tailzie' in the vernacular. This was a body of law which permitted Scottish landowners to predetermine the future inheritance of their own estates (including the possibility of varying the natural line of descent) and simultaneously to restrict the freedom of action that any subsequent owner would then enjoy.[21] Conventional wisdom had it that entail, although in reality only finally confirmed by statute as recently as 1685, was another long-standing national legal peculiarity, linking the Scottish present to a distinctive Scottish past in which the country's landowners had benefited from unusually wide-ranging rights in relation to their own heritable property. Yet the practice was not without its drawbacks, and had increasingly attracted criticism. Entail clearly hindered economic development at a time when most eighteenth-century landowners, influenced by

19 Ibid., p. 119.

20 John Robertson, *The Scottish Enlightenment and the Militia Issue* (Edinburgh, 1985).

21 Erskine Douglas Sandford, *A Treatise on the History and Law of Entails in Scotland*, 2nd edn (Edinburgh, 1842), pp. 1–42.

Enlightenment ideas, were seeking to improve agricultural productivity; the onerous terms imposed by their predecessors frequently prevented current proprietors from pledging land as collateral in return for mortgages or other necessary investment. The remedy, of course, was new parliamentary legislation at Westminster to relieve some of these peculiarly Scottish burdens, with the so-called Montgomerie Act of 1770 among the most important measures.[22]

About the origins and usefulness of entail in particular, already discussed in detail twenty years earlier by the well-respected Scottish legal historian Sir John Dalrymple (whose contribution Stuart knew, because he dutifully hymned it as a 'comprehensive and learned treatise'), the *View of Society*, which given its primary concern with feudal tenures could hardly ignore the question, was quite clear that the device had indeed had ancient roots. These manifestly tied it directly to the emergence of feudal property rights in their classic form deep in the early medieval period: 'The use of entails,' Stuart claimed, 'which was not unknown in the Anglo-Saxon times, and the succession which obtained in allodial estates, must have contributed very much to the establishment of the perpetuity of the fief.'[23] Nor did Stuart doubt that something very like the law of entail, which was still operative in eighteenth-century Scotland, had originally had a formative impact on medieval social relations, tending to reinforce the natural authority of those in possession of heritable property and the considerable respect in which they were typically held by their contemporaries. Indeed, it was the obvious presence of mature feudal relationships in the ninth and tenth centuries, elevating the status and potency of proprietors in society, which most clearly hinted that something like the full set of legal rights associated with heritable ownership would already have needed to be present at that juncture: 'The general tendency of the fief to this ultimate step, and the immense power of many of the Anglo-Saxon nobles,' he suggested, 'seem also to confirm the idea, that the existence of its perpetuity might, in some cases, be known in the Anglo-Saxon times.'[24]

In the years before the *View of Society* was written, the same deep interest in the legacy of medieval property law had also found a focus in two sensational Scottish judicial processes which eventually – though only on appeal to the House of Lords in London – determined the contested successions to the dukedom of Douglas in 1769 and the earldom of Sutherland in 1771, together with their considerable estates

[22] Brian Bonnyman, 'The 3rd Duke of Buccleuch, Adam Smith and the Entail Act of 1770', *Scottish Archives* 6 (2000), pp. 101–9.

[23] Stuart, *A View of Society in Europe*, pp. 356, 373. Dalrymple's study, *An Essay Towards a General History of Feudal Property in Great Britain* (London, 1757), contained a lengthy and detailed chapter entitled 'History of Entails' (pp. 155–87). This gave an account of entails as a late departure from original feudal practice, emerging in England only in the last part of the thirteenth century and in Scotland no earlier than the end of the fifteenth. Modern legislative attempts to loosen the restrictions on owners imposed by this comparatively recent development, essentially only a product of feudalism in its decline, were also portrayed favourably. Curiously, Stuart's discussion ignored Dalrymple's sophisticated argument, merely asserting his own entirely different interpretation, consistent with his other claims about early feudalism, in which entail had purportedly existed in Anglo-Saxon England.

[24] Stuart, *A View of Society in Europe*, p. 356.

and entitlements. The first case had revolved around the extraordinary attempts by rival claimants to present convincing evidence to the courts, partly gynaecological and partly circumstantial in character, that the ostensible teenaged heir could not be his childless uncle's legitimate successor because he was not in fact his mother's biological son, while the second had seen an unashamedly grasping uncle insisting that he rather than his orphaned niece should be recognised as the lawful heir to her deceased father. Both cases attracted rapt public attention through extensive newspaper coverage, as copious quantities of aristocratic dirty linen were washed in public and celebrity legal teams fought doggedly for their clients.[25] Stuart had much to say, as we shall see, about the historical status of women in general, but he also clearly recognised the need to explore the specific question of female inheritance – acutely relevant because the right of a young woman to succeed to an aristocratic title and patrimony had been the specific bone of legal contention, in the event successfully upheld by the Lords, during the long-drawn-out Sutherland case. Stuart's account of this subject made it very clear that, although female inheritance had not been a feature of the first medieval law codes, women's ability to hold heritable property in their own right had received early entrenchment, with the result that female heirs had soon been fully accommodated within the feudal system:

> As the original rudeness of the barbaric nations yielded to successive improvements, as manners softened, and the arts of peace were cultivated, the propensity to add to their emolument, and to contribute to their pleasure, grew stronger. If they could not march to the field, and charge an enemy at the head of their vassals, they might perform these offices by substitution. An approved warriour might discharge, for the female possessor of a fief, the military duties to which it was subject. A right to succeed to feudality was, by degrees, acknowledged in the sex; and, when invested in the grant, they were to exert all its civil rights. Though they deputed its military command, they could sustain its honours and prerogatives. They were to hold courts, and exercise jurisdiction in ordinary fiefs; and, while they attended to these cares in noble ones, they were also to assemble with the peers, in the great assemblies of the state in every country of Europe, to deliberate, to vote, and to judge. Neither the military service incident to every fief, nor the obligation of attending the assembly of the peers or the council of the nation incident to fiefs, which were noble, could prevent the advancing condition of the women.[26]

In other words, in its classic form feudal law had given to medieval society a profound respect for the rights and status of women, which Stuart's eighteenth-century readers themselves increasingly recognised as the mark of a civilised society benefiting from broad-ranging and enlightened improvements.

[25] T. B. Simpson, 'The Douglas Cause', *Scottish Historical Review* 33 (1954), pp. 37–9; 'Obituary – Duchess-Countess of Sutherland', *Gentleman's Magazine*, new series: 11 (1839), pp. 310–12.

[26] Stuart, *A View of Society in Europe*, pp. 35–6.

*

That women formed an increasingly important market for works of history as the eighteenth century progressed, as well as a potentially fruitful subject, was something that clearly informed Stuart's thinking when writing the *View of Society*.[27] In this respect, however, his approach was entirely consistent with that of his rivals. Hume, in the wry and subsequently-suppressed essay 'Of the Study of History', had recognised this seminal trend as early as 1741, making it the basis for a teasing literary polemic targeted at a distinctly gendered audience:

> There is nothing which I would recommend more earnestly to my female readers than the study of history, as an occupation, of all others, the best suited both to their sex and education, much more instructive than their ordinary books of amusement, and more entertaining than those serious compositions, which are usually to be found in their closets.[28]

Thereafter, Hume's own *History of England* successfully accommodated what he had rightly identified as a significant cultural development, not least by crafting an innovative authorial style which freely borrowed aspects of the novelist's art – in itself a shrewd strategy, given that it was the tastes and enthusiasms of female readers in particular that contemporaries believed lay behind the growing literary profile and commercial profitability of imaginative fiction.[29] Part of Hume's attempt to render historical writing more compelling to the kind of women who immersed themselves in novels involved the adoption of strongly sentimental postures, characterised by enhanced levels of emotional engagement between individuals, and an emphasis upon the concerted development and open display of affective and humanitarian sensibilities: the intention was evidently to solicit the reader's empathy with the feelings and perceptions of historical figures, women at least as much as men.[30] Hume's friend Robertson had shown how far these techniques could be exploited in the *History of Scotland*, notably in a brilliant reimagining of Mary, Queen of Scots, previously a much-criticised symbol of Catholic superstition and tyrannical ambition, but now depicted far more favourably as a star-crossed sentimental heroine – a vulnerable victim of malice and misfortune with whom it was all but impossible not

[27] The desire to foreground specifically female historical experiences would reach its logical conclusion the year after the *View of Society*'s appearance, in the Edinburgh-trained physician William Alexander's *The History of Women, From the Earliest Antiquity, To the Present Time*, 2 vols (London, 1779). See Mark Salber Phillips, *Society and Sentiment: Genres of Historical Writing in Britain, 1740–1820* (Princeton, 2000), pp. 163–5.

[28] David Hume, *Essays, Moral and Political* (Edinburgh [1741]), p. 73.

[29] Jacqueline Pearson, *Women's Reading in Britain, 1750–1835* (Cambridge, 1999); Ellen F. Gardiner, 'Elusive Presences: Women Readers of the Eighteenth-Century Novel' (unpublished Ph.D. thesis, State University of New York at Stony Brook, 1989).

[30] Mark Salber Phillips, '"If Mrs. Mure Be Not Sorry for Poor King Charles": History, the Novel and the Sentimental Reader', *History Workshop Journal* 43 (1997), pp. 111–31; G. J. Barker-Benfield, *The Culture of Sensibility: Sex and Society in Eighteenth-Century Britain* (Chicago, 1992); R. F. Brissenden, *Virtue in Distress: Studies in the Novel of Sentiment from Richardson to Sade* (London, 1974).

to perceive an emotional connection, as Robertson hoped, when even at the moment of her final doom she still 'maintained the magnanimity of a Queen, tempered with the gentleness and modesty of a woman'.[31] For all his intellectual suspicion of Hume and intense personal loathing for Robertson, therefore, Stuart, in working out how best to appeal to female readers, had much to learn from the successful examples they had provided.

Certainly his aggressive use of sentimentalisation means that in places Stuart's writing appears almost to have been designed to see how much further Robertson's experiments in emotional manipulation could be pushed. In a later work, the *History of Scotland from the Establishment of the Reformation till the Death of Queen Mary* (1782), when he too was engaged in embroidering a suitably tear-jerking account of the luckless queen's turbulent life, Stuart even seems to have recognised that this relentless focus on inducing in the susceptible reader a palpable sense of intimate personal engagement with past individuals actually ran the risk of bringing the responsible historian into conflict with the more conventional scholarly obligation to maintain distance and preserve impartiality. As he reflected – not entirely convincingly – on the difficult ethical balancing act which arose when describing in breathlessly novelistic terms the sensational murder of Mary's second husband, Henry Darnley, by the earl of Bothwell, the man who would shortly become her third:

> It is with pain that History relates such cruel events; but while she melts with human woe, it is her province to be rigorously just. Her weeping eye is the indication of an instructive sorrow; and while her bursting heart, mourns over the crimes, the calamities, and the wretchedness of ages that are past, she records them with fidelity as a lesson to succeeding times.[32]

Nevertheless, in the *View of Society* there were also many passages where Stuart, exploiting the notion that it might have been easier to express elemental feelings and natural emotions in earlier and less advanced stages of society than in highly-evolved modern conditions, unmistakably erred in the direction of sympathy and sentimentality, deliberately pressing his female readers in particular to identify themselves with the experiences of their predecessors in the Middle Ages, especially in contexts where historical relations between men and women, amongst the most obviously timeless of human situations, were involved.

The eternal impulses of romantic love, for example – inextricably linked with chivalric themes – predictably allowed Stuart to connect the concerns and anxieties of his eighteenth-century female audience with those of women living in the barbarian kingdoms. For it was literally undeniable, he suggested, that:

[31] William Robertson, *History of Scotland*, 2 vols (London, 1759), ii, p. 135; Karen O'Brien, *Narratives of Enlightenment: Cosmopolitan History from Voltaire to Gibbon* (Cambridge, 1997), ch. 4.

[32] Gilbert Stuart, *History of Scotland from the Establishment of the Reformation till the Death of Queen Mary*, 2 vols (London, 1782), i, p. 202.

> the sexes, in every period of society, are important to each other; and that the member of a rude community, as well as the polished citizen, is susceptible of tenderness and sentiment. He is a stranger, indeed, to the metaphysic of love, and to the fopperies of gallantry; but his heart cannot be insensible to female attractions. He cannot but be drawn by beauty; he must know a preference in the objects of his affection; and he must feel and experience, in a certain degree, at least, that bewitching intercourse, and those delightful agitations, which constitute the greatest charm of cultivated life.[33]

Closely linking the 'rude' past to the 'polished' present, Stuart thus coaxed his women readers to believe that the human male in all periods – their own as well as the golden era of knights in shining armour and damsels in distress – had been consistently impelled by an entirely natural yearning for female attention, devotion and affection. Might an eighteenth-century woman not hope to feel the same frisson of excitement, the same quickening of the pulse, the same sense of power and worth, if an honourable modern man, just like his medieval forebears, indicated his sincere interest in them?

It was necessary to this argument that it should be seen that, as chivalric culture had evolved, women had at all times played a pivotal role in its elaboration, not merely as suitable objects of male adoration but even as the prime motivation for the full range of knightly endeavours:

> The emulation of his equals, the example and admonitions of his chief, and the company of the ladies, from whose number he was to select the accomplished fair one, to whom he was to ascribe all his sentiments and his actions, inflamed in him the passion for war, infused into his mind a zeal for religion, and instructed him in all the arts of a respectful gallantry.[34]

The virtuous behaviour that had resulted when medieval men strove for female approval was again cast in strongly sentimental terms, allowing Stuart to imply that the knightly code of conduct had embodied a series of desirable moral values that in their own time the Georgian women who read the *View of Society* might themselves be happy to endorse:

> While it was to guard the sexes from frailty, it invigorated the sense of justice; and, in a period of disorder and confusion, taught the knight to be strenuous in vindicating the wrongs of the injured. The weak and the oppressed, the orphan and the widow, had a particular claim to his protection. To disobey their call, was to infringe a law of chivalry, and to incur dishonour and infamy. He seemed, in some measure, to be entrusted with the power of the magistrate; and the fashion of the times made him forward to employ his arm, and to spill his blood in the cause of innocence and virtue. Thus war, gallantry, and devotion conspired to form the character of the knight. And

33 Stuart, *A View of Society in Europe*, pp. 12–13.
34 Ibid., p. 57.

> these manners, so lofty and so romantic, were for ages to give a splendour to Europe, by directing the fortunes of its nations, and by producing examples of magnanimity and valour, which are unequalled in the annals of mankind.[35]

By such means women were being asked to see themselves not only as having been substantially responsible for the creation of chivalric culture in the early Middle Ages, but also as retaining a capacity for imposing a considerable measure of necessary civilisation and refinement upon men – a key aspiration of eighteenth-century sentimentalism, which further exaggerated the conventional assumption that exemplary displays of female virtue (as, more disturbingly, of female vice) had a particularly powerful formative influence over masculine attitudes and behaviour.[36] This feature of his writing, of course, held out the delicious prospect to Stuart's women readers that they too could hope to mould and moderate men's conduct in their own world, rendering their husbands, brothers and sons more refined, more sociable and better fitted for life in an age of sentiment:

> The knight, while he acquired, in the company of the ladies, the graces of external behaviour, improved his natural sensibility and tenderness. He smoothed over the roughness of war with politeness. To be rude to a lady, or to speak to her disadvantage, was a crime which could not be pardoned. He guarded her possessions from the rapacious, and maintained her reputation against slander. The uncourteous offender was driven from the society of the valiant and the interposition of the fair was often necessary to protect him from death. But the courtesy of the knight, though due in a peculiar manner to the female sex, extended itself to all the business and intercourse of civil life. He studied a habitual elegance of manners. Politeness became a knightly virtue; it even attended him to the field of battle, and checked his passions in the ardour of victory.[37]

*

In an earlier work, Stuart had already declared his firm conviction that the roots of modern British constitutional liberties could be traced back to the German woods. As he had written in *An Historical Dissertation Concerning the Antiquity of the English Constitution* (1768): 'If I have made it appear, that the parts which compose our constitution arose more immediately from the forests of Germany, I have answered my intention.'[38] This was not in itself an unusual assertion. Indeed it was something of a commonplace of eighteenth-century Anglophone political writing to insist that the freedom which had purportedly characterised pre-Norman England, and which many assumed still existed under the Hanoverians, had been transplanted by

35 Ibid., pp. 65–6.

36 Philip Carter, 'An "Effeminate" or "Efficient" Nation? Masculinity and Eighteenth-Century Social Documentary', *Textual Practice* 11 (1997), pp. 429–43 (esp. pp. 439–40).

37 Stuart, *A View of Society in Europe*, pp. 66–7.

38 Gilbert Stuart, *An Historical Dissertation Concerning the Antiquity of the English Constitution*, 2nd edn (London, 1770), p. 290.

the Anglo-Saxons from their original tribal homelands where popular assemblies and the common law had first entrenched the spirit of liberty among the people.[39] Among the very different authors who had already made this point were Samuel Squire, Bishop of St David's, in *An Enquiry into the Foundation of the English Constitution; or, An Historical Essay upon the Anglo-Saxon Government Both in Germany and England* (1745), the future American revolutionary James Otis in *The Rights of the British Colonies Asserted and Proved* (1764), the ardently Anglophile French philosopher Montesquieu in *De L'Esprit Des Lois* (1748), and, stretching as far back as the argument in James I's reign over the respective contributions of the monarchy and parliament to England's constitutional development, the lawyer John Selden in *Jani Anglorum Facies Altera* (1610).

Nonetheless, this claim, though always consistent with mainstream Hanoverian Whig ideology at its most smug and self-satisfied, also had special partisan resonance for those committed to more radical forms of Whiggery. Moreover, as Otis's appropriation of it illustrates, it enjoyed particular currency from the 1760s onwards among those who feared that their own liberty was in jeopardy and who suspected that modern British governments had more in common with the eleventh-century conquerors who had attempted to restrict the people's freedom beneath a 'Norman Yoke' than with the Anglo-Saxons who had introduced and entrenched it. Stuart, whose dislike of Robertson and his conservative Edinburgh coterie (who were closely tied to the established Church of Scotland and subservient to whoever happened to be in power in London) also had a sharp ideological edge, fully shared those anxieties: he was, after all, a close associate of the radical Whig politician David Steuart Erskine, eleventh earl of Buchan, another enemy of Robertson (Buchan denounced the pragmatic and calculating Principal to his face for his 'Apologies for Tyranny and Cruelty'), and of Buchan's brother Henry Erskine, effective leader of the opposition in Scotland by the 1780s, for whom Stuart would write anti-government propaganda over the last few years of his life.[40] As a result, especially by 1778, with the divisive American war at its height and party feelings inflamed, it is difficult not to think that Stuart's decision to assert so emphatically the German antecedents of English constitutionalism was also implicitly positioning him as a critic of the motives and intentions of George III's ministers.

Yet the *View of Society* clearly offered an opportunity to amplify and deepen this ideologically-charged Teutonism in other ways, with Stuart now at pains to suggest that not only specific political forms but even broader attitudes and outlooks – the basic values of the English before the arrival of the Norman oppressors – had had their origins in the remote past in the wild and primitive terrain beyond the Rhine:

[39] Reginald Horsman, 'The Origins of Racial Anglo-Saxonism in Great Britain Before 1850', *Journal of the History of Ideas* 37 (1976), pp. 391–410 (esp. pp. 389–90); S. Kliger, *The Goths in England: A Study in Seventeenth – and Eighteenth-Century Thought* (Cambridge, MA, 1952).

[40] Steven Shapin, 'Property, Patronage and the Politics of Science: The Founding of the Royal Society of Edinburgh', *British Journal for the History of Science* 7 (1974), pp. 7–41 (quotation at p. 28); Zachs, *Without Regard to Good Manners*, pp. 177–83.

> When the inhabitants of Germany sallied from their woods, and made conquests, the change of condition they experienced produced a change in their manners. Narrow communities grew into extensive kingdoms, and petty princes, and temporary leaders, were exalted into monarchs. The ideas, however, they had formerly entertained, and the customs with which they had been familiar, were neither forgotten nor neglected. The modes of thought and of action which had been displayed in their original seats, advanced with them in to the territories of Rome, continued their operation and power in this new situation, and created that uniformity of appearance which Europe everywhere exhibited.[41]

This was another way in which the attractions of chivalric culture, so lovingly painted elsewhere in the *View of Society*, could be exploited to serve Stuart's specific purposes. For it was the Teutonic roots of knightly codes of conduct that allowed them to be linked directly to the peculiar social environment in which the precious spirit of freedom had first been distilled:

> Arms, gallantry, and devotion, were to act with uncommon force; and, to the forests of Germany, we must trace those romantic institutions, which filled Europe with renown, and with splendour; which, mingling religion with war, and piety with love, raised up so many warriours to contend for the palm of valour and the prize of beauty.[42]

It was from here, then, that medieval England had acquired its special political blessings. And it was these that had eventually been recapitulated – crucially, *not* simply invented – in 1215, when Magna Carta finally articulated 'the constitutional freedom that had distinguished this fortunate island from the earliest times'.[43]

Not content to present this convergence merely as a happy historical coincidence, however, Stuart actually contended that knighthood, chivalry and political liberty had all originally gone hand in hand, each reinforcing the others. For it had been normal, he suggested, for the early knights, imbued with the chivalric ideals of honesty and justice, to act as political representatives on behalf of the wider population. They had provided, in other words, the first glimmerings of the parliamentary model that the English in particular had gradually perfected:

> Like all the other barbaric tribes who made establishments, the individuals among the Goths who wore swords, assembled originally in the councils of the nation; and when the disadvantages of crowded and tumultuous assemblies were uniformly felt, it is natural to conclude, that the deputies of the people were called to represent them.[44]

Under the Anglo-Saxons the continuation of freedom had evidently relied upon the

41 Stuart, *A View of Society in Europe*, p. 45.
42 Ibid., p. 46.
43 Ibid., p. 101.
44 Ibid., p. 324.

prevalence of knighthood and knightly culture, since this was what had limited the encroachments on liberty that would otherwise have been possible for an ambitious king. Indeed, it was the political participation of men steeped in chivalry that had helped make the ruler of England more *primus inter pares* than potential tyrant:

> His condition, so far from being despotic, was every moment exposed to danger and insult. He might be deposed for a slight offence. He was elected to his office. And, his coronation-oath expressed his subjection to the community, and bound him to protect the rights of his subjects. The Anglo-Saxon laws are proofs, that, instead of governing by his will or caprice, he was under the controul of a national assembly.[45]

However, Stuart seems to have been acutely aware that this account of medieval constitutional history, grounded in the importance of feudal notions of knighthood and chivalric duty, turned on its head not only the orthodox European historiography of Robertson, but also the notorious claims of Hume about Britain in particular. After all, the latter had argued in the *History of England* that the relative liberty in which eighteenth-century people contentedly basked was the product of recent historical processes, many of them strikingly mundane and most of them also highly contingent: what it was not was the legacy of far-sighted Anglo-Saxon political idealists who had somehow managed to anticipate the Hanoverian House of Commons by more than a thousand years.[46]

Accordingly, Stuart considered that it was in order to add a note on this very point, effectively smearing Hume's critique of ancient constitutionalism by tying it to the controversial writings of the seventeenth-century historian and Royalist apologist Robert Brady:

> To give completeness to the spirit of my present volume, it is sufficient for me to assert the antiquity of the commons, in opposition to an opinion of their late rise, which a modern historian, of great reputation, has inculcated, with that hardiness which he displays in all his writings, but with little of that power of thought and of reasoning which does honour to his philosophical works. Mr Hume, struck with the talents of Dr Brady, deceived by his ability, disposed to pay adulation to government, or willing to profit by a system, formed with art, and ready for adoption, has executed his history upon the tenets of this writer.[47]

Stuart's resolute Teutonism, like so much else in the *View of Society*, thus once again had a powerfully argumentative quality that was carefully attuned to the immediate circumstances in which it was conceived. By resituating feudalism, knighthood and chivalry in an early medieval past inhabited by Anglo-Saxon people familiar with

[45] Ibid., p. 325.

[46] Eugene F. Miller, 'Hume on Liberty in the Successive English Constitutions', *Liberty in Hume's History of England*, ed. Nicholas Capaldi and Donald W. Livingstone (Boston, 1990), pp. 53–104.

[47] Stuart, *A View of Society in Europe*, p. 327.

proto-parliamentarianism and committed to political liberty, he was able to suggest an attractive alternative to the influential account of the Middle Ages offered by a recently-deceased historian whom many contemporaries – especially those of a strongly Whiggish bent – worried had been simply a sly Tory friend of ministerial despotism, even a craven Jacobite stooge for modern absolute monarchy.[48]

Writing more than a decade after the *View of Society* had first appeared, John Pinkerton (a controversial antiquarian with his own even more bizarre theories about the Germanic origins of modern English-speaking people) complained that chivalry, for all the scholarly attention devoted to it in the eighteenth century, remained 'An institution much misunderstood'.[49] Pinkerton does not seem to have had Stuart's work particularly in mind – though he certainly knew the author, claimed to have profited from reading his book, and elsewhere referred fondly to his having enjoyed illuminating personal conversations with 'the late ingenious Dr Stuart'.[50] But his assessment of the general state of the field was surely correct, and to this lack of clarity there can be no doubt that Stuart's thoughts on chivalry, peculiar and deeply contentious as they plainly were, had contributed more than their fair share. 'The writer was prone to controversy,' observed another subsequent commentator, this time the anonymous man responsible for the preface to the posthumous second edition of the *View of Society* when it appeared in 1792.[51] As we can now appreciate, this was a diplomatic understatement by any reasonable standard. Yet as the decision to create a new edition of his work several years after his death also confirms, interest in Stuart's scholarship, and in particular his highly distinctive vision of medieval European society, was actually increasing through the last two decades of the eighteenth century.

When the Edinburgh advocate George Wallace had published his *Thoughts on the Origin of Feudal Tenures, and the Descent of Antient Peerages in Scotland* (1783),

48 These common contemporary aspersions, cast by Thomas Jefferson amongst others, have long been discredited: Ernest C. Mossner, 'Was Hume a Tory Historian? Facts and Reconsiderations', *Journal of the History of Ideas* 2 (1941), pp. 225–36.

49 John Pinkerton, *An Enquiry into the History of Scotland, Preceding the Reign of Malcolm III, Or the Year 1056*, 2 vols (London, 1789), ii, p. 138. On Pinkerton's conviction that the Pictish inhabitants of ancient Scotland were of superior Germanic rather than base Celtic stock, see Colin Kidd, 'Teutonist Ethnology and Scottish Nationalist Inhibition, 1780–1880', *Scottish Historical Review* 197 (1995), pp. 45–68 (esp. 51–4). That Pinkerton's arguments for the 'Gothic' identity of the Picts relied heavily upon fanciful pseudo-translations of Scottish toponyms has hardly helped his subsequent reputation, while the clearly racist assumptions now make his scholarship look positively disreputable.

50 Pinkerton, *An Enquiry into the History of Scotland*, i, pp. lix, lxxvii.

51 Gilbert Stuart, *A View of Society in Europe, in Its Progress from Rudeness to Refinement*, 2nd edn (Edinburgh, 1792), p. iv. Following the first edition of 1778, published in London by John Murray and in Edinburgh by John Bell, which was immediately followed by a Dublin edition, what was misleadingly called the 'second edition' on its title-page but was really just a reprint appeared from Murray in London in 1782 and then again in 1783. A true second edition, supplying the lengthy French and Latin quotations in the original text – supposedly 'inconvenient to almost every reader' (p. v) – with complete English translations, had to wait until 1792 and the enterprise of the Edinburgh publisher James Robertson.

covering large parts of the same ground, he had failed even to mention the *View of Society*; since it is inconceivable that Wallace was not familiar with Stuart's very recent intervention, the only plausible conclusion is that he must have decided that it deserved to be passed over in pregnant silence.[52] During the next decade, nonetheless, the work's profile grew inexorably. Indeed, by the end of the century no fewer than three translations of the *View of Society* had appeared in other European languages, and as late as 1813 another new English edition would be made available.[53] This was evidently testament to certain of its more enduring qualities, which ultimately helped Stuart's work successfully transcend the controversies and preoccupations of the late 1770s in Scotland that had given it such a unique and problematic character. For the depiction of the feudal system as the very foundation of a stable and successful European civilisation throughout the Middle Ages, which had so marked it out from other contemporary studies, had undoubtedly become more rather than less attractive to the public with each passing year. Above all, Stuart's unerring focus on the Germanic origins of medieval and modern society turned out to appeal viscerally to those readers who would soon enthusiastically embrace the Gothic aesthetic of the Romantics, which – in the form of Sir Walter Scott's historical novels like *Ivanhoe* (1820) and *Quentin Durward* (1823), whose leading protagonists were doused in the intoxicating liquor of chivalric heroism – would eventually sweep all before it.[54] In this sense Stuart's greatest misfortune may not in fact have been his failure to acquire the professorial chair at Edinburgh. It was to have been a man before his time – a frustrated scholar of the late Enlightenment who did not live to see his writings about the Middle Ages, which actually spoke more compellingly to the next generation than to his own, finally realise their significant but latent potential.

52 Stuart, now in London, exacted revenge for the calculated insult. In an assessment published in the *English Review* 2 (July 1783), pp. 33–40, Wallace's book was savaged for its slavish attachment to 'the opinions of Dr. Robertson' on medieval history and thus for its author's 'improper doctrines' and 'perpetual mistakes' (pp. 33–4). Since this periodical was Murray's latest venture, Stuart was his amanuensis and the Robertson fixation is, of course, wholly inimitable, the anonymous critic's identity is not hard to guess.

53 A complete German translation was published at Leipzig in 1779, a French translation at Paris in 1789 and another at Basel in 1797. Longman in London and Bell in Edinburgh produced the English version of 1813.

54 Alice Chandler, 'Sir Walter Scott and the Medieval Revival', *Nineteenth-Century Fiction* 19 (1965), pp. 315–32.

2

Creating a 'Medieval Past' for the Swedish Orders of Knighthood

Antti Matikkala

ORDERS OF KNIGHTHOOD (also called orders of chivalry) were first founded in the early fourteenth century and rapidly spread across Europe. Initially these bodies enabled princes to reward service and to promote the loyalty of knights. The orders were important carriers of chivalric tradition, surviving from an era when knighthood had a crucial military role, past the various changes which saw the renegotiation of the place of knights in society, into the early modern period and beyond. From the 1680s a new wave of monarchical orders (focused on the authority of a king or prince) appeared, often veiled in an antiquated disguise of chivalry. These were instituted in order to serve particular national and diplomatic needs in different parts of Europe, and they soon developed into multi-class orders of merit. In terms of institutional development, the case of the orders of Sweden that emerged in the early eighteenth century provides a particularly apt example to consider the way in which chivalry was used to understand the medieval past, and the way in which history was appropriated to provide authority to that present. The Swedish orders, which were principally marks of honour and merit, became a fully-fledged system of pre-modern orders reflecting the concerns of the eighteenth century, while at the same time looking back to the imagined past. The structure of these new orders was based on contemporary French examples, but they also drew heavily on European literature on knighthood and regional motifs from the history of the Baltic region. In a wider sense, the study of the invented past of the Swedish orders tells us about changing attitudes towards historical writing and research, as well as royal and national uses of the past in the search for prestige and glory.

The first three of the modern Swedish orders of merit – the Orders of the Seraphim, the Sword and the Polar Star – were established in 1748. While the Polar Star was presented as a completely new achievement, the other two were given an antiquity that was a deliberate attempt to evoke the authenticity and honour of a long descent from the chivalric medieval past. The senior order was deemed to be 'the age-old Swedish Order of the Seraphim [...] since the dignity of an order is largely dependent on its age', and the military order was called 'the old Order of the Sword', with origins alleged to emanate from the Livonian Order of Sword Brothers. This essay examines how a 'medieval past' was constructed for these Swedish orders. It will first consider how contemporary early modern European writing on knighthood contributed to ideas of the fourteenth-century origins of the Order of the Seraphim; second, how Swedish historical scholarship contributed to those ideas by stretching its origins to the thirteenth century; and, finally, how the fabricated medieval history of the Swedish orders was eventually deconstructed and the consequences of this.[1]

In order to understand the extent of the confusion created by these early modern authors, it is necessary first to briefly outline the relevant facts of the medieval history of the orders, as known to us from current research. D'Arcy Boulton, an established expert on the orders of knighthood, has argued that there is no evidence that any monarchical order existed before 1325, and that no evidence has yet been uncovered for the existence of the Order of the Seraphim before 1748. As such he classifies this order, bearing this name in seventeenth-century antiquarian literature, as a fictive order: that is, a fabricated order with an imagined history.[2] There are, of course, references to the kings of Sweden creating knights from the 1270s, but this is quite distinct from banding them together in a formal body.[3] Until the nineteenth century, some conflation existed between the 'ancient' origins of the Order of the Seraphim and the evidence relating to the early history of Swedish knighthood and dubbing of knights. For example, the earliest reference to a collar with depictions of the heads of angels, which is said to have been given in conjunction with dubbing to knighthood, appeared in 1551 in the will of a Danish nobleman. According to this will, the nobleman's father, Henric Knudsen Gyldenstierne (d. 1517), had received such a collar ('then Guldkæde meth the Engle-Hoveder uthi') at the coronation of King John (Hans) as the king of Sweden in 1497.[4] Later this collar was deployed by historical writers as evidence of a special order of knighthood.

Military-religious orders of knighthood were, of course, an established feature of life in medieval Scandinavia, although very little documentation survives to illuminate their early history. The Order of St John (the Knights Hospitaller) had houses in Denmark, Sweden and Norway. The Teutonic Knights had not only held land in mainland Sweden since the 1260s, but had also established a commandery in Årsta by 1308 (which was sold in 1467) and governed the island of Gotland between

1 For an earlier general discussion of the Swedish pre-1748 'orders of knighthood', which includes some misunderstandings, see Karl Löfström, *Sveriges riddarordnar* (Stockholm, 1948), pp. 97–236.

2 D'Arcy Jonathan Dacre Boulton, *The Knights of the Crown: The Monarchical Orders of Knighthood in Later Medieval Europ. 1325–1520*, 2nd edn (Woodbridge, 2000), p. xi n. 1; D'Arcy Jonathan Dacre Boulton, 'The Monarchical (and Curial) Orders of Knighthood before the Reformation: A Reassessment in the Light of Recent Research', *Les Ordres de Chevalerie: Colloque de la Fondation Singer-Polignac*, ed. André Damien (Paris, 1999), pp. 90 n. 20, 125.

3 On the dubbing of knights in Sweden and Norway until about 1400, see Karl-Erik Löfqvist, *Om riddarväsen och frälse i nordisk medeltid: studier rörande adelsståndets uppkomst och tidigare utformning* (Lund, 1935), pp. 245–79. For the later dubbings, see Karl-Erik Löfqvist, 'Från medeltidens riddarslag till nya tidens riddarutnämningar', *Rig* 22 (1939), pp. 1–16.

4 Oligero Jacobæus, *Muséum regium* (Hafniæ, 1696), p. 70.

1398 and 1408.[5] A new military order was established by the bishop of Riga in 1202, the *Fratres Milicie Christi de Livonia*, known as the Order of Sword Brothers. The Sword Brothers followed the Templar rule and wore the Templar habit with a distinguishing sign: a red cross and a sword, one above the other. In the seal of the order, the sword is depicted as pointing downwards.[6] By a papal bull of 1232, the Sword Brothers were urged to take part in the defence of the Christian faith in Finland against the infidel Rus'ians, but there is no evidence to suggest that they actually did so, and it seems likely that the order did not control any Scandinavian land of its own.[7] However, owing to the central role of the Baltic metropolis Reval/Tallinn, it is likely that there was some kind of contact, 'although the Brothers may never have set foot in' Finland, as John H. Lind has argued.[8] In 1642 Joseph Micheli Márquez in his *Tesoro militar de cavalleria* claimed that there was a further Swedish-founded military order, the Order of the Knights of St Bridget, but despite this being repeated by many subsequent authors, there is no evidence that the order ever existed.[9]

The history of the Order of Sword Brothers as an independent entity was brief: it was subsumed into the Teutonic Order in 1237, becoming its autonomous Livonian branch, the Livonian Order. Even its Scandinavian connections were slight. Prosopographical work on its membership during the period 1237–1562 reveals only one member from Denmark, Sweden and Finland respectively, and some of the information regarding these men is uncertain.[10] One of them, the Swede Johan Elofsson, still styled himself in the 1280s and 1290s as *frater milicie Christi de Liuonia* and *frater de ordine militum Christi*, but his position in the Teutonic Order remains unclear and he is not mentioned in the records of the order.[11]

As a consequence of the Livonian War, the Livonian Order was dissolved in 1561.

[5] Christer Carlsson, 'The Religious Orders of Knighthood in Medieval Scandinavia: Historical and Archaeological Approaches', *Crusades* 5 (2006), pp. 131–42; Birgitta Eimer, *Gotland unter dem Deutschen Orden und die Komturei Schweden zu Årsta* (Innsbruck, 1966). For contact between the Teutonic Order and Finland, see Walther Hubatsch, 'Der Deutsche Orden und Finnland', *Turun Historiallinen Arkisto* 28 (1973), pp. 78–87.

[6] Barbara Bombi, 'Innocent III and the Origins of the Order of the Sword Brothers', *The Military Orders, Volume 3: History and Heritage*, ed. Victor Mallia-Milanes (Aldershot, 2008), pp. 147–53; Friedrich Benninghoven, *Der Orden der Schwertbrüder: Fratres Milicie Christi de Livonia* (Köln, 1965), pp. 54–5.

[7] John H. Lind, 'The Order of the Sword-Brothers and Finland: Sources and Traditions', *Vergangenheit und Gegenwart der Ritterorden: die Rezeption der Idee und die Wirklichkeit*, ed. Zenon Hubert Nowak and Roman Czaja (Toruń, 2001), pp. 159–64; Carlsson, 'Religious Orders of Knighthood in Medieval Scandinavia', p. 131.

[8] Benninghoven, *Orden der Schwertbrüder*, pp. 370–1; Lind, 'Order of the Sword-Brothers and Finland', p. 163.

[9] Hans Cnattingius, 'The Order of the Knights of St. Bridget', *Annales Academiæ Regiæ Scientiarum Upsaliensis – Kungl. Vetenskapssamhällets i Uppsala Årsbok* 2 (1967), pp. 5–35.

[10] *Ritterbrüder im Livländischen Zweig des Deutschen Ordens*, ed. Lutz Fenske and Klaus Militzer (Cologne, 1993), pp. 19–21. The supposed knight from Finland was Hermann Fleming, who has not been identified in any greater detail. Fenske and Militzer argue that his belonging to the Finnish branch of the family is 'probable' because his first name was common in this family. Ibid., pp. 223–4.

[11] Ibid., pp. 203–4; Bengt Hildebrand, 'Johan Elofsson (Johannes Elaui, Elefson, Elepssun)', *Svenskt Biografiskt Lexikon* 13 (1950), pp. 409–12.

Concurrently, Sweden began to conquer northern parts of the order's former holdings. In the early seventeenth century the Swedish realm expanded further south and Livonia became part of it in 1629. Sweden held these Baltic provinces until they were ceded to Russia in 1721. Yet despite very fractured and thin Swedish connections to the Order of Sword Brothers and the Livonian Order in terms of membership, their geographical proximity and the fact that Sweden later came to rule their former lands have rendered the orders as fertile sources for the historical imagination of subsequent writers and later founders of orders of merit.

Before turning to discuss the seventeenth-century accounts of the Order of the Seraphim and the Order of the Sword, one has to bear in mind that, compared with recent scholarship, the early-modern understanding of an order of knighthood was imprecise. The first attempt to provide a classification came in 1502 from the Burgundian courtier Olivier de la Marche, who argued that true orders – like the Burgundian Order of the Golden Fleece – had statutes and a limited number of members, while the false ones or *devises* had neither of these qualities.[12] Thus the main distinction was the existence of a corporate system, or the absence of it: the mere distribution of badges or collars did not constitute an order of knighthood. Boulton's elaborate system of classification recognises distinctions between, for example, the 'closed monarchical confraternal knightly orders' and the 'ceremonial pseudo-orders', like the pre-1725 Knights of the Bath. Nevertheless, in the medieval and early modern world, this rigidity did not exist. For example, the Knights of the Bath were collectively styled as 'Knights of the Antient and Honourable Order of the Bath' in 1661, although they were not incorporated by statutes and lacked permanent administration such as officers.[13] John Anstis, Garter King of Arms, who was the main architect behind the foundation of the Order of the Bath in 1725, pointed out in his own rather strict and idealistic definition that besides a sovereign and knights, an order of knighthood must have statutes and insignia, and the power to nominate and elect new knights as well as to assemble and hold chapters.[14] However, the scholarship of many other seventeenth- and eighteenth-century antiquarians did not match that of Anstis, either in regard to definitions or the use and interpretation of sources.

The Swedish orders made their entry into antiquarian writing on knighthood in the second decade of the seventeenth century. The work of the ecclesiastical historian Aubert Le Mire on the origin of orders of knighthood, first published in Antwerp

[12] Olivier de la Marche, 'Espitre pour tenir et celebrer la noble feste du Thoison d'Or', *Mémoires d'Olivier de la Marche*, ed. Henri Beaune and J. D'Arbaumont (Paris, 1888), iv, pp. 161–3; D'A. J. D. Boulton, 'The Middle French Statutes of the Monarchical Order of the Ship (Naples, 1381): A Critical Edition, with Introduction and Notes', *Mediaeval Studies* 47 (Toronto, 1985), p. 173 n. 20.

[13] Boulton, *Knights of the Crown*, Appendix I: 'A Revised System of Taxonomy for Knightly Orders and Related Nobiliary Bodies', pp. 541–6; Antti Matikkala, *The Orders of Knighthood and the Formation of the British Honours System, 1660–1760* (Woodbridge, 2008), pp. 9–10.

[14] John Anstis, *Observations Introductory to Historical Essay upon the Knighthood of the Bath* (London, 1725), pp. 35–6.

in 1609, did not include any Swedish orders. Nor were they included in its later edition of 1638, despite the same Cologne printer having himself in 1613 published a work on orders of knighthood by the Flemish clergyman Frans Mennens, in which two Swedish orders had been profiled – the *Ordo Equitum Seraphicorum* and the *Ordo Eqvitvm Gladii & Balthei militaris*.[15] Mennens did not provide any information about the age or the founder of the Seraphim, revealing only that, following the example of other Christian princes, the kings of Sweden had instituted military orders. According to Mennens, the golden collar of the 'Order of the Seraphim' consisted of cherubim and seraphim as well as Patriarchal crosses, and was adorned with an 'image of God'.[16]

Figure 2.1 The royal arms of Sweden with the arms of the Vasa dynasty as an inescutcheon encircled with a collar of seraphim, based on a misinterpretation of the Swedish coins struck between 1561 and 1568, in Fransicus Mennenius, *Deliciae eqvestrivm sive militarivm ordinvm, et eorvndem origines, statvta, symbola et insignia*, 2nd edition (Coloniae Agrippinæ, 1638), p. 157.

The misunderstandings were not only literal but also extended to illustrations. The woodcut accompanying Mennens' descriptions (see figure 2.1) depicted the royal arms of Sweden – with the arms of the Vasa dynasty as an inescutcheon – encircled with the described seraphim collar without any pendent figure.[17] It is evident that

[15] Avbertvs Miraevs, *Origines eqvestrivm sive militarivm ordinvm* (Antverpiae, 1609); Avbert Le Mire, *Origine des chevaliers et ordres militaires* (Anuers, 1609).

[16] Fransicus Mennenius, *Deliciae eqvestrivm sive militarivm ordinvm, et eorvndem origines, statvta, symbola et insignia* (Coloniae Agrippinae, 1613), p. 158.

[17] Ibid., p. 157.

this illustration was based on a misinterpretation of a pictorial source, probably the Swedish coins that were struck between 1561 and 1568, which depicted the collar of King Eric XIV's so-called Order of the Saviour (*Salvatororden*), a pseudo-order of knighthood. This collar consisted of alternating seraphim heads and emblems of the Vasa dynasty, the latter of which Mennens mistook for Patriarchal crosses omitting the pendent medallion with the image of the Saviour.[18] According to King Eric himself, the collar was composed of *fleurs-de-lys* and angels' heads ('qui liliis et capitibus angelicis constat'), as he wrote in 1565 when planning to decorate the king of France with this order in an unsuccessful bid to become a knight of the Order of

Figure 2.2 A coat of arms, based on the three crowns of Sweden and encircled with a collar of swords, which illustrated the discussion of the 'Order of the Sword and Military Belt' in Fransicus Mennenius, *Deliciae eqvestrivm sive militarivm ordinvm, et eorvndem origines, statvta, symbola et insignia*, 2nd edition (Coloniae Agrippinæ, 1638), p. 159.

[18] Folke Wernstedt, 'Kungl. svenska riddarordnarna: historisk översikt', *Kungl. svenska riddarordnarna*, ed. H. J. S. Kleberg (Stockholm, 1935), i, pp. 22–3, 26; Nils Ludvig Rasmusson, 'Svenska ordensdekorationer på mynt', *Meddelanden från Riksheraldikerämbetet* 9 (1940), p. 123.

St Michael.[19] There is no evidence of Eric XIV's collar having been conferred by him, and the 'order' had no statutes. The collar is depicted in some of his portraits and a more detailed image of it was available in a woodcut of his arms, but this engraving was not known to Mennens.[20] Eric's order would appear to have been a pseudo-order, closely comparable to the Thistle of the king of Scots.[21]

Mennens also published a fanciful achievement of arms (see figure 2.2) which was, according to him, borne by knights of the Order of the Sword and Military Belt. He had little to say about this order, apart from hinting at a pre-Reformation origin by stating that with the change of religion – from Catholicism to Lutheranism – the order slipped almost into disuse.[22] When discussing the Order of the Seraphim, and with reference to the *Historia de gentibus septentrionalibus* (1555) by Olaus Magnus, Mennens wrote about the coats of arms carved on the rocks of the Gäddtarmen/Hauensuoli natural harbour off Hangö/Hanko on the southern coast of Finland. Here he wanted to associate these rock-carvings with the order, to lend credence to the impression of the order's early origins, despite their complete irrelevance to the Seraphim.

In the same year that Mennens published his work, there appeared another work that referenced the Swedish orders: Pierre d'Avity's *Les estats, empires et principautez du monde*. D'Avity further confused matters by claiming that the port of Hangö/Hanko, which he called the 'stately Port of Angoa' ('le magnifique port d'Angoe ville'), was in South Flanders. In the 1615 English translation, the second of the orders was styled as that 'of the Knights of the Sword and Baudricke [...] called Porte-Espees, or Carrie-swords'.[23] Furthermore, earlier works were influential in their recasting in the mid seventeenth century. For instance, despite the fact that Olaus Magnus, the titular Catholic archbishop of Uppsala, had written nothing about the Order of the Seraphim, his work took on a significance to those writing on the order: Joseph Micheli Márquez (1642), Andrea Mendo (1657) and Gilles André de La Roque (1678) all directed their readers to Olaus Magnus as an authority, apparently without having read what he actually wrote.[24]

André Favyn, the French antiquary and advocate in the High Court of

19 Quoted in Hans Hildebrand, 'Heraldiska studier: I, Det svenska riksvapnet', *Antiqvarisk tidskrift för Sverige* 7 (1884), pp. 73, 83–5.

20 Carl Nordenfalk, 'En svensk vapenbok från 1562: ett nytt dokument till de svenska landskapsvapnens historia', *Meddelanden från Riksheraldikerämbetet* 9 (1940), pp. 86–7. John III, the younger brother and the successor of Eric XIV, altered the design of the collar. The seraphim were omitted but it included angels. Leif Tengström, '*Muschoviten ... Turcken icke olijk*': *ryssattribut, och deras motbilder, i svensk heraldik från Gustav Vasa till freden i Stolbova* (Jyväskylä, 1997), ii, pp. 54–62; Torsten Lenk, 'Johan III:s Salvator och Agnus Dei', *Livrustkammaren* 7 (1955), pp. 25–44.

21 For more on this order, see Katie Stevenson, 'The Unicorn, St Andrew and the Thistle: Was there an Order of Chivalry in Late Medieval Scotland?', *Scottish Historical Review* 83 (2004), pp. 3–22.

22 Mennenius, *Deliciae eqvestrivm*, pp. 159–60.

23 [Pierre d'Avity], *Les estats, empires et principautez du monde* (Paris, 1613), 'Origine des ordres militaires', p. 69; [Pierre d'Avity], *The Estates, Empires, & Principallities of the World*, transl. Edward Grimstone (London, 1615), p. 189.

24 Joseph Micheli Márquez, *Tesoro militar de cavalleria* (Madrid, 1642), [p. 92v]; Andrea

Parliament, was one of the writers who 'were not above inventing information when their sources failed them, and later writers (who seldom did any original research) merely passed on these inventions from one work to the next'.[25] This was, of course, not unusual amongst seventeenth-century antiquarians, who did not suffer from the encumbrances of modern disciplinary standards, and who thought nothing of an intuitive best guess in the absence of confirmed fact. It is these embellishments that were inherited as historical truth by nineteenth-century scholars and that are still being unpicked by historians today. Favyn, in his *Histoire de Navarre* (1612), had written about an extensive number of orders but did not mention anything about the Swedish orders. However, in 1620 Favyn published *Le théatre d'honnevr et de chevalerie* (an English edition was published in 1623), where he informed his readers that 'The Order of Sweden, called of the Name of Iesus, or of the Seraphins' was instituted by King Magnus IV in 1334. The source of this information, Favyn revealed, was the Protestant theologian and cartographer Jacob Ziegler (d. 1549). In turn, Ziegler had Swedish sources who included Johannes Magnus, brother of Olaus Magnus and the last functioning Catholic archbishop of Uppsala, who infamously claimed that Magog had been the first king of Sweden. Favyn's illustration of the collar of the Seraphim was more elaborate than that of Mennens, and included an oval medal charged with the Christogram IHS and four nails as a reference to the passion of Jesus Christ. The collar was said to consist of cherubim and Patriarchal crosses in memory of the *siege Metropolitain d'Vpsale,* meaning the metropolitan see of Uppsala, but mistakenly translated as 'the Siedge laid to the Metropolitane City of Vpsala' in the English edition. Favyn then went on to discuss the details of the insignia of this order, the current location of Christ's nails of Crucifixion, and the details of this method of execution.[26] With regard to later references to Favyn, it is worth observing that he did not claim that any evidence regarding the Order of the Seraphim would have been found in a French monastery; these claims emerged half a century later. Although he had not added much 'historical' information, Favyn's elaborations (such as those to the badge of the order) were significant when the order was finally established in 1748.

During and after the Thirty Years' War, the historiography of the non-existent Swedish orders was much affected by the religious bias of the period. Arguments developed over time. Favyn did not write anything about the abolition of the Order of the Seraphim or refer to the impact of the Reformation on the supposed Swedish orders of knighthood. Instead he commented on the reign of King Gustavus Vasa from a Catholic perspective, by stating that the 'misfortune of misfortunes' happened to him at the beginning of his reign, when 'he was infected by the abominable

Mendo, *De ordinibvs militaribvs* (Salmanticae, 1657), p. 16 ; Gilles André de La Roque, *Traité de la Noblesse* (Paris, 1678), p. 384.

25 Boulton, *Knights of the Crown*, p. xii.

26 André Favyn, *Le théatre d'honnevr et de chevalerie* (Paris, 1620), ii, pp. 1365, 1369–72; Andrew Favine, *The Theater of Honour and Knight-hood* (London, 1623), Booke 7, pp. 244, 246–7 [mispaginated 249]; Iacobus Zieglerus, *Qvae intvs continentvr* (Argentorati, 1532), lxxxv–[lxxxv v].

heresy' of Martin Luther, 'the damnable doctrine' by which several countries were poisoned.[27] Pointedly, this comment was omitted from the English translation.

Despite the steadily growing confusion around the Swedish orders and the contemporary tendency to lack a critical approach, there were some early modern scholars who did seek authoritative evidence in their research. When, for example, Jean-Jacques Chifflet was planning a work on all the orders of knighthood in the world (he had already published an armorial of the Order of the Golden Fleece in 1632), he contacted the legal scholar Johannes Cabiljau/Cabeljauw, who in turn wrote to the Swedish Chancellor of the Realm, Axel Oxenstierna, in 1630.[28] First of all, Chifflet wanted to know how certain the existence was of the Order of the Seraphim. He was also curious about the claim that Magnus IV had founded the Order of the Cherubim in 1334, and wished to know upon what evidence this was based. He asked about the Order of the Sword, the completely unknown Order of the Mount of Olives (*Ordo Montis Oliveti*), 'once attributed to the kings of Sweden', and King Eric's Order of the Saviour that was depicted on his coinage. Chifflet requested extensive detail and wished to know about their origins, foundation dates, meetings and rituals, collars, knightly garments, statutes, development and decline. With regard to the chronology of later investigations, it is interesting to note that Chifflet's list of critical queries was published in 1698.[29] However, it appears to have had little influence on antiquarian enquiries.

Occasionally some early modern writers added a new remark or detail that helped to illuminate the shady origins of the idea that the Swedish orders had antiquity. The suggestion that the Order of the Seraphim ceased to be used after the reign of King Charles IX (1604–11), when Catholic practices had been banished, seems to have been first published in Louvan Géliot's armorial in 1635.[30] Several subsequent authors, such as Father Anselme (Pierre de Guibours, *père* Anselme de Sainte-Marie) in *Le palais de l'honnevr* (1663), repeated Favyn's account but added Géliot's gloss about Charles IX.[31] In fact, rather than having abolished an order, Charles IX had a new collar manufactured for him in 1606; the pendent medal included the Hebrew inscription Jehovah, and thus was sometimes referred to as the Order of Jehovah.[32] The Jesuit Father Silvestro Petra Sancta's contribution to perpetuating the mythology of the Order of the Seraphim was to design a new badge, depicting the Virgin Mary, which was published in *Tesserae gentilitiae* (1638).[33]

Others added further embellishments. Count Majolino Bisaccioni wrote in his *Commentario delle guerre successe in Alemagna dal tempo che il re Gustavo di Svetia* of 1642 that the Order of the Sword was the result of strong 'emulation and imitation

[27] Favyn, *Le théatre d'honnevr et de chevalerie*, ii, p. 1369.

[28] Johannes Cabeljavius to Axel Oxenstierna, 16 March 1630, quoted in Johann Arckenholz, *Mémoires concernant Christine, reine de Suède*, 4 vols (1751–60), iv, pp. 300–1.

[29] Antonius Matthæus, *Veteris ævi analecta*, 10 vols (Lugduni Batavorum, 1698–1710), i, pp. 561–2.

[30] Lovvan Geliot, *Indice armorial* (Paris, 1635), p. 141.

[31] F. Anselme, *Le palais de l'honnevr* (Paris, 1663), p. 162.

[32] Löfström, *Sveriges riddarordnar*, pp. 145–7.

[33] Silvestro Petra Sancta, *Tesserae gentilitiae* (Roma, 1638), pp. 637–8.

of that of Livonia'.[34] The same year, Dr Joseph Micheli Márquez, vice chancellor of the Constantinian Order, whose language and outlook was perhaps even more colourful and inflammatory than that of Favyn, published his *Tesoro militar de cavalleria*. According to Micheli Márquez, *La Orden Militar de las Espadas* had been given 'laudable statutes', but the 'splendour of such an illustrious' order came to an end when the kingdom was 'tyranised by Satan with the depraved sect of Luther'. Whether deliberate or the happenchance of printer's error, Micheli Márquez's discussion of the Swedish Order of the Sword was illustrated with the same woodcut bearing the motto 'PRO FIDE SERVANDA' with which he illustrated the Order of the Sword of the Kingdom of Cyprus. It is hardly surprising that when the Spanish Jesuit Father Andrea Mendo published his book on the military orders fifteen years later, he referred to Micheli Márquez and echoed the view that the Lutheran heresy was to blame for the fate of this order.[35] As Sweden was heavily engaged in religious warfare on the Continent, it was natural for the Catholic propagandists to use every opportunity to argue their case.

In the mid seventeenth century, the influence of Continental works discussing these issues became evident in Sweden. The initials IHS – which eventually became part of the insignia of the Order of the Seraphim in 1748 – had first been connected to a Swedish order of knighthood by Favyn. In 1650 Queen Christina proposed the foundation of the Order of the Sun, or the Order of the Name of Jesus, but members of her council preferred the simplicity and potential legacy of the Order of Christina. It was finally decided to name it the Order of Immanuel, but in the end the project was abandoned.[36] In 1655, IHS became part of the badge of the short-lived pseudo-Order of the Name of Jesus (*L'ordre de la Chevalerie du nom de Iesus*), for which statutes were drafted in 1656.[37] The same year, the Swedish professor Johannes Schefferus published a treatise on ancient collars, where he correctly pointed out that Mennens seemed to have been deceived when he mistook the emblem of the Vasa family for the Patriarchal cross. Later, in his posthumously-published treatise on the Swedish royal arms, Schefferus pointed out that in Swedish history nothing relevant had been handed down from the reign of Magnus IV, but considered it certain that neither had Eric XIV instituted the order.[38]

New but equally unsubstantiated claims about sources relating to the Order of the Seraphim emerged in 1670. Compared to the engraving published by Father Anselme, *Norlandz Chrönika* (1670) includes a somewhat simplified woodcut of the

[34] Maiolino Bisaccioni, *Memorie historiche dalla mossa d'armi di Gustavo Adolfo in Germania l'anno MDCXXX* (Venetia, 1642), Libro Primo, p. 18.

[35] Micheli Márquez, *Tesoro militar de cavalleria*, pp. 87v, 93–93v. For the Cypriot order, see Boulton, *Knights of the Crown*, pp. 241–8; Mendo, *De ordinibvs militaribvs*, p. 16.

[36] Löfström, *Sveriges riddarordnar*, pp. 183–6.

[37] Two different badges of this order have been preserved. King Charles X Gustavus gave the badge of the latter type to his son, the future King Charles XI, whose wearing of it has been documented. Rudolf Cederström, 'Karl X Gustavs Jesu Namns Orden', *Livrustkammaren* 1 (1937), pp. 3–6.

[38] Joannis Schefferus, *De antiquorum torqvibvs syntagma* (Holmiae Svecorum, 1656), p. 20; Joannis Schefferus, *De antiqvis verisqve regni Sveciae insignibus* (Holmiae, 1678–[80]), pp. 167–8.

royal arms surrounded by the Seraphim collar. The accompanying text was written by Daniel Gyldenstolpe, secretary to the powerful *Riksdrots* Count Per Brahe. It referred to *Le palais de l'honneur*, published by a monk, and claimed that this order of knighthood, used in Sweden in former times, had been found again among old documents in a French monastery.[39] Alas, Anselme had not claimed to have found any such new information, but only repeated earlier-published accounts. Neither did Elias Ashmole, Windsor Herald, have anything new to add to the story in his history of the Order of the Garter of 1672, but he pointed out that different accounts of the insignia of the Order of the Seraphim made 'the thing yet more uncertain'.[40] He repeated the Siege (properly, metropolitan see) of Uppsala mistranslation, and besides Favyn, his information came from an established set of authorities: Mennens, d'Avity, Petra Sancta, Micheli Márquez and Mendo.[41] Ashmole found 'mention made of another Order of Knights in Sweden, called of the Sword and Military Belt', but frankly admitted that he was 'not yet informed' 'by whom or when this Order was instituted'.[42] His illustration of its collar, which became influential for the design of the insignia of the real Order of the Sword in 1748, was essentially based on Petra Sancta's idea of combining swords and sword belts, but following Mennens, Ashmole replaced the straight blades with curved ones.[43]

The tradition of circulating these embellished accounts flourished, and while some authors began to ask critical questions, their attempts were hampered by new false information. Abbot Bernardo Giustiniani continued along the traditional Catholic lines in his 'chronological history of the true origin of all orders of knighthood' (1672), but represented the Patriarchal crosses as *bottony*, and placed one of them pendent from the collar; the latter 'information' came from Micheli Márquez.[44] By the time the second edition of his work was published in 1692, Giustiniani had become a Knight Grand Cross of the Imperial Order of St George – the so-called Constantinian Order. Significantly, the 1692 edition included a new critical and comparative discussion of the existing literature. Giustiniani pointed out, for instance, that Olaus Magnus had not said anything about the Order of the Seraphim. Nevertheless, Giustiniani decided to call Magnus IV 'Magnus III', introduced through Ashmole the 'famous siege' ('famoso assedio') mistranslation into Italian, and listed eighteen 'sovereign heads' of the Order of the Seraphim. Giustiniani depicted the badge of the Order of the Sword, a pendant from its collar, as being a downward-pointing sword, and thus 'almost equal' to that of the Livonian Sword

39 Sven Almqvist, *Johann Kankel: Pehr Brahes boktryckare på Visingsö* (Stockholm, 1965), pp. 38–9, 43, 133.

40 Elias Ashmole, *The Institution, Laws & Ceremonies of the Most Noble Order of the Garter* (London, 1672), p. 107.

41 For Ashmole's antiquarian scholarship in the European context, see Vittoria Feola, *Elias Ashmole and the Uses of Antiquity* (Paris, 2012), chapter 5.

42 Ashmole, *Institution*, p. 107.

43 Ibid., p. 107. 'Gothorid. Archont. Cosm.'(i.e. Johan Ludwig Gottfried's *Archontologia cosmica*) included d'Avity's description.

44 Bernardo Givstiniano, *Historie cronologiche della vera origine di tvtti gli ordini eqvestri e religioni cavalleresche* (Venetia, 1672), pp. 364–8.

Brothers.[45] However, he did cast some doubt on the information concerning this order, and because 'evident truth' was not available he left the question undecided, while exposing Micheli Márquez's error concerning the insignia of the Cypriot order.[46]

The peculiar idea that Gustavus Vasa had both restored the Order of the Seraphim and established the Order of the Sword appeared in the late seventeenth century. It seems to have been first published by the Italian Calvinist Gregorio Leti, who was known for his anti-Catholic works, in *Il Ceremoniale historico e politico* (1685).[47] Since it was considered self-evident that the orders of knighthood had been instituted for the defence of the Catholic religion, many subsequent authors wrote that Gustavus Vasa had established the Order of the Sword for this purpose against the doctrine of Luther. This was ironic, since it was he who introduced the Protestant reformation in Sweden. After he was elected a Knight of the Order of St Michael in 1543, Emperor Charles V returned his collar as a protest against the election of heretics.[48] In the course of the seventeenth century, the legendary Swedish orders were firmly rooted in the European corpus of antiquarian writing on knighthood. While authors generally passed on the same scant 'information', these accounts were coloured by the religious division between Catholics and Protestants. The Catholics lamented the destruction caused by Lutheranism in Sweden, and publishers in Protestant countries omitted inconvenient comments. Occasional critical questions raised by scholars did not yet bear the fruit of a fully-fledged critical enquiry. Trust in the often-printed word remained strong and the more critical minds, such as Chifflet, did not have the opportunity to penetrate into the question more deeply.

During the 1690s, the 'ancient' orders of knighthood became more topical in Sweden than ever before, both in historical-antiquarian scholarship and in European power-political diplomacy.[49] The issue of evidence for these early orders was first raised by Field Marshal Count Erik Dahlbergh in 1690 when he was preparing his great pictorial work, *Suecia antiqua et hodierna*. He considered that ancient orders would 'be to no slight glory for our fatherland' and provided Claudius Örnhjälm, Historiographer Royal, with transcripts of books, asking his opinion about them. In his first reply, Örnhjälm pointed out that he 'had no knowledge whatsoever' of the Order of the Sword.[50] A more detailed critical scrutiny followed in 1693, but remained unpublished until 1817. It has been regarded as 'a document distinguished by its critical perspicacity' and reliance 'entirely on primary sources'.[51] Although

[45] Bernardo Givstinian, *Historie cronologiche dell'origine degl'ordini militari e di tvtte le religioni cavalleresche*, 2 vols (Venezia, 1692), ii, pp. 640–2, 646.

[46] Ibid., ii. p. 642.

[47] Gregorio Leti, *Il Ceremoniale historico e politico*, 6 vols (Amsterdamo, 1685), iii, p. 638.

[48] Peter Vetter, 'Der französische Ritterorden vom Heiligen Michael (1469–1830)' (unpublished Ph.D. thesis, Rheinische Friedrich-Wilhelms-Universtität zu Bonn, 1979), p. 45.

[49] For a more detailed discussion, see Antti Matikkala, 'Gustaf Adlerfelt, Orders of Knighthood and Charles XII', *Perspectives on the Honours Systems*, ed. Antti Matikkala and Staffan Rosén (Stockholm, 2015), pp. 13–45.

[50] Cnattingius, 'Order of the Knights of St. Bridget', p. 20.

[51] Ibid., p. 21.

Figure 2.3 The insignia of the Swedish orders according to Elias Brenner (1691). The Royal Library, National Library of Sweden.

Örnhjälm did not deny the existence of the 'ancient Swedish orders', he was the first Swedish historian to tackle the question more thoroughly.[52] To begin with, Örnhjälm demonstrated that the Swedish knights appeared 'not to have called themselves after any particular order', nor to have used insignia such as those depicted in the reproductions provided to him by Dahlbergh.[53] Furthermore, he did not believe that those Swedish knights who were known from Swedish historical sources would have been knights of the Order of Sword Brothers. However, even Örnhjälm was

52 Ibid., p. 21.

53 Claudius Örnhjälm, *'Om de äldre Svenska Riddare-orden', Handlingar rörande Skandinaviens Historia 3 (1817), p. 135.*

confused enough to write that when Eric XIV 'renewed the Order of the Seraphim', he replaced the Patriarchal crosses with his family emblem.[54] With the authority of a field marshal, Dahlbergh dismissed Örnhjälm's critical observations and proceeded with the production of the plate, which was completed in 1694. According to it, the Order of the Seraphim was instituted in 1334 or 1343. Dahlbergh's illustration of the collar of the Order of the Sword or the Military Belt was essentially copied from Ashmole. The layout of Dahlbergh's plate followed the one produced by the numismatist Elias Brenner in 1691 (see figure 2.3), but differed in details. Dahlbergh dated all the 'orders' except the Order of the Sword.

In Swedish academia, the first general discussion on orders of knighthood was completed in 1696, when Gustaf Adlerfelt defended a thesis on knights and orders of knighthood under the presidency of Professor Petrus Lagerlöf at the University of Uppsala. Its account of the Orders of the Seraphim and of the Sword summed up much of the existing European and Swedish knowledge, but dismissed the information referring to Gustavus Vasa and Eric XIV.[55] However, Örnhjälm's survey appears to have been unknown to the author. Despite the limited factual contribution, the thesis provided yet another – and significantly both Swedish and academic – point of reference.

The following year, the 'ancient' Swedish orders made their entry into power-political diplomacy in discussions of the court circles in Sweden. After the death of King Charles XI in 1697, when his Garter insignia had to be returned, Jean-Antoine de Mesmes, Count d'Avaux, French ambassador to Sweden and Provost-Master of Ceremonies of the French orders of knighthood, conceived a plan whereby the possible appointment of Charles XII as a Knight of the Garter could be prevented. He proposed that Charles XII should 'restore an ancient Swedish order or [...] establish a new one'.[56] In keeping with the idea that knowledge is power, d'Avaux apparently delighted in playing the civiliser's role. Shortly before the coronation of Charles XII, he reported having heard that Princess Hedvig Sofia had complained that 'the negligence and indolence of the Swedes was extraordinary; that no one had told her that the kings of Sweden had previously had orders; that it was from me that she learned about them. She testified a great desire that the king, her brother, would re-establish them.'[57] However, Charles XII did not do so – probably (or at least partly) in order to maintain an appearance of independence from foreign influence.

Meanwhile, on the Continent, Christian Gryphius observed in 1697 that while many authors had disseminated their views on the Order of the Seraphim widely enough, it had 'no foundation' among the Swedish authors.[58] The same year, Adriaan Schoonebeek pointed out that it was not possible to determine with certainty

[54] Ibid., pp. 139, 152–3.

[55] Peter Lagerlööf (præs.) – Gustavus Carlson Adlerfelt (resp.), *Equites sive de Ordinibus Equestribus Disquisitio* (Holmiæ, 1696), pp. 58–62.

[56] *Négociations de Monsieur le comte D'Avaux, ambassadeur extraordinaire à la cour de Suède, pendant les années 1693, 1697, 1698*, réd. J. A. Wijnne, 3 vols (Utrecht, 1882–83), ii, p. 158.

[57] Ibid., ii, pp. 369–70.

[58] [Christian Gryphius], *Kurzer-Entwurff Der Geist- und Weltlichen Ritter-Orden* (Leipzig, 1697), p. 179.

the year in which the order was founded. With reference to Brenner's engraving, the 1699 French translation of Schoonebeek's work included a discussion of Eric XIV's Order of the Saviour and John III's Order of the Lamb of God. Regarding the former, Schoonebeek wrote that arguments that it was a renewal of the Order of the Seraphim were not at all likely to be accurate, since the collars were totally different – but he lamented that, owing to the negligence of the Nordic authors, 'we do not have certain evidence of the facts'.[59] Indeed, the contribution of Swedish antiquarian scholarship in the form of Brenner's and Dahlbergh's engravings reinforced the historiographical position of the legendary orders, as they endorsed the 'information' about Continental origin.

Similar legends about a medieval origin surrounded the Danish Orders of the Elephant and of the Dannebrog. The latter had been founded in 1671, but according to its history, written by Thomas Bartholin in 1676, it had been established by Valdemar II in commemoration of the occasion when the Danish flag, *Dannebrog*, fell from the sky during his crusade in Estonia in 1219. In 1706, Janus Bircherod argued that the Order of the Elephant originated from the Crusades and considered the possibility that it was founded in 1188.[60] In the context of the longstanding Swedish–Danish rivalry, the desire to stretch the history of the Swedish orders back to the thirteenth century, if not quite surpassing the age of the Danish orders, becomes understandable. Sweden and Denmark had been parts of the Kalmar Union (1397–1523), which was broken in a war that the Swedish regarded as the War of Liberation. Even after this, the two countries had waged war on each other at almost every opportunity. Besides outright warfare, the two northern kingdoms maintained animosity in the field of symbolic politics. The king of Denmark kept the three crowns of Sweden in his coat of arms even after the break-up of the Kalmar Union in 1523, which incited Eric XIV to add the three Danish lions to his. The high ordinal numbers of the Swedish kings, based on the list of mythological kings provided by Johannes Magnus, were also meant to enhance the antiquity of the kingdom. With regard to orders of knighthood in particular, a lengthy dispute of precedence between the kings of Sweden and Denmark as Knights of the Garter had ensued over the position of their stalls in St George's Chapel in 1670.[61] According to Johan Peringskiöld's genealogy of the Swedish kings, which begins with Magog and was posthumously published in 1725, King Magnus III Barnlock (r. 1275–90) established the Order of the Cherubim, with which his son Birger was knighted in 1279, but many subsequent authors, such as Baron Shering Rosenhane in his 1789 roll of Swedish kings, came to favour 1285 as the foundation year.[62]

[59] Adriaan Schoonebeek, *Historie van alle ridderlyke en krygs-ordens*, 2 vols (Amsterdam, 1697), ii, pp. 183, 283; Adrien Schoonebeek, *Histoire de tous les Ordres militaires ou de Chevalerie*, 2 vols (Amsterdam, 1699), ii, pp. 182, 286, 296, 298.

[60] Janus Møller Jensen, *Denmark and the Crusades, 1400–1650* (Leiden, 2007), pp. 321–31.

[61] Matikkala, *Orders of Knighthood and the Formation of the British Honours System*, pp. 192–4.

[62] Joh. Peringskiöld, *Ättartal för Swea och Götha konunga hus* (Stockholm, 1725), p. 74; Shering Rosenhane, *Svea-rikes konunga-längd* (Stockholm, 1789), p. 25.

A failed proposal to establish orders of knighthood had been made in 1738 by a nobleman who belonged to the French-oriented Hat Party, which had gained political power and advocated closer European connections for Sweden. Matters finally moved forward in 1747.[63] A proposal written by Baron Anders Johan von Höpken, but signed by Director General Baron Carl Hårleman, was submitted to the Secret Council in September 1747. It was argued that the senior order should be 'the age-old Swedish Order of the Seraphim' ('den urgamla Swenska Seraphine Orden'), 'since the dignity of an order is largely dependent on its age', and the military order, 'the old Order of the Sword' ('den gamble Swerds Orden').[64] With similar arguments, the Secret Council forwarded the memorandum to the king in December 1747.[65] The argument about the age of the order contributing to its prestige was sound, since the disposition of some of the compendia on orders of knighthood was chronological. For instance, in the 1692 edition of Giustiniani's chronological history of orders of knighthood, the discussion of the Swedish orders preceded that of the Order of the Garter.[66] Therefore, it appeared advantageous for the northern kingdom, which had only recently lost its position as a great power, to attempt to enhance its symbolic status by reviving an ancient order rather than establishing a new one. Accordingly, by the statutes promulgated in 1748, the king of Sweden decided to 'resurrect the Order of the Seraphim, well-known and honoured in the North, and to give it back its former esteem'.[67] The statutes asserted that the Order of the Sword had been 'a decoration for those who had with honour drawn their swords for the Fatherland' from 'the time immemorial'. Therefore, the king decided 'again to take and dedicate it for the same use'.[68] In combination with other French characteristics, such as the *cordon bleu* from the Order of the Holy Ghost, the collar of the new order was based on Favyn's collar and his medal provided the basis for the centre medallion of its cross.

Compared to the warrant of James VII of Scotland and II of England for a patent by which he claimed to revive and restore, but in fact instituted, the Most Ancient and Most Noble Order of the Thistle in 1687, the 1748 statutes of the Swedish orders were quite circumspect with regard to the details of the history of the two senior orders. According to the Scottish warrant, Achaius, king of Scots, instituted the Order of the Thistle 'in commemoration of' his 'signal victory [...] over Athelstan, King of the Saxons, after a bloody battle' during which St Andrew's cross appeared in the heavens. By appealing to 'the general consent of ancient and modern historians' and 'several other authentic proofs, and documents, and records of that Kingdom', James

[63] Tom C. Bergroth, '"En egen Swensk Riddare Orden": Kring instiftandet av ett ordensväsende i Sverige år 1748', *Livruskammaren* (1997–98), pp. 3–90, is a thorough account of the foundation of the Swedish orders in 1748.

[64] Quoted in Ernst E. Areen and Sten Lewenhaupt, *De nordiska ländernas riddarordnar*, 3 vols (Eskilstuna, 1942), i, p. 13.

[65] Ibid., i, pp. 16–17.

[66] Givstinian, *Historie cronologiche* (1692), ii, pp. 639–43.

[67] The king signed the statutes on 21 March but they were antedated to 23 February. Bergroth, '"En egen Swensk Riddare Orden"', p. 26.

[68] *Kongl. Maj:ts Nådiga Förordning Angående Trenne Riddare Orden Gifwen i Stockholm i Råd-Kammaren then 23. Februarii 1748* (Stockholm, 1748).

VII was 'most certain' of the historical information contained in the warrant.[69] Two decades before the foundation of the Swedish orders, in 1725, King George I had decided to 'institute, erect, constitute, and create a military Order of Knighthood' called the Most Honourable Order of the Bath. The institution of this order was also represented as a revival, but – unlike the case of the Thistle or the non-existent Swedish orders – there had been a real practice of creating Knights of the Bath at coronations, which was merely given an elaborate institutional framework in 1725.[70] Overall, this highlights both the early-modern conceptual ambiguity and the use of similar rhetorical strategies by those reviving orders in different parts of Europe that sought to appeal to a real or imaginary past.

The politically motivated institution of the Swedish orders received expedient academic support. However, the scholarly apparatus which accompanied it was less well orchestrated than the publication of Anstis's treatise, *Observations Introductory to an Historical Essay upon the Knighthood of the Bath*, which had appeared in time to coincide with the inaugural installation of the Order of the Bath. Nevertheless, two academic dissertations were directly linked to the institution of the Swedish orders. On 14 December 1748, Johan Pehr Höppener defended a thesis, *Dissertationis historicæ de ordinibus equestribus*, at the University of Lund under the presidency of Professor Sven Bring, who was later ennobled and took the name Lagerbring. The thesis was appropriately dedicated to Count Carl Gustaf Tessin, the *primus motor* behind the foundation and the first chancellor of the Swedish orders. Since the thesis had discussed only foreign orders, Höppener intended to expand it to cover the Swedish orders too. His immediate plans were halted since, on 19 December 1748, Henrik Rosenstierna defended a thesis entitled *Dissertatio historica de ordinum equestrium in Svecia usu antiquo et hodierno* under the presidency of Olof Celsius, professor of history at the University of Uppsala. This thesis was dedicated to Prince Adolphus Frederick, elected heir to the Swedish throne. The nobleman Rosenstierna had no further plans for historical studies and he entered into a military career the following year. Celsius himself was a loyal supporter of the ruling Hat Party, and his appointment to the professorship has been regarded as a political reward.[71] Initially, the foundation of the orders augmented the political power of the nobility: the appointments were to be made in the state council, so the king had two votes and each of the counsellors one. A majority of two-thirds was required. At the accession of Adolphus Frederick in 1751, the king gained full power in his orders.[72]

The discussion of the 'medieval' Swedish orders in the Celsius–Rosenstierna

[69] *Statutes of the Most Ancient and Most Noble Order of the Thistle, Revived by His Majesty King James II of England and VII of Scotland and again revived by Her Majesty Queen Anne* (Edinburgh, 1978), pp. 1–2. The most comprehensive discussion of the 'ancient' origin of the Order of the Thistle is the one by Peter Galloway, *The Order of the Thistle* (London, 2009), pp. 1–39.

[70] *Statutes of the Most Honourable Order of the Bath* (London, 1725), p. iv.

[71] Nils Eriksson, *Dalin – Botin – Lagerbring: Historieforskning och historieskrivning i Sverige 1747–1787* (Göteborg, 1973), p. 24.

[72] Bergroth, '"En egen Swensk Riddare Orden"', pp. 77–80; Areen and Lewenhaupt, *Nordiska ländernas riddarordnar*, i, pp. 29–33, 151–2, 227.

thesis was the most thorough since Örnhjälm. It used the evidence relating to Gyldenstierne's collar and argued that it was the most obvious example of knights of the Order of the Seraphim having been created by the old kings of Sweden. However, the thesis showed that the collar depicted on the tomb of King Magnus Barnlock in the Riddarholm Church in Stockholm had been carved only during the reign of John III. The orders of Eric XIV and of the subsequent kings were connected under the same heading, as if they were part of the story. Despite some attempts at critical analysis, and an admission of the silence of the Swedish sources and the equal uncertainty of the information relating to Magnus IV, the thesis offered timely scholarly support for the revival of the orders. Tellingly, Peringskiöld was considered to be highly skilled. In a similar vein, King Magnus Barnlock was said to have first introduced the *insigne* of this 'most ancient' order. The account of the Order of the Sword surveyed the information about Swedish connections to medieval religious knighthood, mentioning St Bridget's (*Birgitta*) son, Birger Ulvsson, who had been dubbed a Knight of the Holy Sepulchre in Jerusalem in the 1370s; it also referred to medieval authors, according to whom many Swedes would have been admitted to the Order of Sword Brothers. While Celsius did not believe that the Swedish order was derived from the Livonian one, he considered it clear that it had given its name to the recently-established order.[73]

The poet and former royal librarian Olof Dalin, who was ennobled as von Dalin in 1751 and appointed Historiographer Royal in 1755, published the second volume of his history of Sweden in 1750. In this work Dalin, who had no academic degree, effectively combined the legends about the Orders of the Sword and of the Seraphim. According to Dalin, King Magnus Barnlock knighted his three-year-old son Birger as a Knight of the Order of the Sword or of the Cross (*Svärds eller Kors-orden*) in 1284. Dalin traced this order as having been introduced much earlier in Sweden, explaining that it came from Rome, Cyprus and Jerusalem via Prussia and Livonia, or directly from the Holy Land. According to Dalin's description, the insignia of this order consisted of a sword (or two crossed swords), together with a star, a knightly belt, a golden collar and spurs. Furthermore, Dalin was of the opinion that the distinguishing sign of this great order could not have been anything other than cherubim and seraphim.[74] With this description, the government's future official historian offered a more colourful, fabricated version of the history of the newly-established orders, in order to enhance their prestige by connecting them to the Crusader orders of the Holy Land. By providing an elaborate chivalric antiquity, this appeared more appealing than simply writing that a military order of merit had been founded two years ago.

In the meantime, in 1750 Höppener returned to the topic of his dissertation of 1748, when he entered into the service of the Swedish State Archives. The result

[73] O. Celsius (præs.) – Henricus Rosenstierna (resp.), *Dissertatio historica de ordinum equestrium in Svecia usu antiquo et hodierno* (Upsaliæ, 1748), pp. 47–66. The work was published under the title *Schediasma historicum, de ordinum equestrium in Svecia usu antiquo et hodierno* (1749).

[74] Olof Dalin, *Svea rikes historia*, 3 vols (Stockholm, 1750), ii, pp. 289–90.

was an illustrated treatise, more than five hundred pages long, entitled 'Riddare och Riddare Orden' (Knights and Orders of Knighthood), which has remained unpublished.[75] Höppener's manuscript was presented to the Chapter of the Order of the Seraphim on 29 April 1754. At the Chapter meeting, Chancellor Count Tessin announced that, before publication, Höppener must obtain censorship approval from the Chapter. As the Chapter found 'a thing or two' to which to object, Tessin proposed that the Chancery Board would arrange the censorship. The Chapter resolved that the matter would be presented to the king, but effectively the project seems to have ended there.[76] It is likely that Höppener's fairly open critique of the current Swedish honours policy contributed to this.[77]

Höppener admitted that the information about the Swedish men, who had probably carried their arms under the sign of the Order of Sword Brothers, had vanished into the past, but he referred to the earlier-mentioned Johan Elofsson. Although Höppener acknowledged that nothing was known about the founder, laws, establishment or dubbings of 'our old Order of the Sword', he regarded the information about its collar as undeniable and was of the opinion that this order had been founded long before the reign of Gustavus Vasa. While Höppener wrote that the titled knights and badges of the Orders of the Seraphim, the Sword, and of St Bridget were in Sweden before the Reformation, after which they disappeared, he was rather critical in his survey of the existing antiquarian literature on knighthood. He correctly pointed out that in 1670 Gyldenstolpe had been the first Swede to write about the Order of the Seraphim, and he listed the fallacies of Mennens, Favyn and other writers, such as the account of the Hangö/Hanko harbour, the true origin of the collar illustrated by Mennens, and the illustration techniques of Micheli Márquez. Although Höppener admitted the difficulty of proving or disproving statements about the age of the Order of the Seraphim, he was certain that there was no evidence of Magnus IV having established it, and he dismissed the putative historical testimony of the sarcophagus of King Magnus Barnlock.[78]

Höppener went on to consider it more likely that Magnus Barnlock had established the Order of the Seraphim at the time of his coronation (1276), since an item that Höppener interpreted as 'a sign of a titled knight' was depicted on his garment in his seal. Later, this was interpreted as a 'lozenge-formed clasp or jewel'.[79]

[75] It exists in three manuscript copies: Stockholm, The Royal Library, National Library of Sweden, D 257; Uppsala, Uppsala University Library, H 429; and Gustavianska samlingen F 526.

[76] Kungl. Maj:ts Ordens arkiv [The Archives of the Swedish Royal Orders of Knighthood], Protocol of the Chapter, 29 April 1754. I am grateful to Tom C. Bergroth, Curator of the Royal Orders of Knighthood, for providing a photocopy of the protocol.

[77] The higher Commander classes of the Orders of the Sword and of the Polar Star were not opened for non-nobles until 1809. Considering opinions according to which noblemen could become knights, Höppener wondered why should someone 'ennobled by nature and virtue be precluded from the highest reward of virtue'. Johan Pehr Höppener, 'Riddare och Riddare Orden' [hereafter Höppener, 'Riddare och Riddare Orden'], Stockholm, The Royal Library, National Library of Sweden, D 257, fol. 66.

[78] Ibid., fols 133–4, 362–4, 366–81, 389–91, 394–5.

[79] Ibid., fols 381–2; H. Fleetwood, *Svenska medeltida kungasigill* (Stockholm, 1936–47), i, p. 54.

Höppener knew that the Patriarchal crosses were a misinterpretation of the emblem of the Vasa dynasty; nevertheless, he ventured to write about Patriarchal crosses that appeared in the letters and seals of the Eskilstuna Priory of the Order of St John, arguing that the Order of the Seraphim could probably trace its first origin to the 'holy journeys'. Höppener then abandoned his search for the origin of the Order of the Seraphim, which he admitted was 'buried in the deep hiding places of the old age'. When turning to discuss the different interpretations of the insignia, Höppener regarded Favyn and Anselme as being on the 'most reliable ground although they otherwise run on snow'. While being capable of this kind of criticism of earlier antiquarian literature, Höppener still based his arguments on the shakiest of foundations.[80]

Despite such slight attempts at a more critical approach, the legend of the 'medieval' origins of the Orders of the Seraphim and of the Sword lived on; indeed, it fared rather well during the course of the eighteenth century. Gabriel Bethén, who in 1770 published – with the financial support of the Chapter of the Royal Orders of Knighthood – the first work on orders of knighthood in Swedish, still argued that the origins of the Order of the Sword lay in the Order of Sword Brothers, 'as will be better shown'.[81] However, the contemplated second volume of Bethén's work, which would have discussed the Swedish orders, never appeared.[82] The imagery of the medieval Sword Brothers was further invoked in the Order of the Sword when King Gustavus III – on the occasion of initiating a war on Russia – established a new special dignity in 1788 of Knight Grand Cross. Besides a neck badge, an upright silver sword was adopted as the unique insignia of this special class. Its warlike character was enhanced by the stipulation that it could be given only during war to commanding officers after a victory.[83] In his general history of Sweden, Lagerbring maintained the position of his former pupil Höppener, declaring it 'quite likely' that Magnus Barnlock had instituted the Order of the Seraphim, and he regarded Favyn's illustration of the collar as correct.[84]

Two years later, in 1790, Adolf Fredrik Ristell – who had a varied career in the world of culture as royal librarian, author, critic, translator, playwright and theatre director – published a book entitled *Characters and Anecdotes of the Court of Sweden*, after having fled his native country for England following his bankruptcy. Ristell was confident that the Order of the Seraphim was 'the most antient as well as the most honorable', and he assured his readers that this order 'is mentioned and described in Swedish acts so far back as the thirteenth century'. However, he expressed doubts as to whether it was 'of Swedish institution' or had 'been introduced in that country with the many strangers of birth and distinction who frequented the Court of King Magnus Birgersson, on the occasion of the splendid tournaments given by that

[80] Höppener, 'Riddare och Riddare Orden', fols 383–8.

[81] Gabriel Bethén, *Ordens- och Riddare-Historien* (Stockholm, 1770), pp. 51–2.

[82] Bo Bennich-Björkman, *Författaren i ämbetet: studier i funktion och organisation av författarämbeten vid svenska hovet och kansliet 1550–1850* (Stockholm, 1970), p. 320.

[83] Löfström, *Sveriges riddarordnar*, pp. 307–8.

[84] Sven Lagerbring, *Swea rikes historia*, 4 vols (Stockholm, 1769–83), ii, pp. 698, 700 n. 4; iii, p. 278.

magnificent Prince'. In Ristell's story, the order fell 'into disuse' during the union of the three northern kingdoms, until 'King Fredericus re-established this antient Order as well as that of the sword'.[85] 'The Order of the Sword is also very antient in Sweden,' Ristell argued, adding that it 'was introduced perhaps from Livonia and Prussia', and he mentioned an attempt by King Eric XIV 'to restore this Order to its former consideration'.[86]

Following the conventional wisdom, many popular authors continued to give 1334 as the foundation year of the Order of the Seraphim, but in the official discourse, the older origins were preferred.[87] When opening the Chapter of the Orders in November 1794, the younger brother of the murdered King Gustavus III, Prince Carl, Duke of Södermanland, told the assembled knights that the badge of the Order of the Seraphim had already been used in the 'ancient times' ('Forntiden') by King Magnus Barnlock as the 'highest stamp of true merits for the Fatherland', and that 'the age-old' ('urgamla') Order of the Sword, which had acquired a merited and everlasting reputation 'on the shores of Livonia', had been renewed as a Swedish order.[88] However, a more enlightened approach emerged in the late eighteenth century. Jean-Pierre Catteau-Calleville, who had been a pastor in Stockholm, pointed out in 1790 that 'several learned Swedes' had 'exercised their erudition on this point of history', but that it was 'certain that it was king Frederic who, in 1748, gave' the Order of the Seraphim 'its present form, and framed the statutes of it'.[89] Thus, the Age of Reason began to reason that no evidence meant no evidence.

The early nineteenth century witnessed both a new interest in the origins of the Swedish orders, partly occasioned by the change of dynasty, and a new emphasis on the ever more sophisticated use and interpretation of available sources. However, at the same time, the belief in the 'ancient' origin of the Order of the Seraphim and the literal meaning of the royal statutes remained deeply rooted. The duke of Södermanland became king as Charles XIII in 1809, but since he had no surviving children, Jean Baptiste Bernadotte, Marshal of France, was elected heir-presumptive to the Swedish throne in 1810. Although Prince Carl Johan, as he became known in Sweden, was formally a crown prince until 1818, the government of the country was soon effectively in his hands owing to the infirmity of the king. As was later recounted by the royal librarian Pehr Adam Wallmark, who had been entrusted with the task of teaching Swedish to the crown prince, Carl Johan expressed his desire to acquaint himself with the history of the Swedish orders. Since the orders were at the king's disposal and a part of his 'symbolic capital', it was quite natural for Carl Johan

[85] [A. F. Ristell], *Characters and Anecdotes of the Court of Sweden*, 2 vols (London, 1790), ii, pp. 256–8.

[86] Ibid., p. 264.

[87] Hugh Clark, *A Concise History of Knighthood: Containing the Religious and Military Orders which Have Been Instituted in Europe*, 2 vols (London, 1784), ii, pp. 213, 217; John Payne, *An Epitome of History; or, a Concise View of the Most Important Revolutions and Events*, 2nd edn, 2 vols (London, 1795), i, p. 38.

[88] 'Tal, hwarmed Hans Kongl. Höghet Hertigen af Södermanland öpnade Ordens-Capitlet den 24 sistledne November', *Dagligt Allehanda* 271 (1794).

[89] [Jean-Pierre] Catteau[-Calleville], *A General View of Sweden* (London, 1790), pp. 180–1.

to want to know about their history, and Charles XIII commissioned a treatise on the Swedish orders. In particular, Charles was interested in ascertaining whether the Order of the Seraphim was really the one distributed by King Magnus Barnlock at the inauguration of St Clare's Priory in Stockholm. According to Wallmark, it took a great part of the winter of 1811 for him to prepare the treatise. However, the short time allotted to the project did not permit such extensive studies as the topic required. In 1822, Wallmark published a Swedish version of his treatise in a journal he edited, as 'an attempt to reconcile the different views on the age of the Order of the Seraphim'. Wallmark apparently considered his 'historical researches on the ancientness and the first founder of the Order of the Seraphim' still valid in 1843, when he published the French translation of his treatise in the journal of the Belgian Archaeological Academy, of which he was an honorary member.[90]

Wallmark's treatise was rather carefully formulated and fairly critical of earlier accounts. He pointed out that it would always be difficult to determine 'the uncertain time of the foundation of an older order', owing to the fact that earlier authors had often confused different types of knighthood, either from a lack of knowledge of the subject or from a desire to give a greater age to their order.[91] Wallmark was on the right trail when he wrote that, of the current European orders, none was older than c.1350. He considered it natural that the founder of an order should appropriate as much of the past as possible, and he was eager to employ the old forms for the new purpose. In one important point the Swedish and French versions of Wallmark's text differ. Whereas he wrote in the Swedish original that, on the basis of Gyldenstierne's will, 'one wishes to conclude' ('Af detta dokument will man sluta') that the Order of the Seraphim existed in Sweden in 1497, according to the French translation we can conclude this 'with all historical certainty' ('avec tout le certitude historique'). Indeed, Wallmark pointed out that descriptions of the dubbings of knights from the thirteenth to the fifteenth century did not mention anything of the nature of an order to have been distributed.[92] Therefore, the certainty expressed in the French

[90] Clara Wallmark, *Pehr Adam Wallmark: en tidsbild från adertonhundratalets första hälft* (Stockholm, 1914), pp. 59–62; [P. A. Wallmark], *Promemoria rörande Kongl. bibliothekets behof af ökadt biträde för dess samlingars ordnande och katalogiserande: Utdrag ur ett till Hofkanslers-embetet, den 19 sistlidne december afgifvet utlåtande af bibliothekarien* (Stockholm, 1840), p. 11. In a later autobiography, published in 1852, Wallmark revealed that in 1817 he received a request from the Chancery Board to write, on the basis of historical sources, a report on the age of the Order of the Seraphim. Since Wallmark wrote that this request was based on the king's command and caused by the crown prince's wish to receive such a work, it seems likely that he was here mistaken about the year; he was also mistaken in claiming that his French article was published in 1844. P. A. Wallmark, 'Wallmark, Peter Adam', *Biographiskt lexicon öfver namnkunnige svenska män*, 23 vols (Uppsala, 1835–57), xi, p. 462; [P. A. Wallmark], 'Försök att förena de olika meningarna om Serafimer-Ordens ålder', *Allmänna Journalen* 228, 232, 233, 235, 238 (1822), n.p.; P. A. Wallmark, 'Recherches historiques sur l'ancienneté et le premier fondateur de l'Ordre de Séraphins, principal ordre équestre en Suède', *Bulletin et annales de l'Académie d'archéologie de Belgique* (1843), i, pp. 145–6, 148–9, 163.

[91] [Wallmark], 'Försök att förena', *Allmänna Journalen* 228; Wallmark, 'Recherches historiques', p. 148. The original Swedish text has been generally prioritised.

[92] [Wallmark], 'Försök att förena', *Allmänna Journalen* 228; Wallmark, 'Recherches

version gives a misleading picture of Wallmark's views, and speaks to the pliability of argument and veracity.

Preserving important items of clothing as 'a perpetual memorial' of Sweden's warlike past had been given an institutional form with the foundation of the Royal Armoury in 1628. The State Archives had been regulated a decade earlier, but much of the collection was lost in a fire in 1697. The academies founded in the course of the eighteenth century also directed interest in the Swedish past, but there was still a concern for the preservation of manuscripts. In 1815, a committee was founded in Sweden for the publication of privately-owned historical manuscripts, part of a wider interest in preserving and disseminating the national past. It started to publish its series, *Handlingar rörande Skandinaviens Historia*, the following year and was formalised as the Society for the Publication of Manuscripts concerning Scandinavian History in 1817, adding the prefix 'Royal' to its name in 1821. The driving force behind the foundation of this society was Baron Adolf Ludvig Stierneld, a prominent courtier and collector of manuscripts, but also a 'forger on a large scale'.[93] Stierneld's falsifications extended to his own family history and resulted in a claimed descent from an illegitimate son of King Eric XIV. Stierneld had an enhanced interest in the Royal Orders of Knighthood through his son, Algernon, who, in his twenties, began his career in the Royal Orders of Knighthood as herald of the Order of the Sword in 1814–16. He became sub-chancellor *en survivance* in 1818, secretary in 1829 and finally treasurer in 1832, an office which he held until his appointment as a Knight of the Order of the Seraphim in 1838, when he was minister for Foreign Affairs.[94] Stierneld, who had gilded his own pedigree with false gold, wished to apply the same kind of treatment to the orders his son had started to serve as an officer.

The extensive publication activity during the early years of the new manuscript society was not, on the whole, source critical and was marred by the printing of genuine historical manuscripts in conjunction with fabricated sources. The earlier-discussed Historiographer Royal Örnhjälm's 1693 treatise was printed in the third volume of *Handlingar rörande Skandinaviens Historia* in 1817. It was appended to another manuscript, 'Uttåg om then Cherubim och Seraphim Orden', which was said to come from Dalin's collection and was in Stierneld's library when Wallmark consulted it. Wallmark pointed out that its age and authenticity could not be more precisely determined. It is a fanciful account of a tournament, said to have been held in Stockholm in 1285, when knights were dubbed and King Magnus Barnlock instituted the Order of the Cherubim and Seraphim: the king knighted his son Birger and presented him with a golden collar with angels' heads in the presence of a Knight Templar.[95] In fact, the anonymous manuscripts with the claimed Dalin–

historiques', pp. 145–6, 149–50.

93 Paul Sjögren, 'Erland Hjärne om Adolf Ludvig Stierneld som historieförfalskare', *Nordisk tidskrift för bok- och biblioteksväsen* 6 (1980), p. 15.

94 Per Nordenvall, ed., *Kungliga Serafimerorden 1748–1998* (Stockholm, 1998), p. 252.

95 'Uttåg om then Cherubim och Seraphim Orden', *Handlingar rörande Skandinaviens Historia* 3 (1817), pp. 156–62. Stierneld had provided Örnhjälm's 'original letter' for Wallmark, but Wallmark observed that the alternative claim for a foundation year of 1285 seemed to have been inserted afterwards. [Wallmark], 'Försök att förena', *Allmänna Journalen* 228, 233; Wallmark, 'Recherches historiques', pp. 151, 158 n. 1.

Stierneld provenance, which were published in the early volumes of *Handlingar rörande Skandinaviens Historia, were probably written by Stierneld himself around 1800. More manuscripts relating to medieval knights with the* Stierneld provenance were published in 1842.[96] Evidently the chivalric medieval past, however contrived, resonated with the values of early nineteenth-century Sweden.

It was clear for Wallmark that Magnus Barnlock had not established a particular order of knighthood, although there was evidence of his having created knights. As the views of Peringskiöld, Celsius and Dalin were not supported by any historical evidence, Wallmark considered that their testimony lacked authority. Since the dissertation by Celsius was published in the same year that the Order of the Seraphim was 'renewed' and on the occasion of that event, Wallmark considered it plausible that Celsius's patriotism had required him to make the order as old as possible, following the literary mode of the time. However, even Wallmark was confused enough by the story of the French monastery to consider it possible that a collar given by King Magnus II (i.e. IV) to the French noblemen in the suite of his wife, Queen Blanche of Namur, could have survived in France to Favyn's time.[97]

In his conclusions, Wallmark noted that he had demonstrated the insufficiency of the historical evidence that attributed the foundation of the Order of the Seraphim to King Magnus Barnlock in the hitherto generally accepted sense, which would include a special oath, statutes and insignia. Despite legitimately doubting the evidence of Stierneld's false document, Wallmark nevertheless carefully argued that if Magnus Barnlock had given a collar similar to the current one when dubbing knights, he could, in that case, be 'said to have been the first one, who dubbed Knights of the Seraphim'. Wallmark aspired to save a tradition that he considered venerable, since it had been 'propagated by so many excellent men', while also finding a way of reconciling the two different views about the true rise of this knightly dignity.

The interest in the 'ancient' origins of the Order of the Seraphim culminated with *Seraphimer Ordens historia: första tidehvarfvet ifrån år 1285 till år 1748* ('The history of the Order of the Seraphim: the first era from the year 1285 to 1748') by Lieutenant General Gustaf Wilhelm af Tibell, which was published by the Press of the Royal Orders of Knighthood in 1826. The author was a Commander Grand Cross of the Order of the Sword, who was elected an honorary fellow of the Royal Academy of Letters, History and Antiquities in the same year that he published this work on the pre-history of the Order of the Seraphim. Having been ennobled in 1805, af Tibell was created a baron in 1827. The volume produced by af Tibell was in a way a by-product of his work of collecting old Swedish military statutes, which he had begun in 1819.[98]

As af Tibell pointed out, only a few previous authors had sought to separate

[96] P. Wieselgren, 'Rörande medeltidens riddareväsen', *De la Gardiska Archivet eller handlingar ur Grefl. De la Gardiska bibliotheket på Löberöd* (Lund, 1842), xvi, pp. 228–38.

[97] [Wallmark], 'Försök att förena', *Allmänna Journalen* 232, 233, 238; Wallmark, 'Recherches historiques', pp. 155–7, 161, 168.

[98] Inge Jonsson, 'Akademikern Gustaf Wilhelm af Tibell: grundare av Kungl Krigsvetenskapsakademien', *Kungl. Krigsvetenskapsakademiens handlingar och tidskrift* 210 (2006), pp. 52, 54, 61–3.

factual 'historical wisdom' from fanciful supposition based on ancient legends. In this regard, af Tibell found that Höppener's 1754 manuscript and Wallmark's 1822 article were especially useful. When referring to the earlier-mentioned spurious manuscript, 'Uttåg om then Cherubim och Seraphim Orden', af Tibell pointed out that one could not know whether its information was based on older historical documents or merely on ancient folklore. However, following Örnhjälm, he believed that the collar illustrated by Favyn had been changed by Eric XIV, and he dismissed Höppener's correct argument about the origin of Favyn's collar, supporting Wallmark's idea that it might have been based on a real collar. The general regarded the information about the Order of the Sword as nothing more than 'loose stories', not based on any historical information, but he thought that 'a private corporation of Knights of the Sword' ('ett enskildt Svärds-Riddare-Samfund') may have existed in Sweden. Thus, af Tibell's approach heralded a growing tendency that required a more critical methodology, interrogation of sources and clearer definitions.[99]

By the standards of the day, af Tibell's discussion of pre-1748 Swedish knighthood was rather subtle. Out of the 208 pages of his book, 56 were devoted to a list of early Swedish knights. As af Tibell correctly pointed out, the names of some of the orders, such as that of the Garter, had changed. It was also easy for him to find instances of orders that had been revived. However, considering the amount of accurate information readily available, which provided no tenable support for the medieval origins of the Seraphim, the conclusion at which he arrived is astonishing: that Frederic I only *revived* an old institution. Just as the warrant of James VII of Scotland and II of England for 'reviving' the Order of the Thistle had referred to 'the general consent of ancient and modern historians', af Tibell referred to the opinion of 'all foreign authors' with regard to the name and insignia of the Order of the Seraphim. Despite his learning, such was af Tibell's veneration of regal authority that he took the phrases of the royal documents, referring to the revival of an 'age-old' order, in their literal sense. A medieval past provided authenticity and authority to the order, so uncritical assumptions were convenient. Yet, aware of the limitations of his research, af Tibell ended his discussion with a wish that a more skilled hand would correct the flaws of his work and write the history of the following era.[100]

Accounts of the medieval origins of the Orders of the Seraphim and of the Sword had a remarkable longevity. As late as 1725, the conventionally accepted foundation year of the former (1334) was taken back to 1285. Critical voices were ignored and some of the later historians and writers were misled by false evidence. Nobody who had claimed that the origins of the Order of the Sword lay in the Livonian Sword Brothers was able to offer any tenable explanation as to how an order which had been merged into the Teutonic Order and had only slight connections to Sweden could have become a Swedish royal order. The veracity of the legendary Order of the Sword was finally laid to rest by af Tibell, but by publishing his work in 1826 the Swedish Royal Orders of Knighthood still promoted the view that the Order

[99] G. W. af Tibell, *Seraphimer Ordens historia: första tidehvarfvet ifrån år 1285 till år 1748* (Stockholm, 1826), pp. [5], 14–15, 39–40, 97, 99, 119–20.

[100] af Tibell, *Seraphimer Ordens historia*, pp. 9, 133–40.

of the Seraphim had first been founded in 1285. As late as 1880, a standard work on Swedish constitutional law referred to af Tibell and Celsius with regard to the 'older orders of knighthood in Sweden', but was critical enough to point out that no special Swedish Order of the Sword can be demonstrated to have been instituted during the Middle Ages, and that it was also unfounded to claim that Gustavus Vasa would have instituted it.[101]

It was left to the State Antiquarian Dr Hans Hildebrand finally to conclude that the medieval origins of the Order of the Seraphim belonged to the realm of fable, and that the whole approach of the seventeenth-century literature on the orders had been misleading.[102] As a researcher who based his studies on an immense array of material – published and unpublished sources, as well as material heritage – and who subjected research literature and source publications to critical scrutiny, Hildebrand wanted 'to emphasise, once and for all, the absurdity of the claimed high age of the Order of the Seraphim', and he demolished af Tibell's arguments by showing that they were preposterous.[103]

In many respects, the pre-history of 'the most antient as well as the most honorable' Order of the Seraphim, as it was called by Ristell in 1790, was similar to that of the Most Ancient and Most Noble Order of the Thistle. With regard to the latter, Peter Galloway has observed that Mennens and Favyn 'produced accounts that did much to stimulate interest in an Order that never existed'.[104] The same applies to the Swedish orders. While the Order of the Seraphim did not exist before 1748 in any meaningful sense of the word, the cumulating corpus of European literature and the depictions of Eric XIV's collar provided the basis around which the 'ancient' history of the order could be woven in a very loose manner. For the Catholic authors it was convenient to argue for the pre-Reformation origins of the Swedish orders – both because it was considered self-evident that an order of knighthood must have been instituted for the defence of the Catholic religion, and in order to lament the destruction caused by Lutheranism. For their part, some Swedish authors followed to the extreme their patriotic agenda to enhance the dignity of their supposed orders. The story of the 'medieval' Swedish orders of knighthood is thus a combination of misunderstandings, religious propaganda, gradual accumulation of false information, deliberate confusion in concepts, blind belief in the printed word and wilful misinterpretation of historical facts for the sake of the prestige of the kingdom. Yet it is also a story of continuous attempts to deconstruct false information, and thereby a story of the gradual advancement of knowledge, albeit one with many setbacks.

[101] Christian Naumann, *Sveriges statsförfattningsrätt*, 4 vols (Stockholm, 1876–84), ii, pp. 302, 305 n. 1.

[102] Hans Hildebrand, 'Heraldiska studier: I', pp. 73, 84.

[103] Hans Hildebrand, *Sveriges medeltid: kulturhistorisk skildring*, 3 vols (Stockholm, 1879–1903), ii, pp. 211–14.

[104] Galloway, *The Order of the Thistle*, p. 19.

3

'Hung Round with the Helmets, Breast-Plates, and Swords of our Ancestors': Allusions to Chivalry in Eighteenth-Century Gothicism[1]

Peter N. Lindfield

> Methinks there was something respectable in those old hospitable *Gothick* Halls, hung round with the Helmets, Breast-Plates, and Swords of our Ancestors; I entered them with a Constitutional Sort of Reverence, and look'd upon those Arms with Gratitude; and the terror of former Ministers, and the Check of Kings. Nay, I even imagin'd that I here saw some of those good Swords, that had procur'd the Confirmation of the *Magna Charta*, and humbled *Spencers* and *Gavestons*. And when I see these thrown by, to make Way for some tawdry Gilding and Carving, I can't help considering such an Alteration as ominous even to our Constitution. Our old *Gothick* constitution had a noble Strength and Simplicity in it, which was well enough represented by the bold arches, and the solid pillars of the Edifices of those Days. And I have not observed that the modern Refinements in either have in the least added to their Strength and Solidity.[2]

Gothic architecture largely fell out of favour with architects and those commissioning architectural works in seventeenth-century Britain. It was supplanted by Classicism, and this aesthetic preference continued into the eighteenth century. However, the Gothic style remained a monument to Britain's militaristic, medieval and chivalric past, as indicated by the passage above from 1739 in the *Gentleman's Magazine*.[3] The Gothic Revival in Georgian Britain was linked with social, political and religious history, and was charged with various connected

1 Anon, 'Common Sense', *The Gentleman's Magazine* 9 (1739), p. 641.

2 Ibid. The parallels between this and the 'romantic interior' identified by Wainwright are striking: Clive Wainwright, *The Romantic Interior: The British Collector at Home 1750–1850* (London, 1989), pp. 1–5.

3 See also John Bonehill, 'Antiquities', *Paul Sandby: Picturing Britain*, ed. John Bonehill and Stephen Daniels (London, 2009), pp. 154–5.

meanings, including nationalism, dynastic heritage, political freedom, barbarism and rebellion.[4] It was also intimately connected with chivalry's visual language of heraldry, as well as its historic architecture, based, in part, upon St George's Chapel, Windsor, and Henry VII's Chapel, Westminster Abbey, both of which were and remain the chapels for the Most Noble Order of the Garter (founded by Edward III in 1348) and the Most Honourable Order of the Bath (founded by George I in 1725) respectively.[5] However, the Gothic Revival's connection with the ideas, associations and visual language of chivalry is more complex, especially because it jostles with the Revival's other connotations that centre upon barbarity and the debasement of Roman (Classical) architecture. Despite this complexity, a number of important Gothic Revival houses and interiors were erected and created in eighteenth-century Britain. These demonstrate a palpable interest in and visual representation of the architecture, motifs, figures and visual language of chivalry. The extent to which Gothic's chivalric overtone was adopted into mainstream fashionable taste in this period is explored here through the common use of architectural motifs and heraldic imagery, concentrating especially on furniture. This essay explores the tensions between Classicism and the Gothic, assesses the place of chivalry in the eighteenth-century Gothic Revival, and questions how chivalric overtones were incorporated into fashionable consumption.

In the eighteenth century, Gothic architecture was an historic, but simultaneously current, style. It was both sternly criticised and promoted, and was intimately connected with debates over aesthetics, taste and identity. In contrast to Italy, which preserved the remains of ancient Classical architecture revived by Renaissance architects, including Filippo Brunelleschi (1377–1446), Britain's architectural heritage meant that the Gothic style could not be ignored or sidelined because of its omnipresence throughout towns and the countryside. This legacy had a tangible impact upon one of Britain's most important seventeenth-century architects. Sir Christopher Wren (1632–1723) assumed a mostly critical attitude towards medieval architecture and instead advocated Classicism, which can be seen most prominently in his designs for St Paul's Cathedral, London (1675–1710).[6] In March 1662 he became Surveyor of the King's Works.[7] This official position meant that Wren was directly responsible for maintaining a number of Gothic buildings, including Westminster Abbey. And rather than following his preference for Classical architecture, Wren felt it necessary to embrace the Gothic style of architecture so that his repairs and modifications would match the existing medieval fabrics.[8]

4 Samuel Kliger, *The Goths in England: A Study in Seventeenth and Eighteenth Century Thought* (New York, 1972); R. J. Smith, *The Gothic Bequest: Medieval Institutions in British Thought, 1688–1863* (Cambridge, 1987), pp. 71–100.

5 The vault of Strawberry Hill's State Apartment (referred to as the Gallery) and Arbury Hall's Saloon were based upon that in Henry VII's Chapel: see Michael Snodin, 'Going to Strawberry Hill', *Horace Walpole's Strawberry Hill*, ed. Michael Snodin (London, 2009), p. 45; Michael McCarthy, *The Origins of the Gothic Revival* (London, 1987), p. 145.

6 John Summerson, *Architecture in Britain, 1530–1830* (London, 1993), pp. 203–21.

7 Howard M. Colvin, ed., *The History of the King's Works* (London, 1976), v, pp. 19–38.

8 See Arthur T. Bolton and H. Duncan Hendry, ed., *The Wren Society* (Oxford, 1934), xi, pp. 9–31.

An uneasy embrace of the mode is noticeable in Tom Tower above the St Aldate's gate of Christ Church, Oxford (1681–82), where he 'resolved [that] it [the tower] ought to be Gothick to agree with the Founder's Worke'.[9] By eschewing the mixture of architectural traditions and approximating Cardinal Wolsey's architecture, Wren avoided the creation of heterogeneous buildings such as the Classical nave of 1740–43 that Henry Flitcroft (1697–1769) added to the fourteenth-century tower at St Mary's Church, Stoke Edith, Hertfordshire. Wren's handling of Gothic design was conditioned not by a deep-rooted reverence for Britain's national style of architecture and its associations, but by aesthetic awareness and the desire to avoid stylistic conflict.

So whilst Classical architecture was considered sophisticated and appropriate for other modern buildings, such as the Banqueting House in London (1619–22) and the Sheldonian Theatre in Oxford (1664–69), an awareness of the native Gothic style was also important.[10] Gothic, irrespective of its varied reception, was familiar in eighteenth-century Britain.[11] Erecting new houses and, to a lesser extent, follies in the Gothic rather than Classical mode – unlike Wren's Gothic additions in Oxford – was a noticeable and important statement that spoke of particular intentions, including the owner's 'taste', interests and family history, or, on occasion, the lack thereof. To this end, Samuel Kliger, in his seminal study of the Revival, noted that Gothic was part of

> what may be called 'Whig aesthetic' [and] represents an eighteenth-century system of critical apologetics or a new canon of taste in which Tories and Whigs, in accordance with their respective political principles, found themselves divided in their judgements on the qualities in a work of art which constitute beauty.[12]

Georgians were certainly divided about how to interpret Gothic architecture, and this varied reception was dependent upon individuals' understanding of the style.

The revived interest in Gothic design meant that numerous architects who favoured Classical architecture, and not just Wren, were also responsible for designing Gothic structures and interiors. Nicholas Hawksmoor (c.1661–1736)

9 See Arthur T. Bolton and H. Duncan Hendry, ed., *The Wren Society* (Oxford, 1928), v, p. 17. Wren also made repairs in the Gothic style to the Divinity School and Duke Humphrey's Library, Oxford. Oxford, Bodleian Library, MS 907, fols 13–14.

10 Writing of the Sheldonian Theatre, Wren's son remarked that it would have 'been executed in a greater and better Style, with a View to the ancient Roman Grandeur discernable in the Theatre of Marcellus at Rome; but [Wren] was obliged to put a Stop to the bolder Strokes of his Pencil, and confine the Expence within the Limits of a private Purse', Wren, *Parentalia: Or Memoirs of the Family of the Wrens* (London, 1750), p. 335. See also Anthony Geraghty, 'Wren's Preliminary Design for the Sheldonian Theatre', *Architectural History* 45 (2002), pp. 275–88.

11 See Thomas Cocke, 'The Wheel of Fortune: The Appreciation of Gothic Since the Middle Ages', *Age of Chivalry: Art in Plantagenet England 1200–1400*, ed. Jonathan Alexander and Paul Binski (London, 1987), p. 185.

12 Samuel Kliger, 'Whig Aesthetics: A Phase of Eighteenth-Century Taste', *English Literary History* 16:2 (1949), p. 135.

devised sections of All Souls College, Oxford (1716–35), William Kent (c.1686–1748) designed Esher Place, Surrey (c.1733), and James Wyatt (1746–1813) was responsible for a number of Gothic houses, including Lee Priory in Kent (c.1785) and Fonthill Abbey in Wiltshire (1796–1812).[13] The burden of tradition meant that even whilst some commentators and patrons considered the style unfashionable, or even barbaric, it could not be, and was not, entirely ignored.[14] This is because individuals or bodies specifically embraced Gothic so that structures and interiors would convey particular associations, ranging from conformity to chivalry (as at All Souls), and aspects of England's cultural past (as at Fonthill Abbey).

The stylistic heterogeneity resulting from a conscious deviation from current, Classical fashions precipitated discussions on 'taste' – or, rather, on 'correct taste' – by architects, the landed gentry and moral philosophers in British periodicals, including the *Gentleman's Magazine* and the *World*, and larger, single-volume publications. It centred upon the conflict between the 'domestic' legacy of the Middle Ages and the prevailing preference for Classical architecture, partly inspired by the Grand Tour of the Continent. The debate surrounding the taste for Gothic, whilst multi-faceted, sheds light on its historical associations and various meanings. Anthony Ashley Cooper, the third earl of Shaftesbury (1671–1713), explored this in 1711:

> Our *State* [...] may prove perhaps more fortunate than our *Church*, in having waited till a national Taste was form'd, before these [parliamentary] Edifices were undertaken. But the Zeal of the Nation cou'd not, it seems, admit so long a Delay in their Ecclesiastical Structures, particularly their *Metropolitan*. And since a Zeal of this [Classical] sort has been newly kindled amongst us, 'tis like we shall see from afar the many Spires arising in our great City, with such hasty and sudden growth, as may be the occasion perhaps that our immediate Relish shall be hereafter censur'd, as retaining much of what Artists call the *Gothick* Kind.[15]

Shaftesbury presents the choice between Classical and Gothic as absolute, and implies that Gothic is a traditional style, for its retention would not harness a foreign country's architecture. However, most of the forty-seven churches Wren designed for London following the Fire of London in 1666 circumvented this tradition.[16]

[13] See Vaughan Hart, *Nicolas Hawksmoor: Rebuilding Ancient Wonders* (London, 2007), pp. 58–60; Peter N. Lindfield, 'Serious Gothic and "Doing the Ancient Buildings": Batty Langley's *Ancient Architecture* and *Principal Geometric Elevations*', *Architectural History* 57 (2014), pp. 147–9; Peter N. Lindfield and Matthew Reeve, '"A Child of Strawberry": Thomas Barrett and Lee Priory, Kent', *The Burlington Magazine* (2015), pp. 836–42; and John Martin Robinson, *James Wyatt (1746–1813): Architect to George III* (London, 2012), pp. 233–8.

[14] See *Age of Chivalry*, ed. Alexander and Binski, pp. 362–3, 367–81.

[15] Anthony Ashley Cooper, Earl of Shaftesbury, *Characteristicks of Men, Manners, Opinions, Times* (London, 1737), iii, p. 401. 'A Letter Concerning Design' was written in 1711 but not published widely until the 1732 edition of *Characteristics*.

[16] See Howard Colvin, *A Biographical Dictionary of British Architects, 1600–1840*, 3rd edn (London, 1995), pp. 1093–97.

Shaftesbury, consequently, lamented the decline of the Gothic at the hands of Classical architects, including Wren:

> As for Architecture, 'tis no wonder if so many noble Designs of this [Gothic] kind have miscarry'd amongst us; since the Genius of our Nation has hitherto been so little turn'd this way, that thro several Reigns we have patiently seen the noblest publick Buildings perish (if I may say so) under the Hand of one single Court-Architect [Wren].[17]

Both passages, taken from Shaftesbury's 'Letter Concerning Design', highlight the contemporary conflict between Gothic and Classical architecture. They suggest that a stylistic counter-discourse on tradition and cultural expectations was alive at the start of the eighteenth century, and they cement Gothic's status as Britain's historical and traditional form of architecture.

This preference for Gothic architecture in Georgian Britain can be located within political thought. Samuel Kliger suggested this conflict arose because of political influence from the Whigs and Tories, but the situation was less straightforward than his assessment suggested.[18] For example, the Tory politician Sir Roger Newdigate (1719–1806), fifth baronet, should, on the evidence, have been a staunch supporter of Classical architecture. Newdigate encouraged the benefaction of the Pomfret marbles (which formed part of the Arundel collection of ancient Greek sculpture) by the Countess of Pomfret to the University of Oxford in 1755. He also likened Classical architecture to 'Corinthian elegance, [which is] more perfect, more distinct' than the 'considerable scars [... of] Gothic majesty'.[19] Nevertheless, his enduring legacy was the refurbishment and enlargement of the Newdigate family seat – Arbury Hall, Warwickshire (1748–96) – in the Gothic mode, which reinforced his noble family lineage.[20] When trying to understand the adoption of architectural styles, the third earl of Shaftesbury used a cultural approach: he separated the supporters of the two architectural traditions into those who valued Britain's old Gothic architecture for its historical associations, which should be 'retained', and those promoting the hasty adoption of a foreign (Classical) one.[21] This helps explain why Newdigate's Arbury Hall was based upon something more than political affiliation, and why he funded modifications in the Gothic style at University College, Oxford.[22] The intentional adoption of Gothic design could be based upon political thought, but at least equally influential were individuals' interests in the style itself, and the historical past from which it originated and to which it referred.

17 Shaftesbury, *Characteristicks*, iii, p. 400.

18 Samuel Kliger, 'The "Goths" in England: An Introduction to the Gothic Vogue in Eighteenth-Century Aesthetic Discussion', *Modern Philology* 43:2 (1945), pp. 107–17.

19 Warwick, Warwickshire County Record Office, Newdigate MS B2539, fol. 1.

20 Roger Newdigate, *The Correspondence of Sir Roger Newdigate of Arbury, Warwickshire*, ed. A. W. A. White (Stratford upon Avon, 1995), pp. 76–9; McCarthy, *Origins of the Gothic*, pp. 117–20, 128–39 ; Will Hawkes (ed.), *The Diaries of Sanderson Miller of Redway* (Stratford upon Avon, 2005).

21 Cooper, *Characteristicks*, iv, p. 41.

22 Oliver Cox, 'An Oxford College and the Eighteenth-Century Gothic Revival', *Oxoniensia* 77 (2012), pp. 117–36; McCarthy, *Origins of the Gothic*, p. 133.

Nevertheless, regard for medieval architecture and its cultural meanings could be entirely overlooked by some commentators. Alexander Gerard (1728–95) framed the choice between the Gothic and Classical styles in terms of aesthetics in *An Essay on Taste* (1759). Despite failing to establish any universal principles, he unilaterally criticised Gothic:

> The profusion of ornament, bestowed on the *parts*, in *Gothic* structures, may please one who has not acquired enlargement of mind, sufficient for conceiving at one view their relation to the *whole*; but no sooner is this acquired, than he perceives superior elegance in the more *simple* symmetry and proportion of *Grecian* architecture [...] WHERE refinement is wanting, taste must be coarse and vulgar.[23]

Gerard sidestepped the inescapable bond between Gothic architecture and British architectural, political and cultural heritage, as championed by Shaftesbury, and instead concentrated upon Classicism's enlightened principles of refinement and strength.[24] Isaac Ware's entry on Gothic in *A Complete Body of Architecture* (1756) similarly attacked the mode and, together with Gerard's text, is representative of pro-Classical thought in eighteenth-century Britain:

> Gothick: A wild and irregular manner of building, that took place of the regular antique method at the time when architecture, with the other arts, declined. The *Gothick* is distinguished from the antique architecture, by its ornaments being whimsical, and its profiles incorrect. The inventors of it probably thought they exceeded the *Grecian* method, and some of late have seemed, by their fondness for *Gothick* edifices, to be of the same opinion; but this was but a caprice, and, to the credit of our taste, is going out of fashion again as hastily as it came in.[25]

These passages demonstrate that moral philosophers and architects in eighteenth-century Britain legislated against Gothic as a credible taste. The whimsicality of ornament and irregular manner of building were singled out as problematic. Given that architects, designers and commentators shared a common, forceful and well-articulated criticism of medieval architecture, those willing to adopt and adapt the style to erect a new Gothic building in Georgian society certainly required a robust reason to do so.

Despite sustained derision, Gothic architecture possessed powerful and positive associations, which were wholeheartedly embraced during the eighteenth century and ultimately conditioned the very premise of its revival, at least for those interested in, and willing to evoke, ideas connected with medieval England. Gothic remained prominent in Britain's architectural and historical landscape, and endured

[23] Alexander Gerard, *An Essay on Taste* (London, 1759), pp. 122–7.

[24] Ibid., p. 23.

[25] Isaac Ware, *A Complete Body of Architecture: Adorned with Plans and Elevations, from Original Designs* (London, 1756), pp. 19–20.

in buildings that were recast as monuments to events in Britain's past.[26] Westminster Abbey and provincial cathedrals such as Gloucester, Winchester and Worcester provided a Gothic environment for the remains of Britain's medieval monarchy, nobility and knights. Even with the addition of Classically-styled tombs or sculptural decoration such as William Kent's work on the choir screen at Westminster Abbey (1731–33), Gothic architecture and British history remained interwoven and this architectural mode quickly came to represent an established narrative of the nation's past.[27] Topographical surveys from the eighteenth century underscore this point and include Samuel and Nathaniel Bucks' *Perspective Views of the Ruins of the Most Noted Abbeys and Castles of England* (1726–39), and Paul Sandby's *The Virtuosi's Museum; Containing Select Views, in England, Scotland, and Ireland* (1778). The Bucks published numerous volumes on medieval architecture over the course of thirteen years, and sixty-one per cent of the plates in Sandby's *Museum* concentrated on medieval structures. Although lampooned, the various manifestations of Gothic architecture were, as today, inescapable throughout Britain.

Gothic architecture's connection with the residuum of medieval royalty and the knightly class, itself a prominent link to chivalry, was one of its defining boons. But it was also an obstacle to its revival, as these Gothic monuments were mostly Catholic. Between the failed Jacobite risings (1715, 1745 and 1759) and the Catholic emancipation (or Roman Catholic Relief Act of 1829), any association with Catholicism was considered dangerous in eighteenth-century Britain and was a customary attack used in contemporary politics. David Stewart has developed this interpretation by arguing that Gothic architecture had an important political-religious role in the eighteenth century:

> In the context of the '45, ruins stood as a threat or moral reminder to those who would rebuild the past, as [ruined Gothic follies] stood as a sign of Whig power to an opposition that feared the political ruin associated with accusations of Jacobitism.[28]

This potential connection between Gothic Revival architecture and Catholicism, outside the context of ruinous follies, is illustrated by Strawberry Hill (1747–70s), the Gothic villa in Twickenham designed by Horace Walpole (1717–97) and his male associates.[29] In his letters, Walpole appeared to embrace the idea of echoing the styles of Catholicism when creating his 'little Gothic castle'. Parts were staffed with appropriately monastic imagery: 'I was going to tell you that my little house is so monastic, that I have a little hall decked with long saints in lean arched windows and

[26] Seventeenth – and eighteenth-century responses to surviving medieval buildings are explored in B. Sprague Allen, *Tides in English Taste 1619–1800: A Background for the Study of Literature* (New York, 1958), ii, pp. 47–9.

[27] See Julius Bryant, 'Exempla Vertutis: Designs for Sculpture', *William Kent: Designing Georgian Britain,* ed. Susan Weber (London, 2013), pp. 554–9.

[28] David Stewart, 'Political Ruins: Gothic Sham and the '45', *The Journal of the Society of Architectural Historians* 55:4 (1996), pp. 403–4.

[29] See George E. Haggerty, 'The Strawberry Committee', *Horace Walpole's Strawberry Hill,* ed. Michael Snodin (London, 2009), pp. 80–6.

with taper columns'.[30] Even before entering the house, this Catholic air was tangible. Passing through the great north gate:

> the first object that presents itself is a small oratory inclosed with iron rails; in front, an altar, on which stands a saint [actually a de-winged angel] in bronze; open niches, and stone basons for holy water [...] On the right hand is a small garden called the abbot's garden.[31]

Yet, despite the clear and sustained allusions to Catholicism and Catholic nomenclature, Walpole ever so slightly distanced his house and its interior from Rome. The Tribune, based upon the Chapter House at York Minster, for example, had 'all the air of a Catholic chapel – bar consecration'.[32] So whilst the Tribune looked, felt and gave the impression of being Catholic, it was not.

Eighteenth-century landowners – both aristocrats and merchants who possessed country house estates in imitation of aristocrats – erected Gothic eye-catchers, or follies, on their country house estates. A number had Gothic structures, particularly castles, designed and constructed as 'new ruins'. Their style and ruinous condition directly implied age and could convey extra symbolism, including the destruction of the Gothic past and, in particular, that the present had overcome tyranny, Catholicism and Jacobitism. However, at the same time, Gothic follies, houses, castles and interiors were designed and created in non-ruinous states by people on all points of the political spectrum. So, despite its Catholic ancestry, Gothic design was widely adopted, and as such the erection of habitable Gothic structures and interiors in Georgian Britain suggests that Gothic's link with Catholicism was not overly problematic for contemporaries.

Indeed, the Gothic was fundamental to mid-eighteenth-century aesthetic theories, in particular the Picturesque. Edmund Burke (1729–97), whose *A Philosophical Enquiry into the Origin of our Ideas of the Sublime and Beautiful* was published in 1757, offers an important interpretation of the related, though distinct, aesthetic theory of the sublime. In his later work, *Reflections on the Revolution in France* (1790), he sheds light on the apparent conflict between the popularity of Gothic and its supposedly tainted association with Catholicism, by connecting Catholic and Protestant England in a continuum:

30 Horace Walpole, *The Letters of Horace Walpole*, ed. Paget Jackson Toynbee (Oxford, 1903), ii, p. 374.

31 Horace Walpole, *Description of the Villa of Mr Horace Walpole, the Youngest Son of Sir Robert Walpole Earl of Orford, at Strawberry-Hill, near Twickenham. With an Inventory of the Furniture, Pictures, Curiosities, &c.* (Strawberry Hill, 1784), p. 2.

32 Horace Walpole, *Horace Walpole's Correspondence with Horace Mann* 5, ed. W. S. Lewis, Warren Hunting Smith and George L. Lam, *The Yale Edition of Horace Walpole's Correspondence*, xxi (Oxford, 1960), p. 306. Walpole's flirtation with Catholicism was noticed in his lifetime. Thomas Rowlandson satirised Strawberry Hill's Catholic associations in *The North Entrance of Strawberry Hill* of 1789 by depicting a procession of monks approaching the villa. Even more explicit was Rowlandson's *Nuns at Prayer in the Tribune at Strawberry Hill* of c.1805, in which the Tribune is represented as a Catholic chapel and includes nine nuns at prayer in front of an altar loosely based upon the Tribune's furniture.

> So tenacious are we of the old ecclesiastical modes and fashions of institution, that very little alteration has been made in them since the fourteenth or fifteenth century adhering in this particular, as in all things else, to our old settled maxim, never entirely nor at once to depart from antiquity. We found these old institutions, on the whole, favourable to morality and discipline; and we thought they were susceptible of amendment, without altering the ground [...] and after all, with this Gothic and monkish education (for such it is in the ground-work) we may put in our claim to as ample and as early a share in all the improvements in science, in arts, and in literature.[33]

Catholic England was Gothic, and, out of conservatism, so was Protestant England. Thus, at the dissolution of the monasteries, the surviving buildings remained Gothic. Iconoclasm may have irrevocably altered their internal and external decoration and furnishings, but Gothic continued as a Protestant style. Moreover, it has more recently been shown that Gothic architecture survived the English Reformation at the hands of local builders. Sir Howard Colvin argued that: 'Gothic in the seventeenth century was still a living style, one which was practised in the towns as well as in the country.'[34] The intentional selection and incorporation of Gothic motifs into sixteenth – and seventeenth-century structures can be seen in the west front and hammer-beam roof at Burghley House in Lincolnshire (1577), and in the tracery windows of the Great Hall at Lambeth Palace in London (1660).[35] In Oxford the specific retention of Gothic is explicitly articulated by the details incorporated into what are otherwise the Classical library and chapel at Brasenose College, added between 1656 and 1666. And, as recognised by John Newman, much of the new architecture in early seventeenth-century Oxford was Gothic, 'both out of unthinking conformism and, as the schools [*sic*] quadrangle and convocation house most strikingly illustrate, by deliberate choice for visual consistency'.[36] These examples reveal that in the face of Classicism, Gothic architecture was practised because of its incontrovertible connection with tradition, patronage and association. It was these associations that contributed to what has been identified as the mania of the Gothic Revival in the 1750s and early 1760s.[37]

Gothic architecture's robust bond with the Goths was at the root of its negative reception in eighteenth-century Britain, especially for the supporters of Classical architecture.[38] Nevertheless, the Goths were simultaneously held up as a people who possessed freedom from an over-powerful monarch, which the Whig party in the

[33] Edmund Burke, *Reflections on the Revolution in France, and on the Proceedings in Certain Societies in London Relative to That Event* (London, 1790), pp. 148–9.

[34] Howard Colvin, 'Gothic Survival and Gothick Revival', *Essays in English Architectural History* (London, 1999), p. 221.

[35] The deliberate use of Gothic architecture in the sixteenth and seventeenth centuries is explored in Giles Worsley, *Classical Architecture in Britain: The Heroic Age* (London, 1995), pp. 175–95.

[36] John Newman, 'The Architectural Setting', *The History of the University of Oxford*, ed. Nicholas Tyacke (Oxford, 1997), p. 169.

[37] Anthony Coleridge, 'A Reappraisal of William Hallett', *Furniture History* 1 (1965), p. 12.

[38] See Cocke, 'The Wheel of Fortune', pp. 185–6.

eighteenth century wished to emulate.[39] Property, rather than the inherited right to rule as king, was central to their politics.[40] Walter Harris articulated the eighteenth century's perception and framing of the Goths as the fountainhead of liberty in 1749:

> THE Gothick Constitution once prevailed over all the Countries of Europe; and was introduced by those Northern Swarms, who, with a wonderful rapidity, over-ran France, Spain, the Netherlands, Italy, &c, and settled such a Government of Liberty, wherever they exerted their conquests.[41]

Also arguing for the existence of this 'Gothick constitution', Sir John Gonson indicated in 1728 that 'we in *Great-Britain* have still happily preserved this noble and ancient *Gothic* Constitution, which all our Neighbours once enjoy'd, as well as we, who are the Wonder and Glory of all the Kingdoms round about us'.[42] Here was a critical idea in the Whig political system and one that attempted to reduce the power of the monarch in favour of representation through parliament. When the Scottish Parliament was debating the Terms of Union with England in November 1706, Daniel Defoe, a writer, political pamphleteer and businessman, noted that: 'I conceive, that this nation [Scotland …] may be in danger of returning to that Gothic constitution of government, wherein our forefathers were, which was frequently attended with feuds, murders, depredations and rebellions'.[43] So, whilst the constitution was recognised, the turbulence of the Middle Ages was perceived as a drawback to this 'Gothic' liberty. Defoe was tapping into the desire to distance the violence of the Middle Ages from that which was useful to contemporary society, specifically the contract between king and people. During the eighteenth century the idea of the Gothic constitution was closely associated with architecture, mirroring the connection made in eighteenth-century Britain between Classical architecture and the empires of antiquity. The meaning of architecture can be seen in the work of Richard Temple (1675–1749), first Viscount Cobham, who developed his gardens at Stowe in Buckinghamshire, notably by the erection of numerous buildings. Most of them were in the Classical mode, inspired by temples. However, one well-known example, the Temple of Liberty – otherwise known as Gibbs's Gothic Temple (1741–47) – was an important exception. As the name indicates, the temple was dedicated to liberty and this liberty was intentionally conceived of and represented by and through a Gothic structure. The entry in George Bickham's guidebook to the garden, *The Beauties of Stow* of 1750, emphasises the synonymy between the temple's Gothic architecture and the perception of Gothic liberty:

39 See Smith, *The Gothic Bequest*, p. 2; Kliger, *The Goths in England*, p. 33.

40 Leslie Mitchell, *The Whig World: 1760–1837* (London, 2005), pp. 135–7.

41 Walter Harris, *The History of the Life and Reign of William-Henry, Prince of Nassau and Orange, Stadtholder of the United Provinces, King of England, Scotland* (Dublin, 1749), p. i.

42 Sir John Gonson, *The Third Charge of Sir John Gonson Knt. To the Grand Jury of the City and Liberty of Westminster, &c.* (London, 1728), p. 14.

43 Daniel Defoe, *The History of the Union between England and Scotland, with a Collection of Original Papers Relating Thereto* (London, 1786), p. 314.

> we come to a Gothic building, call'd
> The TEMPLE of LIBERTY.
> *Libertati Majorum.*
> To the Liberty of our Ancestors.
>
> It is an Imitation of a large antique Building [...] It is impossible to make a better Imitation of the antient Taste of Architecture. This is a Kind of Castle, several stories high, which commands the whole Garden.[44]

A similar desire to represent British ancestral liberty can be detected in the seven 'Saxon' deities for the Sylvan Temple at Stowe.[45] Such an impression is emphasised in their poetic description by Gilbert West from 1732:

> Hail! Gods of our renown'd Fore-Fathers, hail!
> Ador'd Protectors once of *England's* Weal.
> Gods, of a Nation, valiant, wise and free,
> Who conquer'd to establish *Liberty*!
> To whose auspicious Care *Britannia* owes
> Those Laws, on which she stands, by which she rose.
> Still may your Sons that noble Plan pursue,
> Of equal Government prescrib'd by you.
> Nor e'er indignant may you blush to see,
> The Shame of your corrupted Progeny![46]

In both these instances, the choice of Gothic architecture and Saxon gods was intended to create strong connections with, and passionate admiration for, the past: a British national past that was born from the imagined perception of Gothic liberty.

As the garden buildings at Stowe demonstrate, the connection between the idea of 'Gothic liberty' and Gothic architecture was realised. Other parallels between Gothic architecture and Britain's history or 'cultural heritage', and in particular the martial and visual qualities of chivalry, were actively explored in the eighteenth century. Henry Fox (1705–74), first Baron Holland of Foxley, built himself a Classically-styled house at Kingsgate in Kent and surrounded it with ruinous Gothic follies and Gothic monuments. One, the Gothic King's Gate, commemorates Charles II's landing there after being shipwrecked in 1683.[47] Another, the monument of Hackendown, or Field of Battle-axes, was erected to mark chivalrous acts. Thomas Fisher, in *The Kentish Traveller's Companion* (1779) described it as 'a building in the stile of remote antiquity, intended to commemorate a battle fought on this spot between

[44] George Bickham, *The Beauties of Stow: Or, a Description of the Pleasant Seat, and Noble Gardens, of the Right Honourable Lord Viscount Cobham* (London, 1750), p. 46.

[45] See Susan Moore, 'Hail! Gods of Our Fore-Fathers: Rysbrack's "Lost" Saxon Deities at Stowe', *Country Life* (1985), p. 250.

[46] Gilbert West, *Stowe, the Gardens of the Right Honourable Richard Lord Viscount Cobham. Address'd to Mr Pope* (London, 1732), pp. 17–18.

[47] Thomas Fisher, *The Kentish Traveller's Companion, in a Descriptive View of the Towns, Villages, Remarkable Buildings and Antiquities* (Canterbury, 1779), p. 174.

the Danes and the Anglo Saxons in the year 853'.[48] The structure's 'antiquae' architecture is Gothic: an arcade is formed from the highly decorative ogee arches found in mainstream Georgian Gothic design (figure 3.1).

Figure 3.1 James Basire I, *The Hackendown Monument at Kingsgate in the Isle of Thanet*, c.1767. K Top Vol 18 30a8. © The British Library Board.

The ogees nod and the pinched quatrefoil on each arch's face is also consistent with mainstream Gothic Revival design. Corresponding to the monument's Gothic and fortified architectural style, a tablet affixed to it records the battle of Hackendown and its chivalric context:

D.M.
Danorum et Saxonum hic occisorurum [*sic*]
Dum de solo Britannico

[48] Ibid., pp. 176–7.

(Milites nihil a se alienum putant)
Britannis perfide et crudeliter olim expulsis
Inter se demicaverunt;
Hen. de Holland
Posuit.
Qui duces, qualis hujus prælii exitus
Nulla notat historia
Annum circiter DCCC evenit pugna
Et pugnam hanc evenisse fidem faciunt
Ossa quamplurima
Quæ sub hoc et altero tumulo huic vicino
sunt sepulta.[49]

The architect Sanderson Miller (1716–80) likewise built a Gothic eye-catcher (1745–47) in view of Radway Grange, his house in Warwickshire, to mark the nearby battle of Edge Hill of 1642, the first major action of the English Civil War.[50] Miller's work, much like the other examples considered in this section, demonstrates how Gothic structures could be used in Georgian Britain to represent and commemorate martial events. Fox's Hackendown monument illustrates how Gothic was used flexibly to commemorate even sites that predated medieval Gothic architecture. Gothic architecture's ability to resonate with a generic past and to elicit other associations such as freedom were also important, as represented by Cobham's Temple of Liberty. The adoption of Gothic architecture, particularly in gardens, was conditioned by its ability to represent Britain's history and culture; chivalry being a major facet.

Gothic's strong association with the ideas and visual language of chivalry was directly incorporated into the Georgian debate over style. Gerard, who was critical of medieval architecture, ridiculed eighteenth-century Gothic for reviving the 'improbable tastes of Chivalry'.[51] According to Gerard we can understand that chivalry, like Gothic, was only acceptable and of interest to a particular sort, which, as he phrased it, had 'not acquired enlargement of mind'.[52] A less negative analysis of Gothic can be found in the writings of Richard Hurd (1720–1808). A churchman who ended up as the bishop of Worcester, Hurd stimulated interest in 'Gothic Romance' and corresponded with, amongst others, Thomas Gray and William Mason, who were notable eighteenth-century antiquaries. In *Letters on Chivalry and Romance* (1762), Hurd directly connected chivalry with Gothic: 'THE ages, we call barbarous, present us

[49] Ibid., p. 177. Translation: 'To the memory of the Danes and Saxons here slain, who were fighting for the possession of Britain (soldiers think everything their own), the Britons having before been perfidiously and cruelly expelled. This was erected by Henry Lord Holland. No history records who were the commanders in this action, or what was the event of it. It happened about the year 800, and that it happened on this spot is credible, from the many bones which are buried under this and the adjacent tumulus.'

[50] See David Watkin, *The English Vision: The Picturesque in Architecture, Landscape, and Garden Design* (London, 1982), p. 50.

[51] Gerard, *An Essay on Taste*, p. 103.

[52] Ibid., p. 123.

with many a subject of curious speculation. What, for instance, is more remarkable than the Gothic CHIVALRY?'[53] He also associated the appearance of castles (Gothic buildings) with the culture of chivalry:

> For the castles of the Barons were, as I said, the courts of these little sovereigns, as well as their fortresses; and the resort of their vassals thither, in honour of their chiefs, and for their own proper security, would make that civility and politeness, which is seen in courts and insensibly prevails there, a predominant part in the character of these assemblies.[54]

Hurd here creates a vivid representation of castle architecture and its associated meanings. Not only architecture but also the objects within could elicit chivalric associations, and the imagined actions of the architecture's historical inhabitants resonated with chivalric ideas.

Figure 3.2 William Kent, *Arthegal Fights the Sarazin Polente,* c.1730s. E.892–1928. © Victoria and Albert Museum, London.

The apparent synonymy of Gothic architecture and chivalry presented here is also conveyed by a number of eighteenth-century engravings, included in literary works to illustrate narratives and particular scenes. William Kent designed thirty-two plates in the 1730s for Edmund Spenser's *The Faerie Queene*, and the frontispiece for

[53] Richard Hurd, *Letters on Chivalry and Romance* (London, 1762), p. 3.

[54] Ibid., p. 11.

Figure 3.3 William Kent, *The Redcross Knight Introduced by Duessa to the House of Pride*, c.1730s. E.876–1928. © Victoria and Albert Museum, London.

Miguel de Cervantes' *Don Quixote*.[55] These important literary works engaged with the idea of chivalry, and Spenser's *The Faerie Queene* was thought especially good in this regard. In 1715 John Hughes, in his six-volume edition of Spenser's works, wrote that *The Faerie Queene* transformed tales of 'Knights, Giants, Castles, and Enchantments [...] into Allegory'.[56] The ability of this poetry to recreate visions of a medieval past was helped in part by 'the time when our Author wrote, the remains of the old Gothick Chivalry were not quite abolish'd'.[57] Kent's *Arthegal Fights the Sarazin Polente* and *The House of Pride* (figures 3.2 and 3.3) are notable amongst his illustrations for *The Faerie Queene* because of the dramatic and central role given to architecture. In both, Gothic structures frame the overtly chivalric narrative and Gothic motifs are scattered across the idiosyncratic castle in *Arthegal Fights the Sarazin Polente*. In a typically Kentian manner, the castle's structure is dominated by Gothic openings (doorways and windows), overly large arrow slits, machicolations, crenellations and bartizans.[58] Even the bridge is shaped according to the Gothic scheme. Kent's *The House of Pride* locates the figures within an equally evocative courtyard that blends both Classical and Gothic architecture, particularly noticeable in the

55 *The Faerie Queene* was first published in 1590 and Kent's illustrations were first included in the 1751 edition. *Don Quixote* was first published in 1605 and 1615, and Kent's frontispiece was first included in the 1742 edition.

56 John Hughes, *The Works of Spenser* (London, 1715), i, p. xiv.

57 Ibid.

58 Kent's Gothic has recently been examined in Roger White, 'Kent and the Gothic Revival', *William Kent: Designing Georgian Britain*, ed. Susan Weber (London, 2013), pp. 246–69.

arcade, and in the background is an improbably proportioned Gothic hall. For the frontispiece to *Don Quixote* (figure 3.4), Kent's composition places a portrait of the author, Cervantes, in front of Gothic arcading, a Gothic clustered column from which a helmet and sword are hung, and a knight on horseback set within a Gothic hall.[59] The architectural language employed by Kent in this frontispiece and in the illustrations for *The Faerie Queene* reveals how Gothic could inculcate and reinforce ideas of chivalry appropriate to chivalric literature. Therefore, the use of Gothic shapes in a repetitive and decorative style in eighteenth-century Britain harnessed Gothic architecture's associations with the medieval past and also chivalry.

Figure 3.4 George Vertue after William Kent, *The Life and Exploits of the Ingenious Gentleman Don Quixote de la Mancha,* 1742. E.36–1996. © Victoria and Albert Museum, London.

The visual connection between chivalry and Gothic architecture (including just its motifs, on occasion) is entirely understandable given that they are both, loosely,

[59] The portrait is based upon a written description of the author, instead of being taken from a visual source. See Nick Savage, 'Kent as Book Illustrator', *William Kent: Designing Georgian Britain,* ed. Susan Weber (London, 2013), pp. 436–47.

coeval. For instance, Edward III founded the Order of the Garter in 1348, and it is to this time that Perpendicular Gothic architecture can be dated. Additionally, some of the most important and spectacular examples of Perpendicular Gothic architecture – Henry VII's Chapel, Westminster Abbey, and St George's Chapel, Windsor – are also chapels for chivalric orders. Horace Walpole helps to explain the connection between Gothic architecture and the medieval past, and in particular chivalry. In a passage from his manuscript 'Books of Materials', Walpole explored the meaning and associative possibilities of architectural styles, specifically Gothic in contrast with Grecian:

> If two Architects of equal Genius & Taste, or one man possessing both, & without the least degree of partiality was ordered to build Two buildings, (& supporting him unlimited in expense) one in the Grecian & one in the Gothic style, I think, the Gothic wd strike most at first, the Grecian would please the longest. But I believe this approbation would in some measure flow from the Impossibility of not connecting with Grecian & Roman Architecture, the ideals of the Greeks & Romans, who invented & inhabited that kind of building. If (which but few have) one has any partiality to old Knights, Crusades, the Wars of York & Lancaster &c the prejudice in favour of ~~Goth~~ Grecian buildings, will be balanced. All this is supposed to be referred to men who think for themselves; it is idle to address any supposition to men who think by Rote.[60]

Knightly exploits and chivalrous conduct, according to Walpole, were central to and clearly represented by Gothic architecture. Indeed, an interest in chivalry's martial aspects would potentially help disarm the mid-eighteenth-century predisposition against Gothic. Walpole also helped to define chivalry's scope in eighteenth-century Britain: he considered heraldry in detail, a constituent part of chivalry. In a letter of January 1776 to Rev. William Cole, a Cambridge antiquary interested in heraldry and medieval architecture, Walpole commented:

> Duke of Lorrain's The arms, or and gules, I thought were those of Lorrain, which I since find are argent and gules. The argent indeed may be turned yellow by age, as Mr Gough says he does not know whether the crescent is red or black. But the great impediment is, that this achievement of a Tufton was performed in the reign of Charles the Second. Now in that reign, when we were become singularly ignorant of chivalry, anachronisms and blunders might easily be committed by a modern painter, yet I shall not adhere to my discovery, unless I find the painting corresponds with the style of the modern time to which I would assign it; nor will I see through the eyes of my hypothesis, but fairly.[61]

Displaying a sound knowledge of heraldic practice, its terms and its practical

60 Farmington, Lewis Walpole Library, MS 49 2615, Vol. 1, fol. 52.

61 Walpole, *Correspondence*, ii, p. 2.

function, Walpole underlined the connection between heraldic practice and chivalric ancestry.

The representation of chivalry through armorial bearings became particularly influential in eighteenth-century architecture and interiors. It is not surprising, given Walpole's letter to Cole from 1776, that his country villa, Strawberry Hill – otherwise referred to as his 'little Gothic castle' that he built 'of my ancestors' – was laden with chivalric overtones conveyed through painted glass and heraldic devices painted on its walls and ceilings.[62] In an extra-illustrated copy of his *Description of the Villa of Mr. Horace Walpole*, Walpole's copious manuscript additions include a detailed record of the house's heraldic ornament. It reads:

> Explanation
> of the different coats of arms
> about the House at Strawberry hill
>
> Over the door on the outside, three shields of Walpole between Robsart & Shorter.
> In painted glass over the door of the little Parlour, All the quarterings of Walpole.
> N.B. there are several panes of Dutch arms & others in painted glass, which have no relation to the Family.
> The Antelopes in the Stairs are the supporters of Lord Orford.
> In the Armory. Fitzosbert, gules, a fess, or, over a bend, argent. This is the first quartering of Walpole. 1275.
> Sr Robert Walpole's arms impaling Shorter, within a garter. 1726.
> Sr Edward Walpole's arms, impaling Crane, within a red ribband. 1660.
> The See of Ely impaling Walpole, for Ralph Walpole Bp of Ely. 1299.
> Vert, a Lion rampant, or, within a garter for St John Robsart, 1445.
> In the Library
> On the Cieling, the Shield of Walpole, surrounded with small shields; the first of which has an old bearing of Walpole, found on an ancient deed, viz. on a field or, a fess between 2 chevrons, checkie of gules & argent: the other shields have the quarterings of the family.[63]

Apart from the arms enumerated by Walpole in this note, which reflected notable figures from his family's past, his intricately decorated castle-villa included unrelated seventeenth-century heraldic glass. The visual overlap between the genuine Walpole arms and unrelated Dutch glass, nevertheless, offered a tangible expression of the chivalric past and, indeed, present, courtesy of Sir Robert's arms encircled by the garter. His father, Sir Robert Walpole (1676–1745), first earl of Orford, was not only from prominent Norfolk gentry but was also Britain's first prime minister. Walpole's

[62] Horace Walpole, *The Letters of Horace Walpole, Earl of Orford* (London, 1840), iii, p. 2.
[63] Farmington, Lewis Walpole Library, MS 49 2523.

Figure 3.5 John Carter, *Hall: the Armoury at Strawberry Hill.* c.1788. The Lewis Walpole Library, Farmington CT, 33 30 cop. 11 Folio, fol. 57. Courtesy of The Lewis Walpole Library, Yale University.

heraldic narrative at Strawberry Hill clearly capitalised upon this to express both his aristocratic pedigree and his connections with chivalry.

In addition to those mentioned above, other parts of the house were adorned with heraldry and bathed in light that shone through heraldically-decorated glass. Of these, Walpole specifically commented upon the armoury (figure 3.5), a vaulted space just off the main staircase at Strawberry Hill, through which access was gained to the library, which was itself a nexus of heraldic imagery. In a letter to George Montagu from June 1753, Walpole complained:

> I cannot leave my workmen, especially as we have a painter who paints the paper on the staircase under Mr Bentley's direction. The armoury [also decorated in part with this paper] bespeaks the ancient chivalry of the lords of the castle, and I have filled Mr Bentley's Gothic lanthorn with painted glass, which casts the most venerable gloom on the stairs that was ever seen since the days of Abelard. The lanthorn itself in which I have stuck a coat of the Veres is supposed to have come from Castle Henningham. Lord and Lady Vere were here t'other day, and called cousins with it, and would very readily have invited it to Hanworth, but her Portuguese blood has so blackened the true stream, that I can't bring myself to offer so fair a gift to their chapel.[64]

The weaponry, armour, heraldry and other artefacts collected for their historical and chivalric significance, housed within a Gothic context, created a vision of medieval chivalry. This effect was amplified when in 1771 Walpole acquired the so-called parade armour of Francis I, king of France, for £52 10s.[65] The gilt armour, located in a specially constructed Gothic niche on the western elevation of the staircase, enhanced the armoury's knightly and chivalrous connotations, which Walpole had developed in his letter to George Montagu in 1753. Walpole consequently employed multiple devices, including objects and the visual languages of heraldry and Gothic architecture, to create and sustain a chivalric atmosphere, particularly within the house.

Walpole's attempt at imprinting chivalric associations upon Strawberry Hill was successful, but this was not the only approach. During the eighteenth century chivalrous connections were evoked in different ways. The architect Sir John Vanbrugh (1664–1726) created buildings using a far more restrained vocabulary of Gothic motifs and heraldry to elicit chivalric connotations. Writing to the duchess of Marlborough in June 1709, he was full of praise for Woodstock Manor in Oxfordshire, particularly because of its historical associations. It was these very associations that he attempted to harness in his own practice:

> I hope I may be forgiven, if I make some faint application of what I say of Blenheim, to the Small Remains of ancient Woodstock Manour. It can't indeed be said, it was Erected on so Noble, nor on So justifiable Occasion; But it was rais'ed by One of the Bravest and most Warlike of the English Kings [Henry II]; And tho' it has been Fam'd, as a Monument of his arms, *it has been tenderly regarded* as the Scene of his Affections. *Nor amongst the Multitude of People, who came daily to View what is raising to the Memory of the Great Battle of Blenheim; are there any that do no eagerly to See* what Ancient Remains are to be found of Rosamonds Bower. *It may perhaps be worth some Little Reflection Upon what may be said, if the Very footsteps of it are no more to be found.*[66]

[64] Walpole, *Correspondence*, ix, pp. 150–1.

[65] Stuart W. Pyhrr, 'The Strawberry Hill Armoury', *Horace Walpole's Strawberry Hill*, ed. Michael Snodin (London, 2009), p. 226.

[66] London, British Library, Add MS 61353, fols 62–3.

Vanbrugh's admiration of 'ancient' Woodstock Manor (together with its 'warlike' patron) influenced the design of the Kitchen Court at Blenheim Palace in Oxfordshire and resulted in the robust crenellations over an astylar arcade. The inclusion of similar Gothic elements into Kimbolton Castle in Cambridgeshire was on an even larger and more impressive scale. In a letter to the earl of Manchester from July 1707, Vanbrugh emphasised the 'Britishness' of his 'castle style' and the implicated expression of chivalry:

> As to the Outside, I thought 'twas absolutly best, to give it Something of the Castle Air, tho' at the Same time to make it regular. And by this means too, all the Old Stone is Serviceable again; which to have had new wou'd have run to a very great Expence; This method was practice'd at Windsor in King Charles's time, And has been universally Approv'd, So I hope your Ldship won't be discourag'd, if any Italians you may Shew it to, shou'd find fault that 'tis not Roman, for to have built a Front with Pillasters, and what the Orders require cou'd never have been born with the Rest of the Castle: I'm sure this will make a very Noble and Masculine Shew; and is of as Warrantable a kind of building as Any.[67]

Very much like the Kitchen Court at Blenheim, Kimbolton's 'castle air' was conditioned by the bold crenellated parapet. The remainder of Kimbolton's exterior made little reference to castle or, broadly, Gothic architecture. However, this parapet was sufficient to impart the 'castle air' upon Kimbolton, and thus emphasises the importance of architectural motifs in conditioning associations. If Horace Walpole's approach was based upon a collection of objects and layering of chivalric imagery, Vanbrugh applied a bold, simplified and masculine architectural skin of motifs to the houses' façades.

A more complete and explicit articulation of the 'castle air' was expressed through the exterior and interior of Enmore Castle in Somerset. John Perceval (1711–70), from 1748 second earl of Egmont, erected and decorated this house in the castle style between 1751 and 1757. Walpole directly addressed Enmore in his *Memoirs of the Reign of King George the Third* (published in 1845) and related its design to Egmont's interest in 'the age of chivalry':

> WHILE men were taken up with the politics of the age, there was a Minister so smitten with the exploded usages of barbarous times, that he thought of nothing less than reviving the feudal system. This was the Earl of Egmont, who had actually drawn up a plan for establishing that absurd kind of government in the island of St. John. He printed several copies of his scheme, and sent them about to his brother peers. [...] Lord Egmont was such a passionate admirer of those noble tenures and customs, that he rebuilt his house at Enmere in Somersetshire in the guise of a castle, moated it round, and

[67] Bonamy Dobrée and Geoffrey Webb, ed., *The Complete Works of Sir John Vanbrugh*, iv (Bloomsbury, 1928), p. 14.

> prepared it to defend itself with cross-bows and arrows, against the time in which the fabric and use of gunpowder shall be forgotten.[68]

Walpole ridicules Egmont's preference for the social and political structures of medieval England and describes his architectural interventions with faint praise. Nevertheless, he also underscores the robust link between architecture and militaristic and chivalric actions. In particular, the defensive architecture evokes illusions within the minds of men willing and ready to defend such 'with cross-bows and arrows'.

It was not just the exterior of Enmore that conjured up such historical impressions. Visited by Rev. Stebbing Shaw in 1788, it is clear that the interior was also designed to evoke the Middle Ages, which Walpole termed the 'feudal period':

> the true representation of those ancient habitations, which, amid the rivalship, animosities, and dangers of feudal times, were the impregnable protection of every potent Baron before the invention of gun-powder and the use of artillery. It is surrounded by a deep foss, which we cross over by a draw-bridge, into the court, a handsome and spacious quadrangle, leading to the hall, a well adapted room, surrounded with a large gallery; the walls adorned with family busts and coats of arms; painted chairs of the same, &c. We ascended into the upper apartments by a curious geometric staircase; these consist of a good breakfast room, an armoury, large and handsomely hung with most of the proper implements of war.[69]

Shaw emphasises Enmore's militaristic and chivalric overtones. As at Blenheim and Kimbolton, this was achieved on the exterior by the introduction of a crenellated parapet. However, Perceval went further by including a moat, drawbridge, and corner and flanking towers. As in Kent's drawing, *Arthegal Fights the Sarazin Polente,* crossed arrow slits complemented the castle architecture, although unlike Kent's illustrations the arch-heads are round and illustrative of greater historical awareness of genuinely medieval architecture. Enmore was based upon a deeper understanding of the form of medieval castle architecture, as it did not need to be composed of architectural components from 'high' Gothic design. Enmore consequently contributed to Perceval's desire to be incorporated within the English peerage (he would only accept the offices of secretary of state and leader of the House of Commons on such a condition). Although an English title was not granted, Enmore helped cement Perceval and the impression of a chivalrous heritage within England.

Much like Strawberry Hill, Enmore's association with the imagined medieval period, and with chivalry in particular, was made explicit in the house's interior. It is noteworthy that Shaw included chairs in his description of Enmore's Hall, and especially that they corresponded with the Hall's decoration. A chair, now preserved in the Victoria and Albert Museum in London, is almost certainly one of those

68 Horace Walpole, *Memoirs of the Reign of King George III* (London, 1845), i, pp. 387–8.
69 Stebbing Shaw, *A Tour to the West of England, in 1788* (London, 1789), pp. 331–2.

Figure 3.6 Anon., *One of a Suite of Windsor Chairs Commemorating the Marriage of John Perceval, 2nd Earl of Egmont, to Catherine Compton*, 1756. W.34–1976. © Victoria and Albert Museum, London.

referred to by Shaw in his description (see figure 3.6); for instance, it is decorated boldly with heraldry as Shaw mentioned.[70] The chair is of an old and British form known as Windsor, but with the noticeable addition of cusping at the cresting around the chair's heraldically-decorated panel. This addition is almost certainly a reference to the tracery windows of medieval architecture. The coat of arms, which alludes to the values of the cult of chivalry, represents the second earl of Egmont and his wife, Catherine Compton (1731–84), who married in 1756. This impaling appears to correspond with the 'family busts and coats of arms' lining Enmore's Hall, as recorded by Shaw.[71] Consequently, the chair's form and decoration are consistent with the combination of Gothic, heraldry and historical styles to represent chivalry, and give some impression of Enmore's lustrous and chivalric interior.

Enmore's architecture and hall chairs are certainly not mainstream in form

70 London, Victoria and Albert Museum, W.34–1976.

71 Shaw, *Tour*, pp. 332.

and decoration. They could not have been derived from thumbing through mid-eighteenth-century pattern books, such as William and John Halfpennys's *Chinese and Gothic Architecture Properly Ornamented* (1752) and Thomas Chippendale's *The Gentleman and Cabinet-Maker's Director* (1754). Instead, Enmore was conceived of as a bespoke and highly individualised expression of medieval, baronial and chivalric culture, much like the bulk of Walpole's Strawberry Hill.[72] Indeed, Perceval was actively involved in designing Enmore, which is demonstrated by a letter from Henry Wilkins, the carpenter:

> As your Lordship is pleased to alter the form of the window from those drawn in the plan your Lordship sent I have drawn all of them semicircular heads with some little difference in the manner of making them, 3 exactly the same dimensions as your Lordship's directions – that is 3 foot wide in the clear and 6 foot 6 inches high. The other, that marked, I have drawn 3 inches wider which I humbly think to be as good proportion as the others. But that I leave to your Lordship's better judgement if yr Lordship like either of these or part of one and part of another or any other yr Lordship is pleased to direct I will take care shall be executed.[73]

He was also concerned with the castle's furniture, which implies that the hall chair now at the Victoria and Albert Museum may have been produced under Perceval's direct instruction. John Gooding, Perceval's bailiff, wrote in 1751:

> I have been with the Upholsterer, and he says, that the Chairs your Lordship mentions, are 7 (l) per Chair, But if they are made of Beech; they will come for about six. Table Bedsteads, made of Dutch Oak, are about 27 (l) or 30 (l). but if made of Deal, will come for about 1=1=8.[74]

Indeed, the Perceval hall chair now at the Victoria and Albert Museum is made of beech and elm, which suggests that the cheaper option was taken. Writing in the same letter, Gooding sought Perceval's directions for an old bed, which added weight to the idea of ancient lineage developed in the castle:

> P.S. In one of the Chambers there is a Bed Stead of Mr Bayntuus, with an old Canopy, and a large Cornish and an old Head Board. There is no Furniture to it, not so much as Curtains, and what Carving there is to the other Parts is to raggid; that provided we could procure stuff of the same sort, it could not well be repaired. I should be glad, if your Lordship would let me know what must be done with it.[75]

[72] The earliest sections of Strawberry Hill, however, relate to the designs published by Batty Langley in *Ancient Architecture: Restored and Improved* (London, 1741–42). Indeed, a design for Strawberry Hill drawn by John Chute can be found on the rear fly-leaf of Walpole's personal copy of *Ancient Architecture*. Farmington, Lewis Walpole Library, MS 49630.

[73] London, British Library, Add Ms 47011, fol. 128.

[74] Ibid., fol. 65.

[75] Ibid.

Enmore provides datable examples of architecture and furniture illustrating the application of chivalric motifs and allusions: Gothic shapes and heraldry were essential to this.

Perceval's contribution to eighteenth-century chivalric design is important, but a stupendous house erected in Wiltshire for William Beckford (1760–1844), a fantastically wealthy owner of Jamaican sugar plantations, overshadows it. Beckford's country house, Fonthill Abbey, ultimately stemmed from his megalomania and desire to achieve immortal fame through the creation of a chapel and mausoleum.[76] This directly contrasted with his family's merchant heritage and source of wealth; his marriage in 1783 to Lady Margaret Gordon, the daughter of the impoverished earl of Aboyne, added aristocratic connections. Fonthill was largely designed by James Wyatt, one of the most fashionable architects in later Georgian Britain, between 1796 and 1812, and thereafter by Beckford himself with the occasional assistance of Jeffry Wyatt (later Wyatville), who worked extensively on Windsor Castle for George IV.[77] Beckford used his fantastic wealth to erect, decorate and furnish what was one of the most spectacular country seats in Britain.[78] Despite its exterior appearance, inspired by the religious buildings of the High Middle Ages, parts of the interior were primarily devoted to the secular aesthetic of chivalry and heraldry. In *Illustrations, Graphic and Literary, of Fonthill Abbey, Wiltshire* (1823), John Britton addressed this conflict between ecclesiastical and secular design at the house by specifically identifying religious and chivalric attributes and their mixture in medieval architecture:

> In the painted windows, sepulchral monuments, and other parts of our antient churches and monastic edifices, heraldical ornaments and insignia have generally constituted a prominent feature; for the chivalry and religion of our fore-fathers seems to have been intimately blended. Whilst the knight or baron was alike distinguished in the field and at the tournament by his appropriate badge and crest, the bishop, abbot, and other eminent ecclesiastics had their respective cognizances. These were variously displayed, and officially employed to identify rank, connection, attribute, and station: heraldry was therefore studied and cultivated in unison with architecture, and the designs of the one were often made subservient, as they were in fact analogous, to the other.[79]

Chivalry and its visual language clearly extended beyond the militaristic, as Britton argued, and possessed ecclesiastical overtones – particularly in aspects of the

76 See John Wilton-Ely, 'The Genesis and Evolution of Fonthill Abbey', *Architectural History* 23 (1980), pp. 40–51.

77 See Hugh Roberts, *For the King's Pleasure: the Furnishing and Decoration of George IV's Apartments at Windsor Castle* (London, 2001).

78 Joseph Farington recorded Beckford's income for 1797 at £155,000. Kathryn Cave, ed., *The Diary of Joseph Farington: September 1796–December 1798* (London, 1979), iii, p. 901.

79 John Britton, *Illustrations, Graphic and Literary, of Fonthill Abbey, Wiltshire* (London, 1823), p. 5.

dubbing rite that were taken from the ecclesiastical rite of king-making.[80] Framing Fonthill as an abbey in both name and external form, consequently, did not dilute its chivalric overtones.

Figure 3.7 *Fonthill Abbey: King Edward's Gallery, Looking North.* Plate VIII from Britton, *Illustrations, Graphic and Literary, of Fonthill Abbey, Wiltshire* (London, 1823), DA690.F6 B7 1823+ Cop. 1 Oversize. Courtesy of the Yale Center for British Art.

Fonthill's interior was, of course, not universally linked with the ideas and visual identity of chivalry, notable in its absence from the library, for instance. However, the *piano nobile* was dominated by two long galleries connected by the central octagon, which certainly illuminated these themes. Heraldry is seen most prominently in King Edward's Gallery at Fonthill (see figure 3.7). The focus of this room is a painting of Edward III, which was 'copied by Matthew Wyatt from one in the vestry of St George's Chapel, Windsor'.[81] Beckford spuriously traced his descent from Edward III, and so a portrait of the monarch at the room's psychological centre was entirely appropriate, from Beckford's perspective, as an ancestral picture. The connection between Edward III (and, indeed, St George's Chapel) was in the founding of the chivalric Order of the Garter. Beckford was certainly not oblivious

[80] See Maurice Keen, *Chivalry* (London, 1990), pp. 73–82.

[81] John Rutter, *A Description of Fonthill Abbey and Demesne* (London, 1822), p. 59.

to this connection, and the room was awash with heraldic allusions to the Garter and its knights:

> the arms of the sovereign founder of the illustrious order of the garter, and seventy-one knights are placed in the frieze of the entablature, from all of whom the present Duchess of Hamilton is lineally descended. They are arranged in the manner of the stall, the earliest dates being placed nearest the central shield.[82]

The Duchess of Hamilton was Beckford's daughter, and this display clearly engaged with the idea of chivalry, its visual language, and family descent. Further heraldic devices were littered throughout the gallery: 'the Latimer cross, and the cinque-foil of Hamilton in relievo, in the panels of the ceiling, on the panels of the cabinets, and other furniture' were intended to create an inescapable association between Beckford and medieval knights.[83] The painted glass in Fonthill's Brown Parlour similarly invoked medieval kings, lords and knights:

1. William the Conqueror
2. William Rufus
3. Henry the first
4. Stephen
5. Henry the Second
6. Richard the first
7. King John
8. Henry the third
9. Edward the first
10. Edward the second
11. Edward the third
12. Richard the Second — Kings of England
13. Robert Fitz Hamon date 1107
14. Robert Consul — Earl of Gloucester 1146
15. Sir Hugh Bardolph
16. John, Lord Montacute
17. Sir Hugh Hastings
18. Lawrence Hastings Earl of Pembroke
19. Sir Reginald Barry Privy Councellor to Henry 7
20. Arthur Prince of Wales Son of Henry 7th
21. Sir Hugh Marville
22. Sir William Tracy
23. Gilbert di Clare Earl of Clare and Gloucester
24. Thomas Despenser Earl of Gloucester 1400
25. Sir Bryan Stapleton 1432
26. Sir John Harsick 1384

82 John Rutter, *Delineations of Fonthill and its Abbey* (London, 1823), p. 37.

83 Ibid. Rutter went as far as to include as an appendix to this work a genealogical table indicating Beckford's (fictive) descent from Edward III (Ibid., appendix C, tables I–III).

27. From an ancient Tomb. Priory Church ... Malvern Worcestershire
28. Alberic de Vere 2nd Earl of Oxford Earl's close Priory, Essex
29. Figures from the Tomb of Edmund Crouchback
30. Do
31. A Knight in Armour
32. A Statue supposed to be Bishop Gardiner's Father[84]

This roll-call of kings, lords and knights represented in Fonthill's Brown Parlour, together with the overt reference to the Order of the Garter in the King Edward's Gallery, demonstrates a sustained and explicit programme intended to imprint chivalry upon the interior of Fonthill.[85]

Plate 1 *Fonthill Abbey: South End of St Michael's Gallery.* Plate IX from Britton, *Illustrations, Graphic and Literary, of Fonthill Abbey, Wiltshire* (London, 1823), DA690.F6 B7 1823+ Cop. 1 Oversize. Courtesy of the Yale Center for British Art.

Beckford's furniture at Fonthill matched this overtly historical and chivalric environment. Pieces included ancient examples thought to be representative of

[84] Oxford, Bodleian Library, MS Beckford c.37, fols 100–1.

[85] See Stephen Clarke, '"The Almost Innumerable Descents of the Owner and his Late Wife": William Beckford's use of Heraldry at Fonthill Abbey', *The Beckford Journal* 20 (2014), pp. 42–61.

medieval furniture and hence entirely appropriate to the interiors.[86] Referring to his plans for a description of Fonthill Abbey, Britton picked out movables made from turned ebony, including pieces referred to as Wolsey chairs, which could be seen at the end of St Michael's Gallery (see plate 1): 'At present I propose to have a ground plan – two other exterior views & 3 or 4 interiors – also the Holbein Cabinet – Wolsey chairs &c – If my powers keep pace with my wishes.'[87] In 1802, whilst in Paris, Beckford was promised such and similarly appropriate furniture: 'the Ebony Tables are nearly finished & I have got the drawing for the Gothic Table – which shall be finished making before your return'.[88] The application of heraldry further emphasised their supposedly ancient material and forms, and increased the allusion to family descent and chivalry; this is articulated by a table originally at the centre of the King Edward's Gallery (see figure 3.7) but now in the hall at Charlecote Park in Warwickshire.[89] The legs bear the Latimer's Cross Moline and corresponded with those in the gallery's ceiling. Numerous vehicles were harnessed to display chivalry and chivalric ideas throughout Fonthill's *piano nobile*, including the overall architectural context, wall decoration (paintings and plasterwork), painted glass and furniture. Heraldry and heraldic devices were central to this decorative and evocative programme, as were Gothic motifs and structural devices (including the fan vaulting in St Michael's Gallery).

Perceval's and Beckford's furniture was clearly appropriate to the chivalric environments that they created. Like Walpole's Gothic Revival furniture for Strawberry Hill, the pieces were not mass produced, and thus were not representative of mainstream fashionable taste and consumption that could be found in typical eighteenth-century country houses. Of course, mainstream fashionable furniture did respond to the Gothic aesthetic, particularly in the 1750s and 1760s, but in a distinct manner. The relationship between these two types of furniture – antiquarian pieces found or designed specifically for interiors, and fashionable pieces supplied according to popular taste – enables a critical assessment of chivalry's popular impact upon Georgian design.

Furniture was a vehicle frequently used to reveal information about its owners and their historical and chivalric interests. Conveyed through style, design, form, decoration and material, such pieces could align with, or directly react against, those ideas created and promulgated by exterior and interior architectural schemes. Movables could be and were used to establish and evoke impressions, including wealth, cultural knowledge, and an awareness of and engagement with current fashionable trends, such as Neoclassicism from c.1765, and the historical. Chivalry is located in the latter. The landed classes in mid-eighteenth-century Britain had a wide range of furniture styles from which to choose, including Classical, Neoclassical, Rococo,

[86] For Fonthill's place in the romantic interior, see Wainwright, *Romantic Interior*, pp. 109–46.

[87] Oxford, Bodleian Library, MS Beckford c.27, fol. 9r.

[88] Oxford, Bodleian Library, MS Beckford c.29, fol. 137v.

[89] The National Trust, inventory number 532954.

Chinoiserie and Gothic, and their choices could feed directly into important allusions evoked elsewhere in the house.

Stylistic choice, especially non-Classical, has come under increasing scrutiny by scholars in recent decades to rectify the traditional focus on Classical design.[90] This has resulted in an important framing of 'different' aesthetics. For example, Chinoiserie has been interpreted as a feminine taste by scholars including Helena Hayward and David Porter.[91] Representative of this aesthetic trend is the Chinoiserie bedroom furniture supplied by William and John Linnell to the fourth duke and duchess of Beaufort in 1754, over which the duchess was consulted.[92] On the other hand, mainstream Georgian Gothic furniture has received comparatively little attention, especially regarding its connection with chivalry.

That variant architectural styles evoked different associations is self-evident, but the question remains to which degree mainstream fashionable furniture was appropriated to harness specific associations. Evidence for this is very rare, but in an exceptional comment on furniture's potential to express ideas or moods, Thomas Whately (1726–72) stated:

> the great effects which have been ascribed to buildings, do not depend upon those trivial ornaments, and appendages, which are often too much relied on; such as, the furniture of a hermitage; painted glass in a Gothic church [...] Such devices are only descriptive, not expressive, of character; and must not be substituted in the stead of those superior properties, the want of which they acknowledge, but do not supply.[93]

Whately's criticism indicates that furniture was used in the eighteenth century to convey mood and impressions to the mind, in much the same way that wallpaper or architecture could, but that it should not be used as the primary vehicle for this. Consequently, it is reasonable to assume that mainstream Georgian Gothic furniture

[90] Michael Snodin and Elspeth Moncrieff, eds, *Rococo: Art and Design in Hogarth's England* (London, 1984); Christopher Gilbert, *The Life and Work of Thomas Chippendale* (London, 1978); David Porter, 'From Chinese to Goth: Walpole and the Gothic Repudiation of Chinoiserie', *Eighteenth-Century Life* 23:1 (1999), pp. 45–58; Michael Snodin and John Styles, *Design and the Decorative Arts: Georgian Britain 1714–1837* (London, 2004).

[91] Helena Hayward, 'The Chinese Influence on English Furniture from the 16th to the 18th Century', *The Westward Influence of the Chinese Arts from the 14th to the 18th Century*, ed. William Watson (London, 1973), pp. 57–61; Helena Hayward, 'Chinoiserie at Badminton: The Furniture of John and William Linnell', *Apollo* (1969), pp. 134–39; David Porter, *The Chinese Taste in Eighteenth-Century England* (Cambridge, 2010), pp. 57–77, 86–7.

[92] Stacey Sloboda, 'Fashioning Bluestocking Conversation: Elizabeth Montague's Chinese Room', *Architectural Space in Eighteenth-Century Europe: Constructing Identities & Interiors*, ed. Denise Amy Baxter and Meredith Martin (Farnham, 2010), p. 130. See also Helena Hayward and Pat Kirkham, *William and John Linnell* (London, 1980), i, pp. 74–5. Linnell's furniture for the Beauforts at Badminton House, Gloucestershire, is now at the Victoria and Albert Museum, London: W.143:1 to 26–1921 (bed); W.55:1 to 24–1952 (dressing table); W.33–1990 (armchair); W.34–1990 (armchair).

[93] Thomas Whately, *Observations on Modern Gardening, Illustrated by Descriptions* (London, 1770), pp. 125–6.

Figure 3.8 *The Refectory, or Chevy Chase Room, St Michael's Mount.* Plate opposite p. 201, *The European Magazine,* September 1812. A88 Eu7. Courtesy of the Beinecke Rare Book & Manuscript Library, Yale University.

had the potential to elicit associations with knighthood, warfare and chivalry, as seen in bespoke non-fashionable furniture at houses like Fonthill.

Fashionable Georgian Gothic furniture was incorporated into rooms designed to evoke chivalric allusions. A prominent example of this can be found in the modifications made by Sir John St Aubyn (1726–72) to St Michael's Mount, Cornwall, in the 1750s. These Gothic revisions played upon both the ancient history of St Michael's Mount and the St Aubyn history. The family had lived seven miles inland at Clowance since the fourteenth century, and the Mount was 'anciently only a monastery, in tumultuous and warlike times a fort and monastery together, since the Reformation a fort only'.[94] St Aubyn's Chevy Chase room was part of this programme of works, and was reproduced as an engraving in *The European Magazine*'s issue for September 1812 (figure 3.8). The hall's name makes reference to the *Ballard of Chevy Chase*, which is based upon the Battle of Otterburn (1388). Recording a great battle fought by the forces of the earl of Northumberland and the earl of Douglas, the *Ballard* is coloured by heroism, courage, and loyalty to the monarch; all qualities central to chivalry.[95] Of the earl of Northumberland's forces, we are told that:

> Then the Persé owt of Banborowe cam,
> With him a mightee meany;

[94] Quoted in John Cornforth, 'St Michael's Mount, Cornwall: A Property of the National Trust and the Home of Lord and Lady St Levan', *Country Life*, 3 June 1993, p. 84.

[95] See Ruth Perry, 'War and Media in Border Minstrelsy: The Ballard of the Chevy Chase', *Ballards and Broadsides in Britain, 1500–1800*, ed. Patricia Fumerton, Anita Guerrini and Kris McAbbe (Farnham, 2010), pp. 251–70.

> With fifteen hondrith archares bold;
> The wear chosen out of shears thre.[96]

Thomas Percy included the *Ballard* in his *Reliques of Ancient English Poetry* of 1765, which, when compared with printed broadsides, possessed 'a romantic wilderness, and are in the true spirit of chivalry'.[97] The *Ballard*'s overtly chivalric narrative – in both form and content – was expressed by the room's decoration and furniture. It was, according to *The European Magazine*:

> ornamented in a style of great ingenuity, namely, with a broad frieze displaying views of the chase.
> Before the hounds the *ferine creatures* fly;
> On coursers fleet the nobles join the cry,
> Which rocks, and woods, reverb'rate to the sky.[98]

Underneath this frieze the decoration turned to favour 'the baronial trophies, and the armorial bearings [… which] are as recognitory of former times and manners'.[99] Above the mantel was a collection of armour, very much like that in the armoury at Strawberry Hill and in Kent's frontispiece to *Don Quixote*, suggesting a shared repertoire of objects alluding to chivalry. The room's collection of furniture was similarly inspired by the historical, and comprised four types of 'Gothic' chair: to the left of the illustration are four 'Glastonbury chairs'; at the back, flanking the chimneypiece, are two ebony chairs; to the right, in the corner, is a tripod chair made from turned limbs; and on the right-hand side is a range of eighteenth-century cabinet-maker's Gothic Revival chairs. The first three types were consistent with the repertoire Walpole collected for his medievalising interior at Strawberry Hill, and also seen at Fonthill.[100] However, the occupied Gothic Revival chair was mainstream and fashionable, with its serpentine arms inscribed with Gothic panelling and its back formed from cusped lancets and reticulations. It accorded with contemporary notions of comfort, particularly in terms of the form of the arms, back and seat. Yet it was Gothic. The combination of Georgian comfort and Gothic aesthetics made the chair entirely appropriate for a room designed to both celebrate and evoke the idea of chivalry as represented in the *Ballard of Chevy Chase*.

A similarly fashionable form of Gothic was deployed at Croft Castle in Herefordshire. The Gothicisation was undertaken by Thomas Pritchard (c.1723–77).[101] However, it was not under the auspices of the long-time incumbent family of

[96] Thomas Percy, *Reliques of Ancient English Poetry: Consisting of Old Heroic Ballads, Song and Other Pieces of Our Earlier Poets* (London, 1765), i, p. 5.

[97] Ibid., p. xxii.

[98] *The European Magazine*, September 1812, p. 205.

[99] Ibid.

[100] See Gabriel Olive, 'The Glastonbury Chair', *Regional Furniture* 8 (1994), pp. 25–41; Clive Wainwright, 'Only the True Black Blood', *Furniture History* 21 (1985), pp. 250–7; Wainwright, *Romantic Interior*, pp. 90–2, 96–7, 106.

[101] Designs for the plasterwork exist in the Pritchard Sketchbook held at the American Institute of Architects in Washington D.C. It is reproduced in Julia Ionides, *Thomas Farnolls Pritchard of Shrewsbury: Architect and 'Inventor of Cast Iron Bridges'* (Ludlow, 1999), appendix.

the Crofts that Pritchard added the veneer of Gothic decoration. Instead, when Sir Arthur Croft (1683–1756), second Baronet, sold it in 1746 to Richard Knight (1693–1765), who in turn gave it to his daughter Elizabeth Knight (d. 1813) and her husband, Thomas Johnes (1727–80), the castle was embellished. In contrast with the Crofts, the Knight family could not trace its line back through generations of the nobility; Richard Knight was a wealthy industrialist who had made a new and large personal fortune by managing a number of ironworks at the heart of the Industrial Revolution.[102] By purchasing a genuinely ancient country seat and adding a further suggestion of age, Knight and his family were attempting to assimilate themselves conspicuously into a culture of which they were not part, even if they could afford it.

The modifications made to Croft were hardly sophisticated and antiquarian, unlike at Strawberry Hill and Fonthill Abbey, but were in the mainstream form of Georgian Gothic. Some of the changes Pritchard made to Croft were conventional – for instance, the addition of sash windows and bays – but what is particularly interesting is the scattering of a thoroughly fashionable (Rococo), yet simultaneously historicising, suite of Gothic details throughout the castle's interior. These external and internal additions can be seen to have strengthened the castle's association with medieval England – a change that negated Knight's and Johnes' traceable connection to this England. Indeed, the Gothic tomb of Sir Richard (1429/30–1509) and Eleanor Croft (d. 1519) survives in St Michael and All Angels Church opposite the castle and embodies all the chivalric associations that the new occupants lacked: Richard fought for Edward IV at Mortimer's Cross (1461), was credited with capturing the Lancastrian Prince of Wales at Tewkesbury in 1471, and was thereafter knighted. Pritchard harnessed the language of chivalry seen in Sir Richard's Gothic tomb and reformed it in his decoration at Croft Castle, but in a fashionable rather than antiquarian form.

Of the modifications to Croft's interior, the Gothic overmantel is the most spectacular and incorporates the Gothic ornament associated with chivalry (see figure 3.9), especially as seen in Kent's illustration, *The House of Pride* (see figure 3.3). The structure's lightened decoration, particularly with the addition of Rococo scrollwork wreaths on the flanking lancets, subverts the mass and rigidity of castle architecture. It demonstrates how this vocabulary of ornament could be introduced into the mid eighteenth century's preference for light Rococo scrollwork decoration. Less frivolous in decoration are the bookcases in Croft's library: the subtle introduction of a quatrefoil frieze Gothicises the whole and thus ties it in with Croft's 'castle air'. Croft Castle's modifications reframed its entrance face to simulate fortified towers, but the most important changes were to the castle's interiors, which gained a fashionable form of Gothic that resonated with the established language of chivalric feats, in particular Sir Richard's.

Other designers were more explicit in the evocation of chivalric ideas and the impression of military fortifications and chivalry (the 'castle air'). More architectural

102 These include the ironworks at Coalbrookdale, Shropshire, and Wolverley, Worcestershire. See Nicholas Penny, 'Richard Payne Knight: A Brief Life', *The Arrogant Connoisseur: Richard Payne Knight 1751–1824*, ed. Michael Clarke and Nicholas Penny (Manchester, 1982), p. 1.

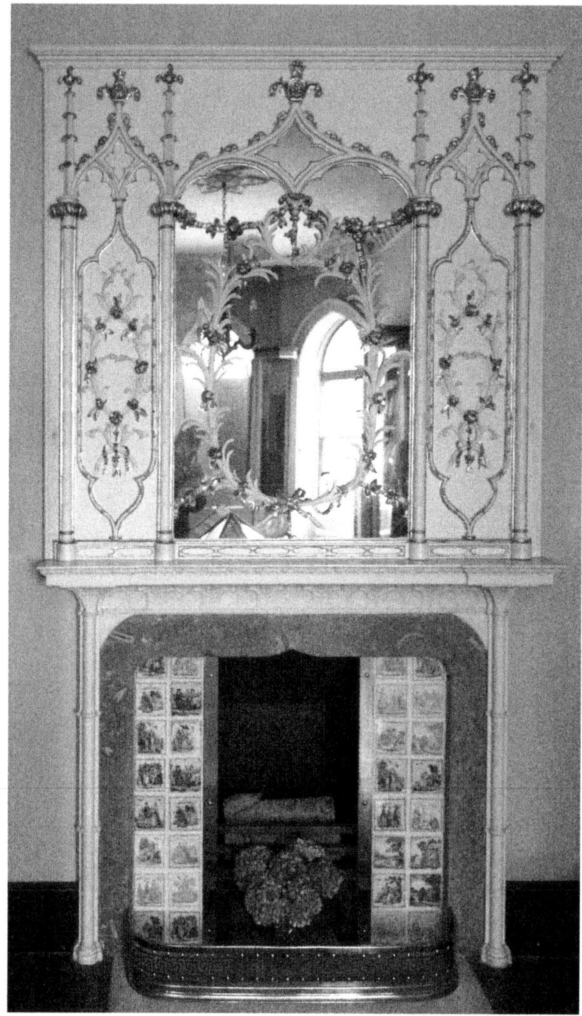

Figure 3.9 Thomas Pritchard, *The Gothic Overmantle at Croft Castle, Herefordshire*, 1765. Author's photograph reproduced by permission of the National Trust.

in form, compared with Croft Castle's modifications, are two designs for hall chairs by John Linnell (c.1703–63) (see figure 3.10). Especially robust, Linnell's designs reveal the practical application of Gothic motifs, including cusping (on panels and the X-frame legs), a blind rose window, and, as seen at Enmore and Fonthill, shields ready to receive arms.[103] The chairs are thus effectively a Gothic revision of the standard hall chair, a set of which was painted by Samuel Cobb in 1752 for Blair Castle in Perthshire, the seat of James Murray (1690–1764), second duke of Atholl. Cobb charged the duke £4 10s for painting 'one Dozn of Hall Chairs with Crest Coronetts Garters & Stars' to represent his knighthood and identity in the language

[103] London, Victoria and Albert Museum, E.29–1929.

Figure 3.10 John Linnell, *Design for a Pair of Gothic Hall Chairs*, c.1750s. E.87–1929. © Victoria and Albert Museum, London.

of heraldry.[104] Despite charging for the 'Garter', Cobb correctly painted the star and badge of the Order of the Thistle, to which Atholl was invested in 1734. The twelve hall chairs thus commemorated Atholl's membership of Scotland's highest order of chivalry. A later set of hall chairs also displayed the Atholl crest and coronet, but – unlike the earlier chairs, which did not reflect chivalry through their form – they were explicitly Gothic, with shield backs pierced by cusped mouchettes (a swept tear-drop shape). Thus, like Linnell's drawing for hall chairs, this later set at Blair Castle combined Gothic forms with heraldry to create a stronger articulation of chivalric imagery.

The examples mentioned here are similar in their form, ornament or decoration, and were explicitly designed to allude to chivalry. Their Gothicism is a clear reference to the visual language of chivalry, as understood and deployed in the

[104] Perthshire, Blair Castle Archives, 697, 1752, Cobb.

Figure 3.11 John Linnell, *Design for a Gothic Pier Glass*, c.1750s. E.170–1929. © Victoria and Albert Museum, London.

eighteenth century. However, the general adoption of Gothic motifs in fashionable furniture at this time was less architectural. Instead, Gothic forms were imaginatively combined to enliven otherwise relatively plain surfaces or to inform furniture's structure. Linnell's design for a Gothic pier glass – of which the form and structure are far more akin to church architecture than military fortifications, in terms of arch formation and the lightness of structure – is representative of this latter approach (see figure 3.11). The panelled column and cusped arcade on Plate XXIX, *Gothick Bed*, the church-window-like cusped astragals partially executed in Rococo scrollwork on Plate LXXI, *Library Bookcase*, and the niche-like pattern on the left-hand leg of the *Sideboard Table*, Plate XXXIX, all from Thomas Chippendale's *The Gentleman and Cabinet-Maker's Director* of 1754, are representative of Gothic's introduction into fashionable furniture. Whilst these designs do not appear to be related to chivalric ideas, their Gothic forms and motifs were, as has been established here, connected by imagination to the idea of chivalry.

Eighteenth-century architecture, furniture and design broadly demonstrate the associative powers of Gothic and its appropriateness for chivalric contexts. Thus, when Henry Emlyn (1728/9–1815) was refurbishing parts of St George's Chapel, Windsor, in c.1785, he chose a Gothic structure for the suite of chairs to be supplied to the chapel.[105] The chair backs were based upon an appropriately chivalric shield, like the second set of hall chairs at Blair, and the splat, or back support, was carved in imitation of Perpendicular Gothic window tracery. However, what is particularly interesting is the prominent placing of the Garter arms on the splat back. Thus Emlyn's chairs reflected the function of St George's Chapel for the Order of the Garter, as well as making reference to the Gothic context. Nods to chivalry in fashionable eighteenth-century furniture were, consequently, imaginatively harnessed.

*

Figure 3.12 Thomas Chippendale (possibly), *Fireplace Flanked by Commedia dell'arte Figures with Overmantle Showing a Gothic Gazebo*, c.1750s. 20.40.1, fol. 73. © Metropolitan Museum of Art, New York, www.metmuseum.org.

[105] Emlyn was the official chapter carpenter between 1784 and 1791. See Jane Roberts, ed., *George III & Queen Charlotte: Patronage, Collecting and Court Taste* (London, 2004), pp. 280–1.

The thoughts of the eminent historian of medieval chivalry, Maurice Keen, apply equally to its evocation in eighteenth-century furniture, architecture and design. Keen wrote:

> Chivalry is an evocative word, conjuring up images in the mind – of the knight fully armed, perhaps with the crusaders' red cross sewn upon his surcoat; of martial adventures in strange lands; of castles with tall towers and of the fair women who dwelt in them.[106]

In eighteenth-century Britain, links were certainly made between Gothic Revival design, heraldry, and the idea of chivalry. Gothic structures, like the term chivalry itself, could precipitate a broad range of associations, both positive and negative. Eighteenth-century houses, interiors and furniture could be specifically commissioned to explicitly imply, or recreate, the idea of the Middle Ages, knighthood and warfare. The characteristics found in this unique furniture were also available in cabinet-makers' pattern-books. Chippendale's *Director*, available and sold to both the landed classes and furniture makers alike, contained designs that were evocative of chivalry and the Middle Ages broadly.[107] Gothicising the prevailing Rococo taste was certainly evident: for example, one third of the plates in each edition of Chippendale's *Director* (1754, 1755, 1762) included designs for Gothic Revival furniture in the Rococo idiom. Although Gothic may not always have elicited chivalric ideas, it certainly could do so – unlike any other style. A manuscript chimneypiece design, perhaps by Chippendale, certainly speaks of 'castles with tall towers and of the fair women who dwelt in them' (see figure 3.12).[108] It appears plausible that the mania for Gothic Revival furniture in mid-eighteenth-century Britain made the visual language of chivalry available to those adopting fashionable tastes, particularly the landed classes keen to assert their ancestry and the newly wealthy merchants and traders who sought to emulate the values of the ranks they wished to join.

[106] Keen, *Chivalry*, p. 1.
[107] Thomas Chippendale, *The Gentleman and Cabinet-Maker's Director* (London, 1754).
[108] New York, Metropolitan Museum of Art, 20.40.1, fol. 73; Keen, *Chivalry*, p. 1.

4

Knights on the Town? Commercial and Civic Chivalry in Victorian Manchester*

Rosemary Mitchell

IN HIS 1838 publication, *Freeling's Grand Junction Railway Company to Liverpool, Manchester, and Birmingham*, Arthur Freeling described the heroic railway-building endeavours of the Liverpool and Manchester Railroad Company, opining that every subsequent railway company should compensate these pioneers, who had undergone all the initial difficulties of this original experiment in modern transportation. However, Freeling continued, this debt would never be repaid: 'There is no chivalry in "Companies".'[1] This opinion reflects the widespread sense in early Victorian Britain that the age of chivalry had passed, and a sense of regret that modern commercial and industrial practices had apparently superseded such a code of conduct. Yet in 1907 the economist Alfred Marshall wrote in the *Economic Journal* about 'The Social Possibilities of Economic Chivalry', arguing that the values of chivalry could be used to recondition and spiritualise capitalism, offering a viable alternative to socialist collectivism.[2] Perhaps the new commercial and civic cultures were not so incompatible with the ideals of chivalry? In fact, the entire Victorian period is characterised by a debate on how to adapt the past – including the medieval past and the values and appurtenances of chivalry – to modern means. Much (though by no means all) of the scholarship on Victorian medievalism has tended to focus on conservative rather than liberal and radical appropriations of the medieval and the chivalric, and on literary and visual ones, rather than on other media.[3] Here some redress is offered in both respects.

* I am grateful to Martin Hewitt and Barbara Gribling for their comments on draft versions of this essay.

1 A. Freeling, *Grand Junction Railway Companion to Liverpool, Manchester, and Birmingham* (London, 1838), p. 12.

2 A. Marshall, 'The Social Possibilities of Economic Chivalry', *The Economic Journal* 17 (1907), pp. 7–29.

3 For instance, M. Girouard's classic *The Return to Camelot: Chivalry and the English Gentleman* (New Haven and London, 1981) does have a chapter on 'radical chivalry', but does not really consider commercial and civic chivalry at any length. Similarly, Michael Alexander's *Medievalism: the Middle Ages in Modern England* (New Haven and London, 2007) does

This essay will explore the incorporation of chivalric concepts, symbols and practices into the commercial and civic cultures of Manchester, demonstrating both how easy and how difficult it could be for Victorian urban elites to appropriate and manipulate medieval chivalry in their attempts to legitimise, romanticise and historicise their public and private lives, activities and environments. As this is an immense subject, two case studies will be used to explore how chivalry became a vehicle for civic and commercial identities: the autobiography of the Manchester engineer and inventor of the steam hammer, James Nasmyth, and the Manchester Albert Memorial and its architectural context, specifically the main façade of the Town Hall.[4] The Nasmyth case study deals with a personal and private appropriation of medieval chivalry by a cosmopolitan and internationally-minded Scot who settled on the outskirts of Manchester, although he did not form part of the civic elite – and it considers the problematic transfer of chivalric and paternalist ideals into the sphere of his commercial and managerial activities. The Albert Memorial study takes us into the very heart of civic Manchester and explores a public and political attempt to adapt medieval chivalry to contemporary civic use in articulating the political and provincial independence of the city.

James Nasmyth's autobiographical life, first published in 1883 and edited by that doyen of industrial biography and self-help literature Samuel Smiles, opens with a telling paragraph:

> Our history begins before we are born. We represent the hereditary influences of our race, and our ancestors virtually live in us. The sentiment of ancestry seems inherent in human nature, especially in the more civilised races. At all events, we cannot help having a due regard for the history of our forefathers. Our curiosity is stimulated by their immediate or indirect influence upon ourselves [...] The gifts of nature, however, are more valuable than those of fortune; and no line of ancestry, however honourable, can absolve us from the duty of diligent application and perseverance, or from the practice of the virtues of self-control and self-help.[5]

Here, Nasmyth establishes a balance and a relationship between past and present which is an underlying theme of the entire autobiography. Nasmyth's self-image is shaped by his consciousness of his family name, and his appropriation and representation of a hereditary and chivalric past to serve present purposes. He cites Burke's *Peerage and Baronetage* as a source which explains how his ancestors

contain a chapter on 'The Working Men and the Common Good' which covers figures such as William Morris, but focuses entirely on literary and artistic medievalism.

4 For a brief account of Nasmyth's life and career, see R. Angus Buchanan, 'James Hall Nasmyth (1808–80)', *The Oxford Dictionary of National Biography*, ed. H. G. G. Matthew and B. Harrison (Oxford, 2004). Recent scholars working on Nasmyth – such as J. A. Cantrell – have naturally focused on his engineering achievements.

5 J. Nasmyth, *James Nasmyth, Engineer: An Autobiography*, ed. Samuel Smiles (1883; this edition, London, 1912), p. 1.

came by their name.[6] Fighting under the royal standard for James III of Scotland – against the treasonous Douglas family – Nasmyth's ancestor was allegedly forced to flee a battlefield and take shelter in a smithy. Here he was working in disguise as a hammerman, when some Douglas partisans approached him suspiciously, calling out 'Ye're *nae smyth*!'[7] Nasmyth and his host fell upon them with dagger and hammer, rallied the royal forces, and secured a victory. The chivalrous hero was accordingly rewarded with a coat of arms featuring 'a hand dexter with a dagger, between two broken hammer-shafts' and the motto 'Non arte sed marte' ('Not by art but by war'). Nasmyth then explains how he has at once retained and modernised this coat of arms:

> In my time, I reversed the motto (*Non marte sed arte*); and instead of the broken hammer-shafts, I have adopted, not as my 'arms', but as a device, the most potent form of mechanical art – the Steam Hammer.[8]

Nasmyth not only included an illustration of the scene in the smithy by his own hand (see figure 4.1), but also featured the original coat of arms in other illustrations in the autobiography.[9] The significance of heraldry to him was perhaps heightened by the fact that his father, an artist by profession, had been in his youth apprenticed to a coachbuilder in Edinburgh: he was employed in 'decorating the panels of the highest class of carriages and painting upon them coats of arms, with their crests and supporters [...] it introduced him to the practical details of heraldry'.[10]

In a study of the shaping of middle-class male identities in the Victorian autobiographies of self-made men, Donna Loftus comments that 'largely without exception, these narratives began with a genealogy that charted the male line, usually from the author's father, identifying the skills and talents the author associated with him in ancestors'; Nasmyth's autobiography, she argues, is 'a particularly exaggerated example' of this tendency.[11] Such autobiographies 'presented an alternative version of heroism in which progress was the result of the small but regular actions of modest men [... who] constructed themselves as the agents of historical change'.[12] While Nasmyth does not deny the necessity of 'diligent application and perseverance' by the individual, it is suggested here that this unusual example of autobiography actually suggests the degree to which at least some of the new industrial men of the nineteenth century wanted to see themselves as the agents of historical

6 Ibid.

7 Ibid., p. 2.

8 Ibid.

9 Ibid., pp. 3, 11, 222.

10 Ibid., p. 22.

11 D. Loftus, 'The Self in Society: Middle-Class Men and Autobiography', *Life Writing and Victorian Culture*, ed. D. Amigoni (Aldershot, 2006), p. 74. For the shaping of middle-class male identities through life-writing see also, for example, R. Gray, 'Self-Made Men, Self-Narrated Lives: Male Autobiographical Writing and the Victorian Middle-Class', *Journal of Victorian Culture* 6:2 (2001), pp. 288–312; R. Gagnier, *Subjectivities: A History of Self-Representations in Britain, 1832–1920* (Oxford, 1991), pp. 171–94; P. Joyce, *Democratic Subjects: The Self and the Social in Nineteenth Century England* (Cambridge, 1994).

12 Loftus, 'The Self in Society', p. 81.

Figure 4.1 J. Nasmyth, 'The Origin of the Name' from J. Nasmyth, *James Nasmyth, Engineer: An Autobiography* (1912 edn), facing p. 310.

continuity as well as change – and their sense of both the urgency and the difficulty of aligning past and present, for the act of appropriating the chivalric past to the modern agenda was not an uncomplicated one.

The themes established here in Nasmyth's description of his earliest ancestor – loyalty to the crown and country, high principles, industrial activity and energy, inventive resourcefulness and so on – are further documented in his succeeding account of his family, which serves paradoxically to root his progressive and modernising activities in a genealogical and chivalric past. Thus the family history includes vigorous involvement on both sides in the seventeenth-century Civil War (considered by some to be one of the last forays of British chivalry), and the persecution for witchcraft of a female ancestor who showed 'the spirit of an experimental philosopher' in her use of spectacles to read her Bible.[13] The suggestion here, that negotiating the relationship of past and present is not an easy one (it is possible to have ancestors who stand for different causes), is further illustrated in his account of his great-great-grandfather, Michael Naesmyth [*sic*]. This ancestor, Nasmyth notes, having lost his 'ancestral property', pursued a career as a 'builder and architect', modelling the modernising tendencies of the engineer himself:

[13] Nasmyth, *Autobiography*, pp. 3–7.

> His chief employment was in designing and erecting new mansions, principally for the landed gentry and nobility. Their old castellated houses or towers were found too dark and dreary for modern uses. The drawbridges were taken down, and the moats were filled up. Sometimes they built the new mansions as an addition to the old. But oftener they left the old castles to go to ruin; or, what was worse, they made use of the stone and other materials of the old romantic buildings for the construction of their new residences.[14]

The balance of past and present is delicately poised in this paragraph: Nasmyth accepts the need for modernisation, but deplores any developments which destroy 'old romantic buildings' or brutally recycle their materials for new constructions. In other words, appropriating the past is a problematic process. His own preference is clearly for modernisation which is 'an addition to the old', an organic development which mirrors his own, carefully graduated version of his family history, in which the medieval knight evolves gradually into the modern man of commerce, retaining the more admirable attributes of his ancestors. Nasmyth records, for example, that his great-great-grandfather's tomb (complete with the coat of arms) carries an additional motto – *Ars mihi vim contra Fortunae* – 'which I take to be, "Art is my strength in contending against Fortune" – a motto which is appropriate to my ancestors as well as myself'.[15]

The theme of appropriate preservation of the past – and, in particular, of one's family heritage – is reiterated when Nasmyth documents his father's career as an artist and an adviser on landscaping. In his youth, he recalls, there was an 'utter want of appreciation of the dignified beauty of the old castles and mansions' (which were often dismantled), but also 'an utter ignorance of the beauty and majesty of old trees'.[16] What initially appears to be merely a celebration of picturesque landscape takes a more significant turn when Nasmyth recollects that his father often created models of old buildings and trees, and on one occasion produced what he called '"The Family Tree", as he required each member of his family to assist in its production. We each made a twig or small branch, which he cleverly fixed into its place as a part of the whole.'[17] This tree is illustrated in the autobiography: the image thus marries the idea of creatively shaping the landscape of the past, incorporating such chivalric items as castles and pedigrees, with intelligent industry. Alexander Nasmyth's hand is 'dextrous', an adjective which both celebrates his craft and recalls the language of heraldry.[18]

The interconnection of pedigree, trees, and the heraldic symbol of the hammer on the family coat of arms is a constant feature in James Nasmyth's self-imaging and his organic adaptation of his medieval heritage to modern purposes. At the end of his career, when he retired from his business, he chose to move south to Kent, seemingly in an attempt to establish himself as a country squire, albeit a decidedly

14 Ibid., p. 8.
15 Ibid., pp. 11–12.
16 Ibid., p. 36.
17 Ibid.
18 Ibid., pp. 37–8.

modern one. The Tudoresque house which he purchased was situated in a neighbourhood which was at once modern and historic:

> The view from it was charming, and embodied all the elements of happy-looking English scenery. The noble old forest trees of Penshurst Park were close alongside, and the grand old historic mansion of Penshurst Place was within a quarter of a mile's distance from our house [...] the railway station, which was within thirty-five minutes' pleasant walk, enabling us to be within reach of London, with its innumerable attractions, in little more than an hour and a quarter.[19]

The association with the medieval manor house of Penshurst is telling. It was the family home of the sixteenth-century poet and soldier, Sir Philip Sidney, who was for many contemporary Victorians the premier model of chivalry: the episode at the Battle of Zutphen, when the dying Sidney shared his water-bottle with another fallen comrade, was frequently depicted in paintings and illustrations.[20] But equally significant is the immediate access to the bustling metropolis of London by the modern transport system. This modernising appropriation of the medieval and chivalric was continued in the house itself, a mock Tudor mansion built in the mid nineteenth century by George Devey.[21] A free reinterpretation of such Tudor mansions as Compton Wynyates and Dorney Court, its asymmetrical façade also reminds the viewer of the nearby garden front of Penshurst Place.[22] Nasmyth tells us that 'from my hereditary regard for hammers – two broken hammer-shafts being the crest of our family for hundreds of years – I named the place "Hammerfield", and so it remains to this day. The improvements and alterations to the house and gardens were considerable.'[23] These alterations included an octagonal workshop, where Nasmyth spent many 'a busy and delightful hour in handling my tools', an activity which brought to mind 'bygone incidents' and 'friends long dead'.[24] Outside, the planting of trees was an important part of the improvement. Their abundant growth meant that:

[19] Ibid., pp. 359–60.

[20] M. G. Brennan, '"Thy necessity is yet greater than mine": The Re-mythologizing in the Literary and Visual Arts of Fulke Greville's Water-bottle Anecdote (1750–1930)', *Sidney Journal* 28:2 (2010), pp. 1–40. The Battle of Zutphen (1586) was an episode during the Eighty Years' War between the Netherlands, supported by England, and Spain.

[21] See A. Ballantyne and A. Law, *Tudoresque: In Pursuit of the Ideal Home* (London, 2011), pp. 149–50 for the architectural history of Hammerfield, which was originally built for the Victorian artist F. R. Lee.

[22] It is therefore not surprising to learn that Devey was also employed in restoration work at Penshurst Place, 'trying to make the new buildings seem at ease in their surroundings by having been built and adapted piecemeal over centuries' – an approach which approximates to Nasmyth's refashioning of his medieval ancestry to create a modern self-image. Ballantyne and Law, *Tudoresque*, pp. 72–3.

[23] Nasmyth, *Autobiography*, p. 360.

[24] Ibid., p. 362.

> they required the judicious use of the axe in order to allow the fittest to survive and grow at their own free will. Trees contrive to manage their own affairs without the necessity of much labour or interference. The 'survival of the fittest' prevails here as elsewhere.[25]

Thus trees were fostered and valued for their picturesque antiquity, but – like the Nasmyth family tree – were subject to the forces of modernity and must be adapted (judiciously) to contemporary use. Similarly, Hammerfield may allude to Nasmyth's medieval ancestry and construct him as a traditional country gentleman, but it must also serve the engineering and astronomical interests of its owner. But what is equally remarkable in this passage is the way in which Nasmyth – while highlighting his own intervention with the axe – nevertheless contrives to make it seem that the trees achieve historical continuity by an organic and evolutionary process (managing their own affairs). Thus we have at once the adaptation of the past for present purposes and an attempt by Nasmyth to deny his own agency in the process of adaptation, rendering it apparently natural and inevitable.

This appropriation of a historical heritage was, however, not limited to Nasmyth's private life: it was also a significant (if problematic) element in shaping his public identity and his understanding of his own profession. The reader of his autobiography is inevitably struck by the fact that Nasmyth's business trips always involved visits to historic sites as well as industrial and engineering works.[26] As he himself said:

> I desired to pass through the most interesting and picturesque places [...] I wished to see the venerable buildings and cathedrals of the olden time, as well as the engineering establishments of the new. Notwithstanding my love for mechanics I retained a spice of antiquarian feeling. It enabled me to look back to the remote past, into the material records of man's efforts hundreds of years ago, and contrast them with the modern progress of arts and sciences.[27]

One such comparison – an appeal to a past pedigree, to medieval chivalry – is particularly revealing. When Robert Bald, the mining engineer, invited the young James Nasmyth to visit his workshop, the Carron Ironworks, to see a 'powerful pumping engine', Nasmyth immediately tells his reader that this establishment is 'near Bannockburn – close to the site of the great battle in the time of Robert the Bruce'. Its medieval chivalric past, however, mingles with its new industrial history, as it is 'classic ground to engineers', being a site 'associated with the memory of Roebuck, Watt and Miller of Dalswinton'. Nasmyth offers a sublime description of the ironworks, reminiscent of the industrial scenes of Joseph Wright of Derby (whom he mentions), alluding to the 'fire-lit halls' and the 'dark, black, smoky

[25] Ibid., p. 363.

[26] A similar mobile mixture of the modern and the medieval is apparent in the promotion by rail companies, in guidebooks designed for the railway traveller, of the heritage sites adjacent to their lines. See M. Freeman, *Railways and the Victorian Imagination* (New Haven and London, 1999), pp. 80–1.

[27] Nasmyth, *Autobiography*, p. 157.

vaults' in a way which might well have reminded the contemporary reader of the Gothic castles of Horace Walpole and Ann Radcliffe.[28] Applauding the 'useful arts' of the ironworks, Nasmyth moves on to recall that:

> I was afterwards greatly interested by a collection of old armour, dug up from the field of Battle of Bannockburn close at hand. They were arranged on the walls of the house of the manager of the Carron Ironworks. There were swords, daggers, lances, battle-axes, shields, and coats of chain-armour. Some of the latter were whole, others in fragmentary portions. I was particularly interested with the admirable workmanship of the coats of mail [...] The beauty and exactness with which this chain-armour had been forged and built up were truly wonderful. There must have been 'giants in those days'. This grand style of armour was in use from the time of the Conquest, and was most effective in the way of protection, as it was fitted by its flexibility to give full play to the energetic action of the wearer.[29]

Nasmyth makes no explicit link between this medieval chain-mail and the 'vast power', 'capability of resistance' and 'moving parts' of the great machines he viewed at the ironworks, nor between the diligent and accomplished craftsmanship of the medieval armourers and the modern ironworkers – yet this is inevitably implied by their narrative proximity. The engineers and ironworkers of Carron are clearly in descent from medieval predecessors, the knights and armourers of Bannockburn – although Nasmyth cannot quite bring himself to articulate this historical continuity.

The same appropriation of a medieval heritage to contemporary industry is much more explicit when, later in life, Nasmyth selected a site for his own engineering workshop at Patricroft, near Manchester, on the Bridgewater Canal. Nasmyth was obviously influenced by pragmatic considerations, one of which was apparently the 'abundance of skilled workmen' in the area:

> I was in the neighbourhood of Manchester, which forms the centre of a population gifted with mechanical instincts. From an early period the finest sort of mechanical work has been turned out in that part of England. Much of the talent is inherited. It descends from father to son, and develops itself from generation to generation. I may mention one curious circumstance connected with the pedigree of Manchester: that much of the mechanical excellence of its workmen descends from the Norman smiths and armourers introduced into the neighbourhood at the Norman Conquest by one Hugo de Lupus, the chief armourer of William the Conqueror.[30]

Drawing on the information provided for him by William Stubbs, a local manufacturer of files, Nasmyth continues with an account of the cottage industry established by Lupus for the manufacture of armoury and weaponry. Even when 'the use of armour was discontinued', Nasmyth tells us, 'the skill that had formerly

28 Ibid., pp. 105–6.
29 Ibid., p. 107.
30 Ibid., p. 206.

been employed in forging chain armour and war instruments was devoted to more peaceful purposes': the making of tools, wire, and even clocks and watches. These 'refined metal-workers' are all the 'direct descendants' of the original Norman settlers.[31]

It would be gratifying to find more explicit evidence that chivalric ideals shaped both Nasmyth's view of his relationship with his employees and his treatment of them – given that he so clearly constructed himself as the direct although modernised descendant of the medieval knightly Nasmyth, and as the contemporary manifestation of Hugo de Lupus. However, Nasmyth predominantly describes his relationship with his workmen in the language of classical economics, presenting his opposition to trade unions, for instance, as his natural preference for a 'free trade in ability' which allowed him to pay differential wages to those of greater promise and talent.[32] As Patrick Joyce points out, such *laissez-faire* economic liberalism 'set limits to the degree and nature of the operation' of the 'new paternalism' of the northern industrial factories.[33] For Nasmyth and his ilk, medieval chivalric ideals were not so easily adaptable to the commercial and industrial environment as they were for contemporary Tory Radicals such as John Ruskin and the Young England group.[34]

Nevertheless, there are occasional signs that Nasmyth evaluated relationships between masters and men in other contexts in the light of feudal traditions. For instance, whilst visiting the factory of the Liverpool engineer, William Fawcett, he noted that Fawcett had a 'peculiar courteous manner [which …] reminded me of some of my father's oldest noble employers, and the representations given of them by some of our best actors'. He continued to note 'the courtly yet kindly manner in which he addressed his various foremen and others', and the 'lasting impression' Fawcett made as 'a most interesting specimen of "the fine old English gentleman, quite of the olden time"'.[35] Here Nasmyth does not directly invoke the medieval code of chivalry, referring instead and no doubt deliberately to the more chronologically nebulous period of 'olden time'.[36] Similarly, he exhibits a certain amount of unease with Fawcett's courtly attitude (note the theatrical allusion, which suggests that he suspects it is an impersonation rather than an authentic expression of nobility). But, nevertheless, this comparison hints at the potential for the industrialist to be

31 Ibid., p. 205.

32 See, for instance, Ibid., p. 209.

33 P. Joyce, *Work, Society and Politics: The Culture of the Factory in Later Victorian England* (New Brunswick, 1980), p. 136.

34 Ruskin's reinvention of the industrialist as a benevolent and paternalist 'merchant' in *Unto this Last* (1860) and other similar texts is well known; John Morrow, in his *Young England: The New Generation* (London and New York, 1999) has argued that the aristocratic pressure group, Young England, was more sympathetic to the idea of commercial paternalists ('The Seigneurs of the Sea', as George Smythe imagined them) than had previously been thought (pp. 133–8).

35 Nasmyth, *Autobiography*, pp. 153–4.

36 P. Mandler, '"In the Olden Time": Romantic History and the English National Identity', *A Union of Multiple Identities: The British Isles, c. 1750–c.1850*, ed. L. Brockliss and D. Eastwood (Manchester and New York, 1997), pp. 78–92; A. Sanders, *In the Olden Time: The Victorians and the British Past* (New Haven and London, 2013).

interpreted as the feudal lord of the modern age. A similar moment of reflection surfaces during his account of a business trip to Russia, where Nasmyth visited the iron foundries and engine works of Francis Baird. Noting that the workmen were all 'serfs, or sons of serfs' given to the Baird family by the Empress Catherine, Nasmyth adds that 'I had rarely seen more faithful and zealous set of workmen [...] They were able and skilful, and attached to their employers by some deeper and stronger tie than that of mere money wages.'[37]

While Nasmyth does not directly represent labour relations in his workshops through a medieval idiom, the contextual culture in which he found himself would have made it difficult for him to avoid at least thinking in these terms. In Books III and IV of *Past and Present* (1842), a celebrated work by a fellow Scot, Thomas Carlyle repeatedly appropriated the language and values of chivalry to the contemporary industrial context.[38] Calling for a new 'noble Chivalry of Work', he urged the 'working aristocracy' of Britain – the new industrial and commercial middle-class elites – to learn from the medieval barons how to offer strong leadership, protect their inferiors, and offer a just division of the rewards of enterprise.[39] One of the models of leadership proposed is William the Conqueror and 'his Taillefers, *Ironcutters*': for Carlyle, William is a model not only of the fair division of the spoils of war, but also of a clear-sighted commitment to 'what *is* really what on this God's Earth' – a man who would have recognised the superiority of the hard-working 'Steam-Engine Captains of Industry' over the effete nineteenth-century aristocracy.[40] This representation of William as a distinctly modern, proto-industrial man of metal is echoed in Nasmyth's autobiographical representation of Hugo de Lupus. Similarly, the engineer's reinvention of his medieval family motto seems remarkably similar to Carlyle's refiguring of the opening line of Virgil's *Aeneid* in a manner which Nasmyth was bound to approve: 'For we are to bethink ourselves that the Epic verily is not *Arms and the Man*, but *Tools and the Man* – an infinitely wider kind of Epic.'[41] The Carlylean echoes in Nasmyth's autobiography seem too many to ignore.

What Nasmyth might have hesitated to express in his prose may well have surfaced in some of his illustrations to the autobiography, in some of which he seems to be experimenting with ways to contemporise the chivalric. Most of these show landscape features, or are technical drawings of his inventions. However, a significant minority are what his contemporaries might well have called 'fancy pictures', evocations of a fairy-tale past, often rather similar to the picturesque work of early-nineteenth-century illustrators such as George Cattermole and George Cruikshank. These illustrations show an ambiguous and possibly subconscious response to the medieval and early modern past, a mixture of fascination with, and fear of, the power of nostalgia, which Nasmyth seems to have managed to organise into an orderly narrative of descent and organic development in his text. In other words, these sketches are exactly that: rough workings for the achievement of an integrated

37 Nasmyth, *Autobiography*, p. 282.

38 T. Carlyle, *Past and Present*, intro. G. K. Chesterton (1843; Oxford, 1932), pp. 141–305.

39 Ibid., p. 280.

40 Ibid., pp. 199, 219–21.

41 Ibid., p. 257.

picture of past flowing into present, of pedigree and progress. Take, for instance, *The Fairies*.[42] This appears to depict the richly adorned Gothic study of an antiquary, and the accoutrements of chivalry are readily apparent – swords hang above the fireplace, heraldic shields appear in the panels of the walls and the stained glass window, a helmet is displayed above the doorway, and the Holbeinesque portraits have coats of arms above their sitters. The room is occupied by what appears to be a fairy court, lit by the hearth fire. The costumes look vaguely sixteenth – or seventeenth-century. In the centre of a ring of fairies, couples dance, whilst under the canopy afforded by the seat of a carved chair sit a king and queen. Other fairies dance on a stool to the sound of a mandolin or guitar, whilst on the antiquary's desk some monastic figures seem to peruse the pages of an enormous book. Nasmyth's fantastical image seems to belittle and distance the past: is it as alien to and inconceivable in the modern world as fairies, as 'long, long ago' as the fairy story? But, as Nicola Bown has shown, the depiction of fairies might well express a number of complex and conflicting anxieties about industrialisation, including, for instance, a sense of human insignificance when compared with the size and power of new machinery.[43] In other words, the drawing might well reflect Nasmyth's attempts, not to dismiss and even ridicule the past, but to negotiate a place for it as the precursor of modernity. This seems to be the implication of one of the comments which the image provoked: Viscount Duncan, to whom Nasmyth sent his drawings, commented that he received much pleasure in contemplating these 'detailed works of art', recalling that 'the same hand and head that executed them invented the steam hammer, and many other gigantic pieces of machinery which will tend to immortalise the Anglo-Saxon race'.[44] The connections made here between the medieval past and the mechanical present, minute details and huge machinery, seem to confirm a reading that these images were not just a private pursuit, but also a site for the negotiation of the relationship between the medieval and the modern. This antiquarian study is a modern workshop for the adaptation of the 'olden time' to the modern context.

Erected between 1862 and 1865, the Manchester Albert Memorial was one of many memorials erected to the memory of the queen's consort after his death in 1861. The debates and controversies provoked by these memorials are revealing of the tensions inherent in the adaptation of chivalric appurtenances and values to Victorian civic and commercial purposes. Whilst the Albert Memorial is remarkable as an uneasy appropriation of chivalry in its own right, its real significance for the civic and commercial culture of Manchester is only fully evident when its situation in front of the Town Hall is considered (see figure 4.2). For the Town Hall, although often seen as a triumphant appropriation of the medieval and chivalric to modern civic and commercial purposes, also represents a struggle to adapt the past to the present. Subtexts can be found in its messages, which show that the process of appropriation of the medieval and the chivalric was not unproblematic. Moreover, when the Memorial and the statuary of the front façade of the Town Hall

42 Nasmyth, *Autobiography*, facing p. 310.
43 N. Bown, *Fairies in Nineteenth-Century Art and Literature* (Cambridge, 2001).
44 Nasmyth, *Autobiography*, p. 311.

Figure 4.2 Thomas Worthington, The Albert Memorial, Manchester, 1862–65. The northern pavilion of the Town Hall and two of its statues can be seen to the right of the Memorial. Courtesy of Paul Burrows Photography Ltd.

are considered in relation to each other, further complications are apparent. These can be read as a debate on medieval and modern chivalry. It is not the intention here to offer exhaustive architectural descriptions of either Thomas Worthington's Albert Memorial or Alfred Waterhouse's extraordinary Town Hall building, which have been examined extensively elsewhere.[45] Instead, this essay will focus on the use of specific features to articulate a brand of modern civic and commercial chivalry,

[45] For the memorial, see A. J. Pass, *Thomas Worthington: Victorian Architecture and Social Purpose* (Manchester, 1988), pp. 42–50; T. Wyke with H. Cocks, *Public Sculpture of Greater Manchester* (Liverpool, 2004), pp. 11–16; C. Hartwell, *Manchester* (New Haven and London, 2001), pp. 143–4. For Manchester Town Hall, see J. H. G. Archer, 'A Classic of its Age', *Art and Architecture in Victorian Manchester*, ed. J. H. G. Archer (Manchester, 1985), pp. 127–61; Hartwell, *Manchester*, pp. 71–88.

which is presented as both a counterbalance and a challenge to the contemporary chivalry of the Prince Consort.

The Memorial itself made uncomplicated and extensive use of chivalry and heraldry to celebrate the prince, drawing on an already established tradition of representing Albert as a medieval knight or king. This tradition dated from as early as 1842, when Albert and Victoria had presided over a costumed ball at Buckingham Palace, dressed as Edward III and his consort, Philippa of Hainault – an event commemorated in Edwin Landseer's 1842–46 painting of the royal pair in their costumes – and continued after his death in images such as Edward Corbould's memorial portrait of 1863–64.[46] In the Manchester Memorial, Matthew Noble's statue of the prince presents him dressed in the robes of the Order of the Garter (which was founded by Edward III). The canopy and base (see figure 4.3) are extensively decorated with Albert's coat of arms and heraldic bearings, as the *Illustrated London News* made clear in an extensive and technically-informed description:

> In the centre of the piers or buttresses are piers carved on stone, representing the arms of England quartered with those of Saxony, differenced with the late Prince Consort's own label of three points argent, charged in the central point gules, alternate with the simple arms of Saxony, emblazoned with foliated bands and arched coronet on a field barry of ten, or and sable. Each shield is surmounted by the peculiar coronet of the late Prince, which differs from the Imperial crown in having eight instead of four arches. They rise from strawberry leaves, and are curved. Each shield is encircled by the garter, with the usual motto, and below, on a label, is the motto 'Treu und Fest'. These armorials are repeated on the eight angle panels of the basement, and in the intermediate panels, of which they are five on each front, are carved the various crests of the late Prince's ancestry.[47]

These chivalric appurtenances – which stress the prince's noble (and German) descent and hereditary right to rule – are, however, supplemented by other features of the Memorial, establishing him as a thoroughly modern and constitutional consort. The four smaller canopies at the corners contain statues of Art, Commerce, Science and Agriculture, of which Albert was seen as the encourager and patron, while lower figures identify branches of the four key activities: Science, for instance, is accompanied by Chemistry, Astronomy, Mechanics and Mathematics. In the

[46] See D. N. Mancoff, '"Albert the Good": Public Imagery and Private Iconography', *Biography* 15:2 (1992), pp. 140–64; and Girouard, *The Return to Camelot*, pp. 111–28, for further coverage of Victoria's and Albert's use of medieval chivalry to shape public and private identities. For Victorian attitudes to and representations of Philippa of Hainault, see R. A. Mitchell, 'The Red Queen and the White Queen: Exemplification of Medieval Queens in Nineteenth-Century Britain', *Heroic Reputations and Exemplary Lives*, ed. G. Cubitt and A. Warren (Manchester, 2000), pp. 157–77.

[47] 'The Manchester Albert Memorial', *Illustrated London News*, 26 January 1867, p. 88. Pass points out that the accuracy of the armorials was ensured by the assistance which Worthington, who was struggling with this aspect of the commission, received from the queen's librarian at Windsor Castle (Pass, *Worthington*, p. 46).

spandrels above the arches of the canopy appear the heads of figures representative of the Arts and Sciences, including Michelangelo, Raphael, Beethoven, Goethe, Schiller and Shakespeare: there is a slight bias towards Teutonic worthies, no doubt a compliment to Albert's German ancestry.

Figure 4.3 Detail of the Prince Consort's crests on the base of the Albert Memorial, Manchester. Courtesy of Paul Barrows Photography Ltd.

However, an examination of the circumstances surrounding the erection of the Memorial reveals a more disrupted relationship between prince and people than this coalescence of armorial bearings and modern attributes suggests. At a meeting of the committee for the memorial in January 1862, the mayor, Thomas Goadsby, complained that the amount collected by subscription so far was 'pitiably small'; it is clear from the discussions that a major cause of the low level of donation was uncertainty about the form the memorial would take. As one committee member put it, 'amounts would depend on the character of the memorial'.[48] Indeed, there was considerable debate on this subject, with practical projects such as a hospital, a school of science and working-class housing all being suggested as alternatives.[49] Such arguments about the form that memorials to the prince should take were

[48] 'The Manchester Albert Memorial', *Manchester Times*, 18 January 1862, issue 215. Of course, a major factor in the lack of contributions to the Memorial fund, particularly by the working classes, was probably the economic hardship caused by the 'Cotton Famine', as many commentators suggest (see, for example, Wyke, *Public Sculpture*, p. 13). The City Council, however, was not slow in demonstrating loyalty to the crown in more economical ways: on 10 November 1862 they voted for the usual loyal address to the queen and the Prince of Wales on the latter's attainment of his majority. *Manchester City Council Proceedings for 1862–1863* (Manchester, 1864), pp. 6–7.

[49] 'The Manchester Albert Memorial', *Manchester Guardian*, 18 September 1862. See also Wyke, *Public Sculpture*, p. 11 and Pass, *Worthington*, p. 42.

not confined to Manchester: there was clearly a sense that a more practical and pragmatic form of memorial than a statue might be appropriate in many provincial communities.[50] For instance, in the *Aberdeen Journal* for 29 January 1862, the editorial called for a memorial expressive of the character of the prince, who was not 'a warrior, or a statesman, or a man celebrated for uncommon achievements' but 'the type and excellence of noble manhood – the exemplar of every duty of good citizenship': for such an individual, 'some work of public utility' would be more appropriate than a statue in his likeness.[51] In other words, citizenship should replace chivalry in the memorialisation of the prince. Indeed, two weeks after this meeting, the Manchester committee was obliged to quash what appears to have been an attempt to appropriate Memorial funds to the erection of towers on the cathedral.[52] A week later, the mayor offered to pay for the Memorial statue, a clear attempt to rectify the apparently stingy response of his fellow citizens.

The letter which announced this contribution was full of oblique reproach. Goadsby suggested that his own preference for a statue had influenced the committee into proposing that form of memorial, although he affected to believe that 'the very generally entertained feeling of my fellow-citizens' in favour of such an effigy also affected the decision. Adding that he wished to 'testify in an especial manner that high appreciation which I entertain for the character of his late royal highness', he continued with significant emphasis:

> It will not, I believe, be doubted that there is no place in Her Majesty's dominions more strongly called upon than Manchester publicly to testify to the memory of the late Prince Consort. The constant interest and anxiety manifested by his late Royal Highness to promote everything calculated to add to the prosperity and happiness of the people of this city, will never be forgotten; and I am unwilling to believe that my fellow-citizens, in carrying out the resolution adopted on the proposition of the Bishop of Manchester, would, under any circumstances, be content with a statue only to his memory [...] I will not doubt that the liberality of my fellow-citizens will enable the committee to secure a memorial of the late Prince Consort worthy of this great city, and adequately to testify the gratitude felt for the services rendered by the great and good man whose untimely loss the nation now deplores.[53]

Evidently, Goadsby doth protest too much, suggesting that Mancunian enthusiasm for celebrating the memory of Albert through the erection of a statue was decidedly muted. While Goadsby's gesture was inevitably welcomed by the committee, his

50 See E. Darby and N. Smith, *The Cult of the Prince Consort* (New Haven and London, 1983), pp. 58–84, for more extensive coverage of other memorials – statues and images – and the debates surrounding their erection.

51 'Monument to the Prince Consort', *Aberdeen Journal*, 29 January 1862, issue 5951.

52 'The Manchester Albert Memorial', *Manchester Times*, 1 February 1862, issue 217, and 'The Manchester Memorial of Prince Albert', *Manchester Guardian*, 4 February 1862.

53 'The Manchester Albert Memorial – Munificent Offer of the Mayor', *Manchester Times*, 8 February 1862, issue 218. This subject was raised again in a report on 'The Manchester Albert Memorial', *Manchester Times*, 8 July 1865, issue 396.

chivalric loyalty to his prince may well have been more cynically received by the wider community. In an article in the radical *Reynolds's Newspaper* published the very next day, the Lord Mayor of London, William Cubitt, was accused of discouraging collections for the sufferers of a colliery disaster because it diverted contributions from 'a gigantic fund for erecting some colossal memorial to the late Prince Albert', which might 'fructify into a baronetage, and eventually a peerage'.[54] In other words, Cubitt was seen to aspire to the sort of armorial bearings which appeared on the Manchester Albert Memorial: his chivalry was perceived as being of a self-interested character and it is quite possible that Goadsby's generosity solicited the same kind of private criticisms.

Goadsby's sense that the people of Manchester were failing in their duty to their prince was echoed elsewhere. On 8 July 1863, an article in the *Manchester Guardian* reminded readers that 'in precise proportion to the amount raised will be the beauty of the memorial', combining an appeal to local pride with loyalty to the crown in a pointed reference to the 'more magnificent' London Memorial, followed by a call for Mancunians to show how appreciative they were of the late prince.[55] A similar reproach is apparent in an account of the progress of the construction of the Memorial two years later. Here the journalist of the *Manchester Times* recorded that, now the pedestal was visible above the hoardings, it could be seen that its upper stages contained six panels:

> These panels are designed to contain the armorial bearings of the Prince, but for the present they will be left in the rough [...] all the decorative carving is to be postponed until the subscriptions approach more nearly the cost of the memorial than they do now. As it advances, it will no doubt arrest attention, and be a permanent reminder to many who pass by that they have not paid a substantial tribute of admiration to the lamented prince. To see the panels of the podium uncarved, and know that they await the sculptor's chisel to cut upon their surfaces the escutcheons of the prince; to see above them a rude string course, and to be conscious that out of the unshapen stone beautiful forms of fruit and foliage ought to be carved [...] to witness all this imperfection, and to elicit the explanation that it means lack of money, would testify to something with which Manchester citizens would not willingly reproach themselves, nor allow visitors to reproach them [...] It rests with the citizens to say how soon the statue and its canopy will be a memorial to be gazed upon with unmingled satisfaction.[56]

This article also reviewed the funding strategies, stressing that it was important that wealthy private subscribers did not entirely deprive working-class contributors of their chance to participate. However, it was largely such well-to-do individuals who did provide over half of the money, some of them being prosperous members of

54 'A Wet Blanket Upon Charity', *Reynolds's Newspaper*, 9 February 1862, issue 600.
55 'The Manchester Albert Memorial', *Manchester Guardian*, 8 July 1863.
56 'The Manchester Albert Memorial', *Manchester Times*, 20 May 1865, issue 389.

Manchester-based German firms.[57] On completion of the Memorial, the committee made a public request to the mayor that – as the Memorial was to 'one who took the greatest interest in those sciences and manufactures which have been the foundation of the success of this district' – the queen should be requested to inaugurate it.[58] Victoria declined to do so, even though she had previously and warmly approved the design of the Memorial.[59] However, the Prince of Wales did ask both to view it and to meet its architect in 1869; Worthington noted significantly that the prince was particularly interested in the heraldic panels of the Memorial.[60]

The occasion of the inauguration of the Memorial was recorded in an article in the *Manchester Guardian* which epitomises the tensions which the history of the monument has so far suggested. The journalist opened with a description of the Memorial which is obliquely critical: he commented on the 'semblance of instability' when viewing it from Queen Street, remarking that two of the buttresses appear to be falling outwards. He adds that the short spire makes it look 'somewhat stunted'. If this seems to hint at the apparently shaky commitment of the city's people to the royal family, the following critique of the armorial bearings adds to that impression. It is initially directed at the account of the Memorial given to the Committee, where the heraldry is (accordingly to this commentator) 'inaccurately described'.[61] While he admits that the Memorial itself is largely accurate in its representation of the prince's arms and those of the German royal families to which he was connected, the writer still finds an error in the arms of Saxony and is critical of the repetition of the same heraldic devices on each façade of the Memorial. Use of the badges of the various orders of knighthood to which Albert belonged would have produced 'more variety'.[62] Thus the Memorial not only represents the rather lukewarm loyalty of Mancunians to their prince, but also a tendency to see his monument – and perhaps he himself – in terms of ancient lineage rather than as a successful Victorian version of the knight: old chivalry rather than new.

The writer's reportage of the speeches only increases the sense of unease. William Fairbairn's characterisation of the people of Manchester as 'a loyal, a liberal and a generous-minded people' who are 'certainly not behind any other city' in attachment to 'the throne and the constitution' is full of subtextual acknowledgements of tensions between national loyalty to the crown and local liberalism and interdependency, between commitment to hereditary monarchy and modernising

57 Wyke, *Public Sculpture*, p. 14. Goadsby, as chairman of the Albert Memorial Committee, made strenuous efforts to solicit further funding from the broader population, presenting a circular to the City Council on 5 July 1865, calling for the collection of a penny in the pound from all rate-payers to allow 'all classes' to contribute to the cost of the Memorial, although on an 'entirely voluntary' basis: it was passed. *Manchester City Council Proceedings for 1864–65* (Manchester, 1865), pp. 198–9.

58 'The Manchester Albert Memorial', *Morning Post*, 5 September 1866, issue 28934, p. 2.

59 Pass, *Worthington*, pp. 46, 48. The invitation to the queen and her reply declining it are recorded in *Manchester City Council Proceedings for 1865–66* (Manchester, 1866), pp. 168–9.

60 Pass, *Worthington*, p. 50.

61 'The Inauguration of the Manchester Albert Memorial', *Manchester Guardian*, 24 January 1867.

62 Ibid.

constitutionalism, between extravagant competition with other cities and preference for the economic reserve of funds for local needs.[63] In the *Manchester Guardian's* account of events, Fairbairn continued with an assertion of the city's contribution to the advance of the 'fine and useful arts' which received 'encouragement' from the prince; a statement which at once acknowledges and undermines the prince's role as cultural and scientific patron. Nor was the mayor's address any less ambiguous. While celebrating the 'good and virtuous prince' and voicing the usual loyal sentiments, it suggested local pique at the non-attendance of any royal personage at the inauguration, and dwelt on how the square in which the Memorial appears would soon contain 'the finest town hall in England', on which 'the face of the statue will look directly'.[64] While the mayor argues that this will allow citizens to reflect on the virtues of the Prince Consort, there is an implication that Albert will also be able to reflect on the power and achievement of Manchester. This sensitivity to the context of the Memorial and how it might resonate with Manchester's strong sense of regional pride and independence had already been apparent in earlier discussions about the location of the monument.[65] One of the proposed sites, the centre of the esplanade of the Royal Infirmary, was rejected for (among other reasons) the fact that it was 'not fitting that the back of a statue, even though it be that of an illustrious Prince, should be turned to the figures of the *savans* Dalton and Watt'.[66] In other words, even the modernising Albert was not to be allowed to trump the achievements of modern scientists (particularly Mancunian ones).

So, for all his creation of a modern constitutional form of monarchy, Albert was still a hereditary prince – as his son's attention to the heraldic panels suggests – and thus a troubling representative of the traditional monarchical order of the Middle Ages for many Mancunians. While the *Manchester Guardian* article on the inauguration of the Memorial merely hinted at this tension in Albert's representation, an article of 27 October 1866 in the *Manchester City News* was considerably more explicit in its expression of the archaic character of the heraldic (and perhaps other) achievements of the Prince Consort. While praising the beauty of the Memorial, the author of the article took exception to 'one little feature':

63 Works which illuminate the politics of Victorian Manchester include M. Hewitt, *The Emergence of Stability in the Industrial City: Manchester, 1832–67* (Cambridge, 1996) and A. Kidd, *City, Class, and Culture: Social Policy and Cultural Production in Victorian Britain* (Manchester, 1985).

64 'The Inauguration of the Manchester Albert Memorial', *Manchester Guardian*, 24 January 1867.

65 See, for instance, *Manchester City Council Proceedings for 1862–63*, pp. 88–9, for 4 March 1863, which records the Council's consideration of a site in Bancroft Street for the Memorial. It was noted that creating a square would give the Memorial a 'commanding and satisfactory situation', but it is equally clear that the improvement of the 'sanitary condition of the district', the free passage of 'constantly increasing traffic', and the 'favourable influence' which the Memorial might have on the character of the architecture built around it were of equal importance to councillors. In other words, the Memorial was to serve progressivist liberal Mancunian agendas (or at least not to obstruct them).

66 'The Manchester Albert Memorial', *Manchester Guardian*, 17 November 1862. The allusion here is apparently to bronze figures of the scientists John Dalton (1766–1844), a Mancunian, and James Watt (1736–1844).

> It may be inevitable and consonant [...] with the exigencies of the style of architecture chosen for the memorial, that the Herald's College should have been so largely used in its ornamentation. Is it impossible that the story of the Prince's life might not have been expressed in other art language than that of the unknown tongues of heraldry?[67]

He continues to describe the blazons of the base as:

> An unintelligible and goblin invention in which, certainly, not one man in ten thousand will be able to discover any significance whatsoever. A memorial to a man essentially of this generation should hardly be made the medium for the study of antiquities [...] shield and visor, armour and battle-axe [...] have become the property of melodrama.[68]

While initially offering a moderate, liberal and meritocratic argument that the Memorial should have celebrated what Albert had done, rather than his descent, the author subsequently revealed a decidedly more anti-royalist and radical perspective in his remarks on Victoria's refusal to attend the inauguration of the Memorial. He commented sarcastically that this absence was because she was 'enjoying herself to such an extent in the darling highlands of Scotland that she cannot fatigue herself. Is the Prince of Wales too "fatigued" too?'[69]

The difficulties and disjunctions surrounding the creation of the Memorial thus illustrate the difficulties inherent in exchanging old chivalries for new. However, once it was built, the appropriation of the medieval and chivalric on the façade of the Town Hall served to situate the prince within a broader chronological narrative of the history of Manchester, climaxing in its modern manifestation as the premier industrial city, and to continue to reveal the difficulties of appropriating the chivalric to modern uses. Charles Dellheim's somewhat underrated work, *The Face of the Past*, long ago identified the adept adaptation of the medieval to 'the values and structures of liberal industrial England' which Alfred Waterhouse's Town Hall epitomises. He stressed that the building was not 'an attempt to imitate an aristocratic style' or an expression of 'nostalgia for an idyllic rural past', but a 'cultural coup' in which 'middle-class, progressive, urban England' appropriated the medieval to its own agenda.[70] This is a largely accurate analysis, and – as many commentators have pointed out – the architect himself was the very first to emphasise the decided modernity of the Town Hall.

[67] 'The Albert Memorial', *Manchester City News*, 27 October 1866.

[68] Ibid.

[69] 'The Albert Memorial', *Manchester City News*, 27 October 1866. Victorian anti-monarchist republicanism was, of course, at its height during the 1860s, following Victoria's grief-stricken withdrawal from public life: see, for instance, A. Taylor, *Down with the Crown: British Anti-Monarchism and Debates about Royalty since 1790* (Chicago, 1999).

[70] C. Dellheim, *The Face of the Past: The Preservation of the Medieval Inheritance in Victorian England* (Cambridge, 1982), pp. 153, 156. A preference for the neo-Gothic from the very start of the project was indicated by a motion at the Manchester City Council meeting of 6 March 1867 in favour of that style (which was, however, withdrawn). See *Manchester City Council Proceedings for 1866–67* (Manchester, 1867), p. 112.

However, the history of the building's iconography reflects the same awkward appropriation of the chivalric as the Memorial and, indeed, the two together may well be said to create a dialogue of difficulties.[71] Facing the Memorial and framing the Albert Square window of the Banqueting Hall, part of the suite of civic function rooms on the first floor of the building, are four statues. They depict John Bradford, a sixteenth-century Protestant martyr; Henry of Grosmont, first duke of Lancaster; Humphrey Chetham, the founder of the school and library; and Charles Worsley of Platt, a Parliamentary general (see figure 4.4). Two of the four – Grosmont and Worsley – are depicted as knights and warriors. Grosmont appears in full armour, with a lion-headed helmet. Other external statues also include medieval and chivalric figures: Thomas de Gresley, the fourteenth-century Lord of the Manor, and Thomas De La Warre, the fifteenth-century Lord of the Manor and founder of the collegiate church, appear on the corner of Albert Square and Princess Street, becoming part of the frieze of figures adorning the Banqueting Hall pavilion.[72] Together, Gresley, Warre and Grosmont illustrate the appropriation of the medieval history of Manchester to its civic and commercial agenda. If one looks to one of the best-known historical works on Manchester available to contemporaries, C. H. Timperley's *Annals of Manchester* (1839), some insight can be gained into contemporary understanding. Timperley records that in 1351, 'Henry "the Good", earl of Derby', became duke of Lancaster with 'the same jura regalia as the earls palatine of Chester had ever enjoyed. The duchy became consequently a petty kingdom, and some of its original regulations are yet in force.'[73] Thus we have Henry the Good facing Albert the Good, a continuity of royal chivalric achievement. But we also have an assertion of Mancunian independency ('a petty kingdom') which would align well with the liberal political tradition of the city. Nevertheless, it is a petty kingdom legitimated by royal authority and ruled by a royal prince.

The two Lords of the Manor perhaps fitted more comfortably in a liberal civic and commercial agenda. Timperley's *Annals* record that in 1301 Gresley granted to the burghers '"the great charter of Manchester", by which it became a free borough'; subsequently, in 1307, he was summoned to parliament and given the Order of the Bath.[74] For Victorian readers, Gresley thus married chivalry and knightly achievement to constitutional and civic government and freedoms. However, this is not Gresley's only significance within the Mancunian narrative: Timperley records in previous pages the advance of knowledge about the manufacture of textiles such as silk and linen in Europe and England, and then states that in 1311 'mention is made of fulling mill at Colne, thus proving the manufacture of woollens in this county

[71] For illustrations and descriptions of the external statuary see Wyke, *Public Sculpture*, pp. 24–30. Dellheim's analysis of the political message of the external statuary is also very useful: *The Face of the Past*, pp. 161–3.

[72] These finalised subjects were suggested to the City Council by Waterhouse after 'lengthy and careful consideration and consultation' with the chairman of the Town Hall sub-committee, as the architect put it in a letter of 17 November 1873: *Manchester City Council Proceedings for 1873–74* (Manchester, 1875), p. 95.

[73] C. H. Timperley, *Annals of Manchester: Biographical, Historical, Ecclesiastical and Commercial, From the Earliest Period to the Close of the Year 1839* (Manchester, 1839), p. 12.

[74] Ibid., p. 12.

Figure 4.4 External statuary (by Farmer and Brindley of London) facing Albert Square, on the northern pavilion of Manchester Town Hall. From left to right: John Bradford; Charles Worsley of Platt; Humphrey Chetham; and Henry of Grosmont, first duke of Lancaster. Courtesy of Paul Burrows Photography Ltd.

by nearly thirty years before the introduction of the Flemish artizans by Edward III'.[75] This entry is sandwiched between Gresley's call to parliament and his death.[76] Thus the knight was also associated with the development of Manchester textile manufacture – which, it is to be noted, does not rely on royal patronage; another assertion of independence similar to those apparent in the discussions about the Albert Memorial. Of course, this message is somewhat subverted by Ford Madox Brown's depiction in the Great Hall of 'The Establishment of Flemish Weavers in Manchester, AD 1363' (1881–82) and (more immediately) by the inclusion of a statue of Edward III over the mayor's private entrance in Princess Street; William Axon, in his *Architectural and General Description of the Town Hall* (1878), deliberately declared that 'Manchester owed so much' to the king because of 'his introduction of the Flemish weavers into this country'.[77] Perhaps the more erudite viewer could be expected to make the connection between Gresley and the emergence of medieval Manchester as a textile centre, and to note that the king was consigned to the side entrance, while the provincial knight enjoyed a much more prominent billing.

[75] Ibid., pp. 10–11.

[76] Ibid., p. 12.

[77] W. E. A. Axon, *An Architectural and General Description of the Town Hall, Manchester* (Manchester and London, 1878), p. 5. In his updated version of Timperley's *Annals*, Axon still implies that the textile industry in Manchester was founded prior to the reign of Edward III: W. E. A. Axon, *Annals of Manchester: A Chronological Record from Earliest Times to the End of 1885* (Manchester, 1886), p. 13.

Moreover, he faces (and faces down) that modern manifestation of royal patronage of commercial and economic progress, the Prince Consort.

Grosmont and Gresley both belonged to the fourteenth century, which was seen by contemporaries as the most productive and attractive period of the Middle Ages. It was the century of Chaucer, John Wycliffe, Edward III and the Black Prince, and it was associated with national cultural, commercial, constitutional and religious progress – as is illustrated clearly by the statue of the Black Prince in Leeds.[78] The statue of Thomas De La Warre can be seen as part of this narrative: Timperley records that he, too, was summoned to parliament (and his foundation of the collegiate church offers a medieval religious dimension to the narrative).[79] If the inclusion of Gresley might be seen to offer a slightly disruptive note in the commercial history of Manchester – is royal patronage *really* responsible for the origins of the Mancunian textile industry? – other statues on the façade offer a similarly destabilising perspective on constitutional advancement. Over the entrance gable appears Agricola, the Roman general 'by whom this district was conquered' (Axon tells us), surmounted and flanked (on the second floor) by the figures of Henry III and Queen Elizabeth.[80] Axon's *Description* does not explain why these two monarchs were included, but Dellheim suggests that 'both of them granted charters that enlarged the scope of local self-government'.[81] This may be the case, but both of them were also rather better known as opponents to the increase of parliamentary authority. While Queen Elizabeth enjoyed a buoyant Victorian reputation (and we may even view her inclusion as an oblique compliment to Queen Victoria, with whom she was sometimes associated), she was nevertheless a monarch who once imprisoned the speaker of the House of Commons.[82] Henry III's reputation in the Victorian period (and, indeed, before and since) was considerably less positive: although parliament was allegedly established during his reign, no one is inclined to attribute this achievement to the king whose emphasis on royal authority led to two civil wars with his barons. Indeed, while Elizabeth carries a sealed charter as well as a short sceptre, Henry sports instead an orb and a decidedly more substantial rod of office, as if to suggest how much more absolutist he was than his female successor.

The inclusion of these two royal figures can thus be read as much as a warning to a royal visitor as a graceful tribute to his or her lineage: a sermon in stone for the Prince Consort in the square. The warlike figure of another knight – Worsley of Platt – could also be seen to contribute to this narrative. Rather an obscure figure now, he would have been recognised by Victorian Mancunians: he has a page in Axon's

[78] See Barbara Gribling, 'Nationalizing the Hero: The Image of Edward the Black Prince in English Politics and Culture, 1776–1903' (unpublished Ph.D. thesis, University of York, 2009).

[79] Timperley, *Annals*, p. 13.

[80] Axon, *Description*, p. 3.

[81] Dellheim, *Face*, p. 161. Wyke, *Public Sculpture*, pp. 25–6, offers a similar explanation, although he comments that it was market privileges specifically which were extended.

[82] See N. J. Watson, 'Gloriana Victoriana: Victoria and the Cultural Memory of Elizabeth I', *Remaking Queen Victoria*, ed. M. Homans and A. Munich (Cambridge, 1997), pp. 79–194. Also M. Dobson and N. J. Watson, *England's Elizabeth: An Afterlife in Fame and Fantasy* (Oxford, 2002), pp. 147–78.

Annals of Manchester and is one of Francis Espinasse's fourteen *Lancashire Worthies* (1874).[83] Like Gresley, the Commonwealth general could be seen as combining chivalry and constitutionalism: a warrior who was also a member of parliament. Terry Wyke points out that Worsley was a replacement for Waterhouse's original suggestion of Charles I: a substitution by the Town Hall building sub-committee which 'underlined the shift in historical emphasis'.[84] Another interesting change in Waterhouse's initial line-up was the replacement of William the Conqueror by the figure of Elizabeth, and the removal of Edward the Elder to the less significant façade overlooking Cooper Street, at the back of the building, to make way for Henry III.[85] The decision to retain Edward, while excluding William I, may well have been dictated both by Victorian enthusiasm for the Anglo-Saxons as icons of freedom, constitutional development and racial vigour and superiority, and by the sense that – as a king who fortified Mercian *burhs* – he was of more local significance than the Conqueror.[86] The same sense of local and liberal priorities is apparent on the central gable of the main façade. Here, the diminutive figure of the patron saint of England and the knight *par excellence*, St George, surmounts (but is also rendered inconspicuous by) the coat of arms for the city, dated 1873.[87]

In the light of the dialogue established here between the sculptures on the Town Hall and the figure of Albert facing them, the speeches made at the banquet celebrating the opening of the Town Hall assume a particular significance. In proposing Victoria's health, the mayor, Abel Heywood, alluded both to the loyal sentiment of Mancunians – who esteemed the queen for 'her *constitutional* rule' – and (once again) to their pique at her non-attendance at a Manchester inauguration. The bishop of Manchester, with rather less than Christian charity, reminded Her Majesty that it 'might not be necessary to appeal to the sentiment of loyalty today, but it might be tomorrow', when it would be 'a matter of regret' to the queen that she had not graced her (nevertheless chivalric and supportive) Mancunian subjects with her presence. He followed this pointed reflection with a stout defence of the cost of the Town Hall as a much better use of money than the similarly expensive purchase of a 'first-class iron-clad' ship for the purposes of war (and specifically the defence of the heathen Ottoman Empire).[88] These were the awkward accents of modern chivalry, which was loyal to Queen Victoria (but only as a constitutional monarch and within the context of local self-government), and liberal with its purse (but for the purposes of civic weal and prestige, rather than in adulation of the princely knight Albert). These civic dignitaries looked to Gresley and Worsley, the civic and commercial knights on the Town Hall, and not to the problematic prince on the Memorial.

[83] Axon, *Annals*, p. 62, and F. Espinasse, *Lancashire Worthies* (London, 1874), pp. 96–115. The fact that Worsley was buried in the Henry VII chapel at Westminster Abbey may have meant that he was seen to offer a democratic challenge to royal authority even after death.

[84] Wyke, *Public Sculpture*, p. 24.

[85] Ibid., p. 26.

[86] See, for instance, B. Melman, 'Claiming the Nation's Past: The Invention of an Anglo-Saxon Tradition', *Journal of Contemporary History* 26 (1991), pp. 575–95, for the Victorian enthusiasm for the Anglo-Saxons.

[87] Wyke, *Public Sculpture*, p. 25; see also Axon, *Description*, p. 3.

[88] Ibid., pp. 45–9.

*

In 1906, Roger Oldham published his *Manchester Alphabet*, an ABC book for children. The illustration 'L for Lord Mayor' offers a view of the back of the mayor, who is standing in the porch of the Town Hall, looking out towards the Albert Memorial, ready to receive some important guests. The tiny figure of the Prince Consort hovers over the dumpy civic dignitary, who carries an incongruous umbrella despite the apparent absence of rain. Perhaps a well-informed adult viewer would recall the long-ago Eglinton tournament of 1839, a Tory chivalric representation rendered ridiculous by the terrible weather, of which the knight sporting an umbrella became the iconic image.[89] This mayor perhaps wears his civic chivalry uncomfortably, or with a liberal independence. On the floor of the porch, the artist has represented the emblem of Manchester, the community-minded and industrious bee, beloved of Bernard Mandeville and a key element in the heraldic symbolism of the Town Hall, but one which expresses a modern, independent, commercial city. In my opinion, it is difficult to better this image in terms of its summary of Victorian Manchester's difficult but definite appropriation and adaptation of the chivalric to modern civic and commercial agendas.

[89] For the Eglinton tournament, see I. Anstruther, *The Knight and the Umbrella: An Account of the Eglinton Tournament 1839* (Gloucester, 1963). For a recent re-evaluation of the political role of its initiator, see A. Tyrrell, 'The Earl of Eglinton, Scottish Conservatism, and the National Association for the Vindication of Scottish Rights', *Historical Journal* 53 (March, 2010), pp. 87–107.

5

'The Dark Side of Chivalry': Victory, Violence and the Victorians*

Barbara Gribling

DURING THE 1870s, 1880s and 1890s, liberals, radicals, popular and academic historians, folklorists and writers of children's books became increasingly critical of medieval chivalry. This essay examines the negative view of the Middle Ages summed up in the Victorian author Louise Creighton's phrase, 'the dark side of chivalry'.[1] The sense that chivalry was a problematic ideal gained strength in the late nineteenth century, in part as a reaction against the more idealised Romantic and Tory visions that had circulated in boys' magazines, art, adventure novels and even re-enactments. These criticisms reflected new discussions about the nature of democracy and the progress of the people, about explorations into the primitive mind and about tensions over proper role models to form the right kind of British man and citizen. This essay explores these alternative darker views of chivalry that appeared in the late Victorian period, arguing that chivalry became a site of reflection and even contestation about the less palatable aspects of the medieval and, by extension, Victorian society.

The late Victorians inherited a dim picture of the Middle Ages from eighteenth-century Enlightenment and Whig narratives. This view was, in part, the creation of the *philosophes*: for instance, in his 1756 *Essai sur les moeurs et l'esprit des nations*, Voltaire portrayed the Middle Ages as a violent and intellectually dark age in contrast to his own time where reason and science triumphed.[2] The progress of civilisation was another Enlightenment theme. Exploration and the growth of empire in the eighteenth century led to a wider interest in categorising present societies and comparing earlier periods unfavourably to their own stage in history.[3] Equally

* I would like to thank Jacqueline Rose, Ludmilla Jordanova, Billie Melman and Peter Mandler for their comments on this essay.

[1] Louise Creighton, *Life of Edward the Black Prince* (London, 1876), p. 185.

[2] Voltaire, *Essai sur les moeurs II, Oeuvres completes de Voltaire,* nouvelle edition, vol. xii (1878).

[3] Alicia C. Montoya, *Medievalist Enlightenment: From Charles Perrault to Jean-Jacques Rousseau* (Cambridge, 2013), pp. 45–7, 62. Montoya's work explores alternative Enlightenment narratives towards the medieval that move away from the negative depictions espoused by the *philosophes*.

influential was the standard Whig version of the Middle Ages. Presenting themselves as the guardians of liberty, the Whigs saw the Middle Ages as a time of oppression, Catholic dominance and barbarism. While Whig narratives admitted the valuable development of institutions such as parliament, these institutions became part of a wider narrative of unfolding liberalism and nationality that saw the Middle Ages as the less advanced precursor to contemporary Britain.[4]

By the early nineteenth century, this darker view was increasingly overlaid by opposing Romantic re-evaluations, both Tory and popular.[5] In 1842, Queen Victoria and Prince Albert dressed as the fourteenth-century English royals, Edward III and Philippa of Hainault, at their medieval-themed costume ball in order to present Victoria's reign as a new golden age. Just three years earlier, in 1839, the Romantic Tory the earl of Eglinton had recreated a chivalric tournament at Eglinton Castle in the west of Scotland. This event drew a crowd of 100,000 and reflected a public fascination with chivalric spectacle.[6] Audiences clamoured to read Sir Walter Scott's novels and to watch their theatrical renditions. Children's stories presented the medieval past as a repository of moral ideas. The reprinting and dissemination of medieval source material such as the *Chronicles of Froissart* fostered a taste for and a trade in medieval tales of adventure.[7] The popularity of these works testified to a focus on real examples of commendable virtue. In periodicals and novels, chivalric heroes such as Edward the Black Prince, the eldest son of Edward III of England and the victor of the battles of Crécy and Poitiers, and Henry V, the hero of Agincourt, were proffered as examples of virtue for children and adults to emulate.[8]

Yet, in the 1830s and 1840s, celebratory depictions of the Middle Ages were being contested and many of these critiques were politically charged.[9] The Whigs,

[4] Peter Mandler, '"In the Olden Time": Romantic History and English National Identity, 1820–50', *A Union of Multiple Identities: The British Isles, c.1750–c.1850*, ed. L. Brockliss and D. Eastwood (Manchester, 1997), pp. 78, 82; Colin Kidd, *British Identities Before Nationalism: Ethnicity and Nationhood in the Atlantic World 1600–1800* (Cambridge, 1999), pp. 79–81; J. W. Burrow, *A Liberal Descent: Victorian Historians and the English Past* (Cambridge, 1981), p. 21. For examples of earlier, non-Whig narratives of 'Gothic' democracy, see R. J. Smith, *The Gothic Bequest* (Cambridge, 1987).

[5] This Romantic focus on emotion and sentiment was not new. A more nuanced reading of eighteenth-century works reveals an Enlightenment interest in sentimentalism. See David Allan's chapter in this volume.

[6] The Eglinton tournament prompted later parodies, including that by Richard Doyle (who would pen cartoons for *Punch Magazine*), offering a comedic take in *The Tournament, or, The Days of Chivalry Revived*. Here he sketched scenes of fumbling modern knights incapable of living up to the lofty standards that, in their minds, this bygone age represented. Richard Doyle, *The Tournament, or, The Days of Chivalry Revived* (London, 1840).

[7] Written by the fourteenth-century author Jean Froissart, the *Chronicles* focused on the deeds of knights during the Hundred Years' War. The *Chronicles* were popular on both sides of the Atlantic into the late nineteenth century. H. P. Dunster, *Stories from the Chroniclers: Froissart* (London, 1847); S. C. Lanier, *The Boy's Froissart* (1878; this edition, London, 1880); H. Newbolt, *Stories from Froissart* (New York and London, 1899).

[8] Barbara Gribling, 'Nationalizing the Hero: The Image of Edward the Black Prince in English Politics and Culture, 1776–1903' (unpublished Ph.D. thesis, University of York, 2009).

[9] Richard Faber, *Young England* (London, 1987), pp. 204–16. For far-left critiques, see Karl Marx and Friedrich Engels, *Manifesto of the Communist Party* (1848; this edition, New

for example, criticised the ideals of Young England, an aristocratic Tory political group that looked to feudal society as a model for social and political relations. They saw the group's attempt to recreate medieval models and promote feudal and chivalric codes as antiquated and elitist in a new age of reform.[10] There was also criticism of Gothic architecture and objects, which were associated with aristocratic exclusivity and Catholicism. Critics of Augustus Pugin, whose 1836 book *Contrasts* and decorations in the new Houses of Parliament epitomised the new Gothic style, reviled the architect for his papist tendencies.[11] More generally, as Peter Mandler has shown, the mass culture revival of the Tudor past from the 1820s to the 1850s was partly a reaction to perceptions of the violent, elitist and Catholic Middle Ages.[12] New print technology such as steam-printing machines aided the dissemination of these competing visions of the medieval past.[13] While this essay will focus on these growing critiques, it is important to remember that the Romantic strain of chivalry continued to be used, promoted and celebrated.

By the late nineteenth century, new elements appeared that led to increased criticism of medieval chivalry. In the 1870s, a new historical scholarship emerged that was generally more critical of Romanticism. Equally significant was a growing political radicalism that was increasingly suspicious of social inequality. In anthropology, there was a budding interest in the primitive and psycho-cultural development, and chivalry was deemed a product of 'primitive mentalities'. New ideas about masculinity intensified criticism of the more bellicose medieval role models. All of these critiques of medieval chivalry filtered into the mass market through popular history texts and historical readers for children. Reflecting changing ideas about politics, character, science, education and war, a range of historians, liberals, radicals and writers all argued that medieval chivalry had become a problematic ideal. By the turn of the twentieth century, the negative aspects of chivalry were a prominent part of the academic and popular dialogue about the medieval past.

Twentieth-century historians have focused their attention on the conservative uses of the medieval past in Victorian Britain, and on how conservative thinkers used chivalry to paint a harmonious picture of the social and political relationships between rulers and those who were ruled. However, in the late Victorian period, liberal thinkers criticised chivalry for promoting a social and political hierarchy that

York, 1908), pp. 35–6; Friedrich Engels, *The Condition of the Working-Class in England in 1844*, trans. Florence Wischnewetzky (London, 1920), p. 293n.

10 For example, see contemporary reactions to Disraeli's Young England novels – *Coningsby* (1844), *Sybil* (1845) and *Tancred* (1847) – in Faber, *Young England*, pp. 204–16.

11 Augustus Welby Northmore Pugin, *Contrasts: or a parallel between the noble edifices of the middle ages, and corresponding buildings of the present day; shewing the present decay of taste. Accompanied by appropriate text* (London, 1836); Corinna M. Wagner, '"Standing Proof of the Degeneracy of Modern Times": Architecture, Society and the Medievalism of A. W. N. Pugin', *Beyond Arthurian Romances: The Reach of Victorian Medievalism*, ed. Jennifer A. Palmgren and Lorretta M. Holloway (New York and Basingstoke, 2005), pp. 11–12.

12 Mandler, '"In the Olden Time"', pp. 78–92.

13 Aileen Fyfe, *Steam-Powered Knowledge: William Chambers and the Business of Publishing, 1820–1860* (Chicago, 2012), pp. 5, 7–11.

impeded the progress of the people. They (like historians in other parts of Europe) became increasingly concerned with the relationship between the people and those in power, and with the people as a political force – both in their own period and in the past.[14] One of the tenets of late Victorian liberalism was that the government should represent the people and not simply the interests of one class.[15] From their perspective, chivalry appeared to promote social and political hierarchy and was the product of a selfish class. Liberal evaluations of the medieval period tended to react against what these writers saw as rosy conservative versions of the relationship between medieval rulers and aristocrats and those they ruled.

The non-conformist liberal historian Samuel Rawson Gardiner typifies the more critical picture of chivalry that developed in the late nineteenth century. Gardiner, most famous for his discussion of Oliver Cromwell and the Stuart monarchy, reflected wider liberal views in his exploration of medieval chivalry in textbooks and histories of the 1870s, 1880s and 1890s. In particular, Gardiner promoted the idea that chivalry was inherently barbaric – its ingrained elitism led medieval knights to attack the lower orders for their own glory. In his 1884 *Historical Biographies*, for example, Gardiner cited the Black Prince's brutal campaign of 1355–56, which ravaged France, as an example of how chivalric heroism harmed 'the people':

> In an age when every gentleman loved fighting for its own sake, and when no gentleman cared for the harm which he might do to peasants and tradesmen, even the Black Prince thought it no shame to march about the country with his English soldiers and their Gascon allies, burning towns and farms, and carrying off what booty was to be found.[16]

It was not merely the French people who had to be worried. Gardiner argued that the elitism of chivalry impeded the constitutional development of the English as well, and he maintained that the medieval peasants and townspeople had limited political voice. While other historians lauded the fourteenth century for the development of the House of Commons, Gardiner saw medieval government as reflecting a primitive and unenlightened form of power relations:

[14] For example, see the work of the French historian Jules Michelet: Bettina R. Lerner, 'Michelet, Mythologue', *Myth and Modernity*, ed. Dan Edelstein and Bettina R. Lerner (New Haven, 2007), pp. 63–71; Paul Viallaneix, *La Voie Royale: Essai sur l'idée de peuple dans l'oeuvre de Michelet* (Paris, 1959), pp. 11–107; Jules Michelet, *Introduction à l'histoire universelle* (Paris, 1831); Jules Michelet, *Histoire de la Révolution* (Paris, 1847–52). See also Michelet's discussion of the people in his own time: Jules Michelet, *Le Peuple* (Paris, 1846). Patrick Joyce has argued that the shift to a mass male democracy involved new kinds of political narratives that focused on giving the people 'a sense of political identity, a sense that enabled politics to go forward' with their leaders: P. Joyce, 'The Constitution and the narrative structure of Victorian politics', *Re-reading the Constitution: New Narratives in the Political History of England's Long Nineteenth Century*, ed. James Vernon (Cambridge, 1996), pp. 187–8.

[15] Jonathan Parry, *The Politics of Patriotism: English Liberalism, National Identity and Europe, 1830–1886* (Cambridge, 2006), pp. 88–9.

[16] Samuel Rawson Gardiner, *Historical Biographies* (London, 1884), p. 59.

> Even the House of Commons, which was pushing its way to a share of power, was comparatively an aristocratic body. The labouring population in town and country had no share in its exaltation. Even the citizens, the merchants and tradesmen of the towns, looked down upon those beneath them without trust or affection. To the warrior knight the labouring man was but an instrument of service to whom no courtesy was due, and who, in war, might be pillaged or plundered without pity, when the defeated knight or gentleman would be received to mercy.[17]

Underpinning Gardiner's discussion was a wider liberal critique of chivalry. The idea that medieval rulers should have been concerned for the people as well as for the progress of the state reflected Victorian discussions about the role of those who governed. Gardiner's critique of the Black Prince's character paralleled the way in which liberal intellectuals of the period espoused the idea that men should sublimate their selfish instincts to act for the good of others.[18] It was the duty of the aristocracy, liberals argued, to live up to their responsibilities to the people, in both their public and their private lives. There was an underlying view among liberals that chivalry had impeded national progress in the past. The picture Gardiner painted of medieval chivalry as a force that prompted aristocrats to neglect their duty to the nation was different from that of his conservative predecessors and contemporaries, who saw chivalry as a vehicle that prompted national success.

One of the most common charges against the rulers of the Middle Ages was that their interest in chivalry induced them to neglect the due administration of the country. This is most clearly seen in the changing images of Edward III and Henry V. In the nineteenth century, both late medieval kings enjoyed reputations as chivalrous heroes. Indeed, at the turn of the century, writers on chivalry such as Sir Tomkyns Hilgrove Turner, in his 1799 *A Short Account of Ancient Chivalry*, pinpointed the age of Edward III as the moment when chivalry achieved its pinnacle, when 'A romantic Nation, was led on by a romantic King'.[19] For others, the late Middle Ages evoked images of great victories in battle and of chivalric orders such as the Order of the Garter. In the Victorian era, Henry V's triumph at Agincourt was celebrated as a heroic feat that served both the king and the nation.

The critical evaluations that emerged in textbooks and history readers of the 1870s, 1880s and 1890s re-examined Edward III's and Henry V's roles as administrators. Previously, Edward III had enjoyed a reputation as a keen administrator and statesman whose reign saw the development of the House of Commons as an institution and whose policies contributed to economic growth through the wool trade. In his widely-read *View of the State of Europe during the Middle Ages* (1818), the historian Henry Hallam declared that Edward III was 'the father [...]

[17] Samuel R. Gardiner and J. Bass Mullinger, *Introduction to the Study of English History* (London, 1881), p. 91.

[18] Stefan Collini, *Public Moralists: Political Thought and Intellectual Life in Britain, 1850–1930* (Oxford, 1991), p. 65; Parry, *The Politics of Patriotism*, pp. 88–9.

[19] Tomkyns Hilgrove Turner, *A Short Account of Ancient Chivalry, and Description of Armour* (London, 1799), p. 23.

of English commerce' and, under his rule, 'commerce now became, next to liberty, the leading object of parliament'.[20] However, by the late nineteenth century more negative visions emerged in textbooks and readers, with some writers arguing that Edward III's governing played little part in the advancement of the nation. These writers suggested that the expansion of trade and the development of the House of Commons were due to the work of the people, rather than to the king's own policies. Thus, in a section called 'Parliament and People', the author of *Philips' Historical Readers* asserted that the House of Commons gained power 'in spite of many arbitrary acts of the king [Edward III]'.[21] Questions were raised as to Edward's effectiveness as a statesman, as well as to his motivations as a ruler, and, in particular, these revisions highlighted the ways in which the king's interest in war had curbed, rather than inspired, national economic development. This marked a substantial change in the understanding and use of the medieval past.

Indeed, in the late Victorian period the conservative view that chivalry sparked national progress came under increasing suspicion. The historian J. R. Green, in his 1874 *A Short History of the English People,* argued that 'no age of our history is more sad and sombre than the age which we traverse from the third Edward to Joan of Arc [...] In the clash of civil strife political freedom was all but extinguished, and the age which began with the Good Parliament ended with the despotism of the Tudors.'[22] Green was an ardent liberal whose *History* proposed a radical new way of looking at the past. His work explored the role of the English people in shaping the nation, by examining their lives and triumphs. The illustrated editions of Green's history further offered an alternative vision of this period by including depictions of medieval peasants and townspeople, rather than focusing exclusively on images of battles and aristocrats. While chivalric exploits like the English victory at the battle of Crécy could encourage pride, Green concluded that it did not contribute to the critical development of the nation in the interests of all its citizens:

> I have preferred to pass lightly and briefly over the details of foreign wars and diplomacies, the personal adventures of kings and nobles, the pomp of courts, or the intrigues of favourites, and to dwell at length on the incidents of that constitutional, intellectual, and social advance in which we read the history of the nation itself. It is with this purpose that I have devoted more space to Chaucer than to Cressy.[23]

The *History* was highly influential, both for its new approach and for its engaging style, becoming one of the most popular history books of the late Victorian era found in schools, libraries and homes throughout the nation.[24] In the wake of the

[20] Henry Hallam, *View of the State of Europe during the Middle Ages*, 2 vols (London, 1818), ii, pp. 469–70.

[21] *Philips' School Series, Philips' Historical Readers: Middle England, Book III* (London, 1884), p. 124.

[22] J. R. Green, *A Short History of the English People* (London, 1874), pp. 216–17.

[23] Ibid., p. v.

[24] Peter Mandler, *The English National Character: The History of an Idea from Edmund Burke to Tony Blair* (New Haven, 2006), p. 93.

Chartist movement of the 1830s and 1840s and the Reform Acts, Green's book reflected a new interest in the role of the people in the development of the nation.

For Green, the institution of chivalry curtailed the political freedom of the English people by oppressing them and hindering their progress.[25] Chivalry was restrictive, argued Green, because it encouraged an abuse of social hierarchy. It drove the nobility and those in positions of power to disregard the progress of the nation and to focus on their own wellbeing, as opposed to the interests of the people. Green's book highlighted this tension between chivalry's oppression and English liberty. In his discussion of the late medieval English monarch King Edward I, Green argued that the Romantic elements of chivalry were not only dangerous and destructive, but also un-English:

> The 'chivalry' so familiar in Froissart, with its picturesque mimicry of high sentiment, of heroism, love, and courtesy – a mimicry before which all depth and reality of nobleness disappeared to make room for the coarsest profligacy, the narrowest caste-spirit, and a brutal indifference to human suffering – was specially of French creation.[26]

While Edward I was able to cast off some of the 'baser influences of chivalry' due to his piety and focus on duty, later kings in Green's narrative were often seduced by chivalry's darker elements.[27]

Rather than uniting the nation and contributing to its success, in these works chivalry was presented as a detrimental force that took the attention of medieval kings and nobility away from the much more important business of governing. Central to these discussions was the king's practice of the chivalric ethos – expressed in elaborate ceremonies and pageants, violent warfare and romantic quests – that were costly in terms of lives and money. In particular, charges of how chivalry inspired knight-errantry – the overpowering desire for romance and adventure – took on a more negative tone in the late Victorian period. From the early nineteenth century, the knight-errant had been lauded in literature about the Middle Ages that focused on the spirit of adventure that chivalry inspired. Editors of medieval chronicles and romances, including the *Chronicles of Froissart* and the Arthurian legends, saw these knights-errant as role models whose brand of chivalry could embolden children and adults to do great deeds for their country.[28]

However, by the mid to late nineteenth century, popular textbook writers and

[25] Anthony Brundage, 'Green, John Richard (1837–1883)', *Oxford Dictionary of National Biography*, Oxford University Press, 2004 <http://www.oxforddnb.com/view/article/11391>, accessed 22 February 2014. Brundage refers to Green's interest in exposing 'oppressive oligarchic structures the English people had to liberate themselves from'.

[26] Green, *A Short History*, p. 176.

[27] Ibid.

[28] Dunster, *Stories from the Chroniclers: Froissart*; Newbolt, *Stories from Froissart*, pp. xxviii-xxix; Lanier, *The Boy's Froissart* (1878; this edition, New York, 1895), p. v; Sidney Lanier, *The Boy's King Arthur being Sir Thomas Malory's History of King Arthur and his Knights of the Round Table edited for boys* (New York, 1880), p. xxii. American Sidney Lanier based *The Boy's King Arthur* on Sir Thomas Malory's work.

historians (like Green and Edward Freeman) began to recast chivalry and its result, knight-errantry, as a negative practice where kings and nobles (like Don Quixote) went wrong-headedly in search of adventures and glory, neglecting the more important matters of the nation.[29] The author of the history series *Philips' Historical Readers* proclaimed that:

> [t]he Edward of the great French war was essentially a *knight-errant*. Thus he was personally daring, delighted in dangerous adventure, and won splendid victories; but [...] he was without the foresight of a great general or statesman, and reaped no permanent benefit from the matchless prowess of his armies.[30]

This view was echoed in the historian Freeman's 1869 examination of William Longman's *Life and Times of Edward the Third* for the *Fortnightly Review*. Freeman compared the policies of Edward III and Henry V, remarking that the earlier king's knight-errantry was 'at the expense of suffering millions'.[31] In contrast, Henry V enjoyed a better reputation: 'It was not as a knight-errant that he made war, but as a general and a statesman of the highest order, as a King worthy to wear the crown of the Great William and the Great Edward.'[32]

The liberal critique of chivalry in the late nineteenth century echoed wider criticism of conservative uses of the chivalric past. The Primrose League (founded in 1883), a popular organisation dedicated to promoting conservative ideology, adopted chivalric insignia and terminology, and its members were given chivalric ranks including knights and dames. The denunciation of knight-errantry may also have been a condemnation of these conservative modern knights, who took up the call of chivalry in pursuit of lofty ideals that the liberals saw as ridiculous and antithetical to their own ideas about the rights and privileges of the people.

Political drawbacks were just a part of the increasing perception of a dark side of chivalry. The work of the churchman Arthur Penrhyn Stanley helps us to examine critical discussions of chivalry from religious and moral perspectives, something that reflected wider debates about character, gentlemanliness and Christian

[29] For example, the author of *Longmans' 'Ship' Historical Readers* concluded that Edward III 'was a brave man, but he was often led away by the love of fame to carry on wicked and useless wars [...] His very success did harm, for it made English-men look to winning battles rather than to cultivating the more peaceful arts, which alone can make a nation great.' *Longmans' 'Ship' Historical Readers: Stories and Biographies, Book IV, From the Norman Conquest to the Year 1485* (London, 1893), p. 115.

[30] *Philips' School Series, Philips' Historical Readers: Middle England, Book III*, pp. 100–1.

[31] Edward Augustus Freeman, 'Review of Longman's Life and Times of Edward the Third', *Fortnightly Review* (London, 1869), p. 589; see also Elaine Hadley on the *Fortnightly Review* in *Living Liberalism: Practical Citizenship in Mid-Victorian Britain* (Chicago, 2010), p. 125.

[32] Freeman, 'Review', pp. 589–90. Here Freeman is referring to William I and Edward I. In the late nineteenth century both kings enjoyed reputations as statesmen and legislators. For example, Freeman's 1888 book on William depicted the king as the quintessential statesman directly influencing 'the laws and constitution of England'. Edward Augustus Freeman, *William the Conqueror* (London, 1888), preface.

brotherhood in the 1850s and 1860s. A prominent member of the Anglican church who was canon of Canterbury Cathedral and later dean of Westminster, Stanley wrote and spoke on a number of theological topics throughout his life, produced memoirs and penned a biography of his mentor, the Rugby headmaster Thomas Arnold.[33] In his public lectures and resulting book, *Historical Memorials of Canterbury*, Stanley ruminated on the applicability of chivalry as an ethos for modern men.[34]

In the *Memorials*, Stanley broached the negative rendering of chivalry through a discussion of the life of one of chivalry's main heroes, Edward the Black Prince. Canterbury Cathedral housed the Black Prince's tomb, which was a testament to the fourteenth-century prince's life as a warrior – the effigy showed the Black Prince as a sleeping knight, fully armed, while his shield, coat armour and sword were placed above the tomb as a reminder of Edward's chivalric prowess. In the nineteenth century, the Black Prince was known as one of the heroes of the chivalric age and his victories in the first half of the Hundred Years' War (Crécy, Poitiers and Nájera) were celebrated as much as Henry V's triumph at Agincourt. For Stanley, the honour code of the medieval knight was a key influence on Victorian gentlemanly conduct. Yet the Black Prince could not transcend the values of his age. Contemplating his deeds, Stanley wrote 'that the evil as well as the good of chivalry was seen in him'.[35]

There are two particularly significant aspects to Stanley's criticism. The first concerns the Black Prince and his father's warmongering: 'We shall never again see a King of England, or a Prince of Wales, taking advantage of a legal quibble to conquer a great neighbouring country, and lay waste with fire and sword a civilised kingdom, from mere self-aggrandisement.'[36] Stanley argued that this approach to war was unchristian and that it was the duty of men now to move away from unhallowed warfare and show 'Christian wisdom and forbearance'.[37] In this view, chivalry appeared to provoke men in the fourteenth century to seek out war for self-promotion and unjustified ends. It was the Christian duty of modern gentlemen knights to learn from the dark side of medieval chivalry and prevent such 'unjust' wars from occurring.

Second, Stanley stressed the Black Prince's elitism, a theme dwelt upon by historians such as Gardiner. The core problem with medieval chivalry, Stanley believed, was that its values were only promoted by and towards a particular class:

> it is our further privilege and duty to extend those feelings towards the classes on whom he [the Black Prince] never cast a thought, to have towards *all* classes of society, and to make them have towards each other; and towards ourselves,

[33] Arthur Penrhyn Stanley, *The Life and Correspondence of Thomas Arnold*, 2 vols (1844); Arthur Penrhyn Stanley, *Westminster Sermons: Sermons on Special Occasions Preached in Westminster Abbey* (New York, 1882).

[34] See the chapter on Edward the Black Prince in Arthur Penrhyn Stanley, *Historical Memorials of Canterbury* (1854; this 2nd edition, London, 1855), pp. 97–144.

[35] Ibid., p. 123.

[36] Ibid.

[37] Ibid.

> the high respect and courtesy, and kindness, which were then peculiar to one class only.[38]

For Stanley, the dark side of chivalry did not prevent it from being used by modern Britons. Rather, the good qualities of chivalry should be extended to all people, while the negative aspects were something for modern men to surpass. Stanley's stance on chivalry may have reflected his own ideas about inclusivity at a time of turbulence in the church. The late 1840s and early 1850s saw an increased division between high and low churchmen. As a broad churchman, Stanley championed contemporary chivalry as a unifying code of conduct that encouraged tolerance towards others. While he was pro-chivalry, he stressed that chivalry's negative aspects should be a warning to modern men and suggested that the gentleman knight should bring forth the positive elements of chivalry, while leaving some of its darker medieval features behind:

> It is a well-known saying in Shakespeare, that – 'The evil which men do lives after them; The good is oft interred with their bones.' But it is often happily just the reverse, and so it was with the Black Prince. His evil is interred with his bones; the good which he has done lives after him.[39]

Overall, Stanley promoted chivalry as a potentially universal Christian mode of conduct that could unite men. In 1865, the clergyman and novelist Charles Kingsley, in a sermon on faith before Queen Victoria, summed up this view:

> Some say that the age of chivalry is past: that the spirit of romance is dead. The age of chivalry is never past, as long as there is wrong left unredressed on earth, and a man or woman left to say, 'I will redress that wrong, or spend my life in the attempt.'[40]

Stanley encouraged his readers to bring forward the good elements of chivalry while leaving the undesirable aspects firmly in the past.

In contrast, the popular anthropology writer J. A. Farrer perceived chivalry to be an ethical relic from humanity's uncivilised past, and his work focused on the brutal violence of chivalry. New ideas in the 1870s, 1880s and 1890s about anthropology and the ways in which societies developed influenced how both chivalry and the medieval period were understood. The discovery of 'prehistory', early fieldwork and the expansion of empire led to a renewed interest in the 'primitive'.[41] In 1879 Farrer's book, *Primitive Manners and Customs,* proved popular both with the public and with prominent folklorists, including the eminent Scottish anthropologist Andrew Lang. These folklorists were interested in categorising ancient and modern peoples

38 Ibid., p. 125.

39 Ibid., p. 123.

40 Charles Kingsley, 'Faith', preached in December 1865, in *The Water of Life and Other Sermons* (1867; this edition, London, 1879), pp. 143–52.

41 Virginia Zimmerman, *Excavating Victorians* (Albany, 2008); B. Van Riper, *Men Among the Mammoths: Science and the Discovery of Human Prehistory* (Chicago, 1993).

and classifying civilisations as 'savage' or 'civilised'. In his book, Farrer sought to explore 'ancient barbarism' and the practices of early peoples, exposing how these practices were the product of a 'primitive mind'.[42] While Farrer's focus was on charting the origins of modern-day superstitions, his book offers interesting clues to his position on chivalry.

In Farrer's 1882 article in the *Gentleman's Magazine* on 'Warfare in Chivalrous Times', he linked anthropology and chivalry, presenting the practice of chivalry as a stage in human psycho-cultural development.[43] In his piece, Farrer argued that chivalry was an antiquated ethos that had no place in modern conceptions of warfare or heroism. Farrer used evidence of chivalric brutality to argue against what he saw as the more common adulation of medieval chivalry found in many other popular accounts:

> there never was a period like that handed down to us as the period of chivalry, when the motives for wars as well as the incentives of personal courage were more mercenary; when war itself was more brutally conducted; when the laws in restraint of it imposed by the voice of morality or religion were less felt; or when the consequent demoralisation was more widely spread.[44]

He argued that its violence made chivalry a particularly problematic ideal that should be criticised rather than emulated.

Citing both British and European examples, Farrer suggested that it was the medieval mindset that made 'wars break out so frequently and last so long'. He pinpointed two causes – the desire for gain and a mania for fame that plagued the medieval period and resulted in violence. Farrer split chivalry and religion, arguing that the military ethos of chivalry defined the movement when Christianity was 'powerless to place any check whatever on the atrocities connected with the gratification of the war spirit'.[45] He asked his readers not to be blinded by the great deeds of chivalric characters, nor to ignore the more negative aspects underlying these deeds – what he termed its 'darker features'.[46] These features included a lack of attachment to king and country, little desire for peace, and the desire to kill; for Farrer these were the hallmarks of an uncivilised society. The model of medieval warfare, he argued, was a far cry from the more enlightened conduct found earlier in the civilisations of ancient Greece and Rome.[47] While writers like Stanley recognised the dark side of chivalry but encouraged modern readers to adopt and universalise its good points, Farrer's anthropological critique took a different view, seeing chivalry as a dark age of the mind in which a primitive world-view and brutal violence predominated. In a revised version of his *Gentleman's Magazine* article, published in his book *Military Manners and Customs*, Farrer highlighted chivalry's destructive legacy, where

42 J. A. Farrer, *Primitive Manners and Customs* (London, 1879); Richard M. Dorson, *History of British Folklore: The British Folklorists, A History*, 3 vols (London, 2001), i, p. 198.

43 J. A. Farrer, 'Warfare in Chivalrous Times', *Gentleman's Magazine* 252 (1882).

44 Ibid., p. 615.

45 Ibid., p. 622.

46 Ibid., p. 623.

47 Ibid., p. 622.

earlier 'primitive' medieval military customs still played a part in modern war and contributed to its brutality.[48]

Wider debates about masculinity and violence also led to a new focus on the negative aspects of chivalry in the educational sphere. From the early Victorian period, chivalry had been promoted as a code of conduct for men and boys. Adapted and lauded by politicians and in public schools, chivalry was used to educate young boys on how to be muscular, robust warriors for nation and empire.[49] Medieval heroes were promoted as role models as they were thought to exemplify a robust and hardy masculinity. Indeed, chivalry became so entrenched in ideas about imperial boyhood that it was taken up as a banner by Baden-Powell in the Boy Scout movement. Baden-Powell harnessed chivalric imagery in two of his scouting manuals, linking hardy and robust character building to creating successful citizens for the empire.[50] In his 1908 manual, *Scouting for Boys*, he likened Scout leaders to medieval knights: 'the knights of old were the patrol leaders of the nation, and the men-at-arms were the scouts'.[51] The cover of Baden-Powell's *Young Knights of the Empire* (1916) shows a cowed dragon inside a cage engraved with Scout mottos, while a Boy Scout in armour looks on.

This muscular, robust chivalry was promoted in a variety of media. Tales of heroic knights circulated in adventure novels and magazines, such as the *Boy's Own Paper*, *Child's Champion* and *Young Folks*, depicting hardy and rugged medieval heroes fighting for king and country.[52] These works also encouraged boys to adopt the tenets of chivalry and live up to their standards as if they were modern-day knights. So rooted was this advice about modern-day chivalry for men that contemporary newspapers had regular cartoons parodying attempts at chivalry in public and domestic settings. In an 1899 cartoon in the *Big Budget*, Mr Smith, an Englishman, resolved to be chivalrous after reading about the absence of chivalry in

[48] J. A. Farrer, *Military Manners and Customs* (London, 1885), pp. 31–3, 64.

[49] *Young England* magazine had numerous articles in the late Victorian period on chivalry: 'Schoolboy Chivalry', *Young England*, 1 August 1891; 'Nineteenth Century Chivalry', *Young England*, 1 October 1887, p. 455. For discussions of public school chivalry, see Mark Girouard, *The Return to Camelot: Chivalry and the English Gentleman* (New Haven and London, 1981), pp. 163–76; J. A. Mangan, 'Athleticism: A Case Study of the Evolution of an Educational Ideology', *The Victorian Public School: Studies in the Development of an Educational Institution*, ed. Brian Simon and Ian Bradley (Dublin, 1975), p. 155. Rob Boddice has shown how the drive for muscular masculinity and games in public schools came from the boys and their parents. Rob Boddice, 'In Loco Parentis? Public-School Authority, Cricket and Manly Character, 1855–62', *Gender and Education* 21:2 (2009), pp. 159–72.

[50] Robert Baden-Powell, *Young Knights of the Empire: Their Code, and Further Scout Yarns* (London, 1916); R. S. S. Baden-Powell, *Scouting for Boys: A Handbook of Instruction in Good Citizenship* (London, 1908).

[51] Baden-Powell, *Scouting for Boys*, p. 240.

[52] For example, see 'Edward the Black Prince, the Boy who Won a Battle', *Boy's Own Paper*, 31 May 1879; 'Prince Edward and his Prisoners', *Child's Champion*, 1 July 1881; 'Sir Claude the Conqueror. A Story of English Chivalry', *Young Folks*, 1 October 1881.

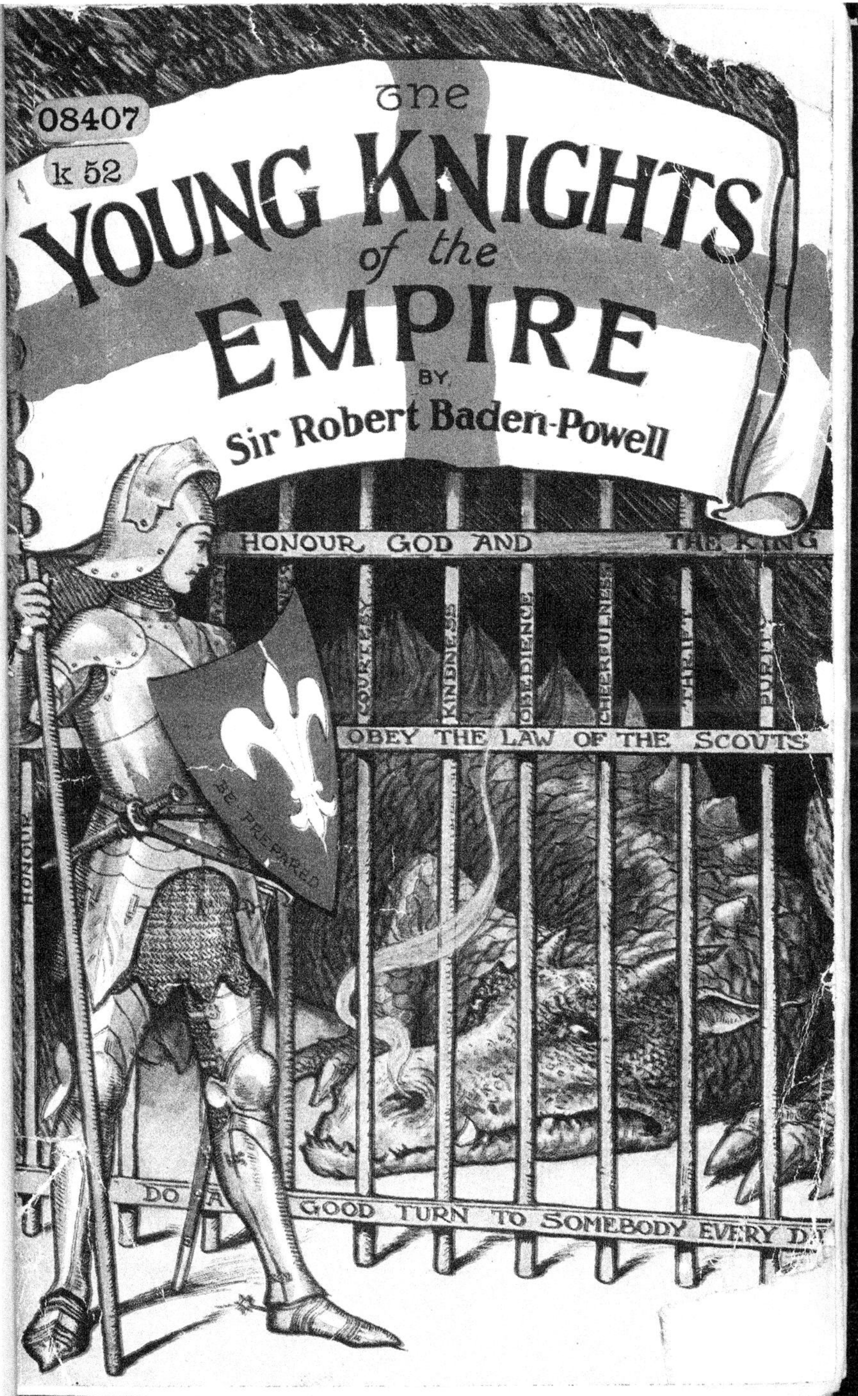

Figure 5.1 Cover of Sir Robert Baden-Powell's *Young Knights of the Empire*, 1916. © The British Library Board. GRC 08407.k.52.

IS CHIVALRY DEAD?

1. SMITH had been deeply impressed by an article he had read on "The absence of chivalry in England;" in fact, so much so that he determined to do his best and be gallant at the first opportunity. "Excuse me, madam," said he, "but you appear heavily burdened. May I help you across——"

2. But he never finished his remarks. "Help me acrorst where, you thief? Warnt ter steal me parcels, do yer? An' me a pore lone woman from the country, too. Garn!——

3. "Yer hort to be ashamed o' yerself. But I am up ter yer low, blaggardish, thieving tricks, you scoundril, &c., &c." And when that last piece of chivalry had been successfully annihilated, she said:

4. "That man must find someone easier ter fool thin a woman wot's turned sevinty-six cum the sixth! Wheer's that 'bus?"

Figure 5.2 'Is Chivalry Dead?' *Big Budget*, 21 January 1899. © The British Library Board. GRC 1899 LOU.LON 671.

England'. However, his attempt to be courteous was thwarted: when he tried to help a woman with a bag, he was mistaken for a thief.[53]

As a result of the late-nineteenth-century Education Acts, a flood of new children's textbooks from the main publishing houses found their way into the classrooms and homes of Victorian children. The Acts (1870–93) extended education to all children between the ages of five and eleven, and by 1891 had made education free of charge.[54] They also showcased a new kind of curriculum: one that focused on creating good citizens. These changes in teaching pedagogy influenced discussions of chivalry and illuminate how the chivalric ethos was being challenged as a model for Victorian boys.

A survey of children's textbooks and readers from the late nineteenth century reveals a more critical approach to medieval chivalry.[55] The *Philips' Historical Readers* (1878–84) and *Britannia History Readers* (Book 1, c.1902) were two of the more popular history series that emphasised the negative aspects of chivalry. Underpinning these books is the concept of change and progress. The author of *The Britannia History Readers* argued that chivalry declined in the fifteenth century: 'as men became more civilized and life grew wider and fuller, they found other ways of spending their lives than in constant fighting for personal glory'.[56] The author suggested that equally important progress occurred in legal and criminal proceedings, which meant that knights were no longer needed to keep order, while advances in military technology, such as the introduction of gunpowder, made way for a different style of fighting.[57] Authors also saw chivalry as the cause of knightly violence during the Hundred Years' War. The *Philips' Historical Readers* (1884) further presented the gloomy side to chivalric knighthood: 'the laws of chivalry bade the knight be courteous to belted knight but they said nothing about the masses of the people; and this long war was one scene of cruelty and suffering to the wretched inhabitants of the devastated land'.[58] *Cassell's Historical Course for Schools* (1884) noted:

> the war was bad for England too, as such wars of aggression almost always are [...] The English nobles ceased to think about the improvement of the laws and condition of their country, but grew quarrelsome, heartless and bloodthirsty [...] they oppressed the poor.[59]

[53] 'Is Chivalry a Failure? By a Knight of the Day', *Funny Folks*, 6 April 1889; 'Is Chivalry Dead?', *Big Budget*, 21 January 1899; 'Chivalry Nowhere', *Judy*, 11 November 1885; 'The Reward of Chivalry', *Illustrated Chips*, 13 August 1892.

[54] Of course, Ellen Ross' *Love and Toil* illustrates that many working-class children, as family providers, could not attend school. Ellen Ross, *Love and Toil: Motherhood in Outcast London, 1870–1918* (Oxford, 1993), p. 149.

[55] For more on the production of history texts, see Leslie Howsam, *Past into Print: The Publishing History in Britain 1850–1950* (London and Toronto, 2009).

[56] *The Britannia History Readers, Book IV, Men and Movements in European History* (London, 1901), p. 86.

[57] Ibid.

[58] *Philips' School Series, Philips' Historical Readers: Middle England, Book III*, p. 107.

[59] For example, see *Cassell's Historical Course for Schools: The Simple Outline of English History, Book II* (London, Paris and New York, 1884), p. 83.

Chivalry was thus perceived to be a catalyst for violence.

Depictions of chivalry, the chivalric ethos and the age of chivalry in these texts clearly drew on the ideas of Green and Freeman.[60] Indeed, the focus on the history of the people and on how chivalry as a code of conduct promoted violence towards other classes is apparent in all these works. Here the age of chivalry (and the chivalric ethos) was slotted into a wider narrative of unfolding liberalism and development where British children could chart their progress. Thus young school children were told to praise their heroic past, but also to reflect on how their heroic future was different and more advanced.[61] While some authors suggested jettisoning chivalry altogether, others suggested that chivalry (without its 'medievalness') could be helpful. In her biographical textbook, *Life of Edward the Black Prince*, Louise Creighton presented the Black Prince as the quintessential chivalric hero whose life illustrated both the nobility and brutality of the chivalric ethos.[62] According to Creighton, 'the sack of Limoges shows us the dark side of chivalry. We must not blame the Black Prince too severely for it. In sacrificing the innocent inhabitants of a whole city to his revenge, he was only acting in accordance with the spirit of the age in which he lived.'[63] The author of *The Britannia History Readers* suggested one solution: 'though the outward form was debased and then passed away, the spirit of chivalry remained as an ennobling and elevating power'.[64] The remnants of chivalry could be found in the refined manners of the English gentleman, if one could cast off its more primitive aspects.

Equally revealing is an exploration of how the reputations of medieval heroes of chivalry inform us about later changes in models of masculinity.[65] Children's textbooks in the late Victorian period were often organised into gradations by education level, reflecting new curriculum standards and educational reforms. It was thought that younger children in the early stages of education benefited from learning history through stories and 'important' characters, and thus textbook series included a number of books dedicated to primary pupils that focused on these aspects.[66] *Cassell's Historical Readers* (1882) outlined their view:

[60] *Cassell's Historical Course for Schools: The Class History of England, Book III* (London, Paris and New York, 1884), preface.

[61] *Philips' School Series, Philips' Historical Readers: Middle England, Book III*, front matter: 'In this Series of Historical Readers the aim has been to present clearly and accurately all that children can well understand of the events which led to the founding and making of our nation, tracing step by step its progress onward to its present proud position – the first among the nations of the world.'

[62] Creighton, *Life of Edward the Black Prince*, p. 55.

[63] Ibid., p. 185.

[64] *The Britannia History Readers, Book IV*, p. 86.

[65] Stephanie Olsen's work on late-Victorian intellectuals and religious promoters offers an excellent assessment of the continuance of an intellectual and polite masculinity in the late Victorian period: Stephanie Olsen, *Juvenile Nation: Youth, Emotions and the Making of the Modern British Citizen, 1880–1914* (London, 2014).

[66] Peter Yeandle, 'Englishness in Retrospect: Rewriting the National Past for the Children of the English Working Classes, c.1880–1919', *Studies in Ethnicity and Nationalism* 6 (2006), pp. 14–15; Peter Yeandle, *Citizenship, Nation, Empire: The Politics of History Teaching in England, 1870–1930* (Manchester, 2015). See also Stephen Heathorn, *For Home, Country,*

In these Fifty Stories children will become familiar with the chief actors and the most attractive incidents of English history. Being designed for a First Reading-book in History, its aim is not to crowd the mind with facts, but to excite a living interest in men and women whose historical position the pupil will hereafter trace. It is hoped that the subjects of these stories will become fixed points, around which a fuller knowledge of the course of history may gather.[67]

While later books offered a more comprehensive understanding of historical movements and events, the emphasis on key characters – the great men of history – remained.

Who were these heroes from the golden age of chivalry? In textbooks and readers, Edward III and his son Edward the Black Prince were repeatedly described as chivalric characters.[68] However, by the late Victorian period, this designation had more negative connotations. Textbooks and children's literature focused on the character of these royals and, in particular, how their adherence to the chivalric ethos meant they did not adhere to modern manly standards of conduct. For example, *The Warwick History Readers* (1895) described Edward III as angry and unmerciful after the siege of Calais (a French city of strategic importance that the king had laid siege to for almost a year before it surrendered).[69] According to the reader, Edward asked that six citizens be brought out as retribution and that they 'should be taken away, and that their heads should at once be cut off'.[70] Only his wife Queen Philippa's intercession stopped their execution.[71] *Philips' Historical Readers* depicted an enraged Edward III sentencing the citizens of Calais while his wife, Philippa, pleaded for their lives. When examining Henry V's victory at Agincourt, the author of *Cassell's Historical Course for Schools* saw the English king's victory as marred by the violence that followed: 'It was a most glorious victory, though its fame was sullied by the slaughter of all the prisoners, according to the cruel custom of those days.'[72]

By the late nineteenth century, the muscular and robust form of masculinity epitomised by Edward III, the Black Prince and Henry V was coming under

and Race: Constructing Gender, Class, and Englishness in the Elementary School, 1880–1914 (Toronto, 2000).

[67] *Cassell's Historical Readers: Stories for Children from English History for Standard III, Book I* (London, 1882), front matter. This notice was replicated in *Cassell's Historical Course for Schools: Stories from English History, Book I* (London, Paris and New York, 1884), front matter.

[68] This was most explicitly stated in *Philips' School Series, Philips' Historical Readers: Middle England, Book III*, pp. 99–100, 121; Creighton, *Life of Edward the Black Prince*, pp. 31, 60, 94.

[69] The story of Edward III's actions at Calais came from Froissart's *Chronicles*.

[70] *The Warwick History Readers First Book of Simple Stories Part I* (London, 1895), p. 61.

[71] For more on Philippa of Hainault's Victorian afterlife, see Rosemary Mitchell, 'The Red Queen and the White Queen: The Exemplification of Medieval Queens in Nineteenth-Century Britain', *Heroic Reputations and Exemplary Lives*, ed. Geoffrey Cubitt and Allen Warren (Manchester, 2000), pp. 157–77.

[72] *Cassell's Historical Course for Schools: The Class History of England, Book III*, p. 166.

Figure 5.3 'Edward and the Citizens of Calais' from *Middle England* (*Philips' Historical Readers*), 1884, p. 117. © The British Library Board. 12200.c.21/5.

attack from religious groups and intellectuals, who endorsed a more refined kind of man.[73] Adventure novels, boys' magazines echoing the rhetoric of politicians, and the ethos of public schools did not shy away from war; indeed, these stories were seen as crucial in inspiring future knights of the empire. The development of a robust manliness was intimately connected with ideas about empire. While Kelly Boyd highlights an imperial setting for tales of adventure, magazines and novels often placed such stories in a different temporal setting. In these, the late Middle Ages became a time of chivalric boyhood and its hardy heroes were presented as models for contemporary consumers.[74] By contrast, textbooks and history readers

[73] Olsen, *Juvenile Nation*. Olsen argues that religious and social groups in the late nineteenth century used 'informal' education such as youth societies, magazines and books to promote polite, moderate, religious and intellectual manliness to all classes.

[74] Kelly Boyd, *Manliness and the Boys' Story Paper in Britain: A Cultural History, 1855–1940*

simultaneously questioned, even as they described, the behaviour of these rugged chivalric heroes. Rather than emulate the behaviour of these heroes, young boys were now urged to consider their violence. *Pitman's King Edward History Reader* asked young children to assess Edward III's actions at the siege of Calais: 'Would the English King have been right if he had killed the six men?'[75]

The chivalric ethos proved to be a more problematic concept for those promoting a new kind of man. Chivalry was still usable, but not medieval chivalry. Instead, modern boys were to cast off this old form of chivalry that promoted violence and embrace a new one that emphasised modesty and moderation. While the victors of Crécy and Agincourt were deemed important, young boys were warned to follow different heroic role models; modern men, who were more restrained, like Horatio Nelson or the duke of Wellington.

The darker visions of chivalry surveyed in this essay became commonplace by the time the Eton schoolmaster Francis Warre Warre-Cornish wrote a defence of the ethos in his 1901 book, *Chivalry*, published in the *Social England* series.[76] Warre-Cornish's recognition of the dark side of chivalry as the dominant vision illustrates a dramatic shift in the way it was perceived by the end of the Victorian era. He argued that historians such as Green and Freeman saw the 'fantastic ceremonialism of chivalry [as] nothing but an empty pageant and a cloak for social immorality'.[77] Their views, he asserted, had swayed a generation of students of history who 'can see nothing in chivalry but the exaggeration of the military spirit, a childish ceremonialism, and the degradation of the family by an unnatural code of gallantry'.[78] However, he suggested that modern audiences look at the *good* of chivalry as well. The code helped keep violence in check and had a civilising effect on medieval knights. For Warre-Cornish, chivalry, although flawed, played a key part in the progress from savagery to civility. He shows how much the dark side of chivalry framed ideas about the medieval past and about the Victorian present. While many late-Victorian authors bemoaned the rosy-tinted perception of chivalry and sought to revise it, by the early twentieth century Warre-Cornish responded to criticisms of this darker image that he saw as a predominant yet problematic reductionism.

The new attacks on chivalry that emerged in the late nineteenth century thus provided a rebuff to the Romantic depiction of medieval chivalry. The diverse approaches to chivalry by the Victorians speak both to the ambiguity of the Middle Ages in Victorian culture and to the perceived viability of this past. Chivalry became a rallying point, not just for those seeking to celebrate the Middle Ages but also

(Basingstoke, 2003), pp. 123–52. There is an extensive literature on empire and masculinities. For some key works, see: J. A. Mangan, ed., 'Benefits Bestowed'? *Education and British Imperialism* (Manchester, 1988); Graham Dawson, *Soldier Heroes: British Adventure, Empire and the Imagining of Masculinities* (London, 1994); Joseph Bristow, *Empire Boys: Adventures in a Man's World* (London, 1991).

75 *Pitman's King Edward History Reader* (1902–05; this 2nd edition, London, 1925), p. 105.

76 F. W. Warre-Cornish, *Chivalry*, ed. Kenelm D. Cotes (London, 1901). The *Social England* series sought to present a fuller picture of English society, beyond 'politics and wars'.

77 Ibid., p. 13.

78 Ibid., p. 369.

for those wishing to articulate their own concerns about politics, character and the mind. The debates about the dark side of chivalry, which increased in prominence in the late Victorian period, may have their own historical legacy in present-day perceptions of the medieval past as a 'dark age'.

6

Daze and Knights: Anachronism, Duelling and the Chivalric Ethic in Nineteenth-Century Italy*

Steven C. Hughes

IN A CRITICAL scene of Marchese Filippo Crispolti's 1899 anti-duelling novel *Un duello*, three young Roman noblemen gather around Iacopo Gelli's *Codice cavalleresco Italiano*, or the *Italian Code of Chivalry*, as they fill in the blanks of a formulaic text of challenge:

> The undersigned, feeling himself offended by words pronounced by You at the *Circolo del Tevere* [a social club] has requested *Baron Emilio de Teufelsberg* and *Sir Giacomo Letarghi* to ask You for a retraction or reparation according to what you think most opportune for the tutelage of your honor. The above named gentlemen, having accepted this mission, should be considered by You as representatives armed with full powers by the undersigned.[1]

Whatever the literary merits of Marchese Crispolti's book – and they are many – this passage aptly illustrates the pervasive authority and extraordinary success enjoyed by Iacopo Gelli's *Code of Chivalry* in Italy. First appearing in 1886, his code quickly became the standard handbook of 'honourable' behaviour for Italian 'gentlemen', and by 1926, the year of its fifteenth edition, it had sold over 55,000 copies and could be found in both Austrian and Spanish translations.[2] Other editions would follow in 1932, 1935 and 1943, and a reprint of the 1926 version would appear as late as 1981. In addition to guiding potential duellists, Gelli's book was used as expert testimony during criminal trials dealing with duels and was cited in published debates of gentlemen seeking to discredit their adversaries with erudite arguments over points of honour. Gelli's stature was no less impressive among the military, and in 1920 his book was adopted by the *Comando della Scuola di Guerra* and recommended to its

* Much of this essay was written as a Fulbright Senior Scholar and Visiting Scholar with the American Academy in Rome.

1 Filippo Crispolti, *Un duello* (Milan, 1899), pp. 112–13.

2 Athos Gastone Banti, preface to Iacopo Gelli, *Codice cavalleresco Italiano* (Milan, 1926), pp. xiv, xix.

students as basic reading.[3] Likewise, in his 1907 book of advice to military cadets, E. Filiberto Iviglia argued that: 'In order to negotiate and resolve any chivalric affair *[vertenza cavalleresca]* it will be necessary to consult the golden *[aureo]* code of chivalry of cavaliere Gelli.'[4] Gelli and his chivalric code became the primary arbiters of honour, which served to propel and guide the *duellomania* that followed the creation of Italy as a country in 1861, with no fewer than 3,513 duels reported between 1879 and 1894.[5] Various duelling codes had appeared to try to control, as well as legitimise, this 'plague of duels', but it was Gelli who came to the fore: a fact recognised in his tenure first as secretary and then as president of Florence's prestigious *Corte permanente d'onore*, which made decisions on cases from all over Italy. By 1926 Gelli claimed to have personally intervened in more than seven thousand *vertenze,* or chivalric disputes of honour.[6]

It seems redundant to point out the primacy of chivalry as a sanctioning concept in Gelli's code, but it is argued here that Gelli's stress on chivalry – most obvious in the title – was one of the factors accounting for his book's extraordinary success, for it tied into the popularity of medieval – or supposedly medieval – images of knighthood as a model of masculinity among elites in the new country of Italy.[7] The point is reinforced by the fact that Gelli's only real competition among the various duelling codes published after unification came from General Achille Angelini, who was, as we shall see, even more obvious in his affinity for images of chivalry, and particularly medieval chivalry. Indeed, it is clear that in nineteenth-century Italy, an imaginary but powerful 'chivalric community' was created; 'an elite honor group that borrowed the concept of chivalry and knighthood as a lexicon of proper behavior that suited its sensibilities and purposes.'[8] Interesting in this regard is that, with the important exception of Germany, chivalry was not so obviously central to the duelling ethic elsewhere.[9] For instance, the most important duelling code for France in

[3] Comando della Scuola di Guerra, *Norme riguardanti le vertenze cavalleresche ed i giurì d'onore* (1920). This is a typewritten booklet, a copy of which can be found in the Biblioteca Nazionale di Roma, Sala Manoscritti, Duello 0.9.I.2.

[4] E. F. Iviglia, *Il vero gentiluomo modern* (Cassone, 1907), p. 106

[5] Steven C. Hughes, *Politics of the Sword: Dueling, Honor, and Masculinity in Modern Italy* (Columbus, 2007), pp. 114–15.

[6] This is according to his friend, Athos Gastone Banti, who wrote the preface to the 1926 edition of Gelli's code, p. xxii. Gelli was often cited chapter and verse in public *vertenze*; on occasion people wrote to him for his opinion as an authority, and his letters were also used as evidence. See, for instance, *Vertenza Conte Ivan de Vargas Machuca-Principe Altieri. La Narrazione* (Rome, 1930). See also *Questione d'onore: Panattoni-Simonelli* (Pisa, 1886), pp. 13–15.

[7] I would add that Gelli's mantle of chivalry was not the only reason his book came to dominate the world of honour in Italy. For the others, see Steven C. Hughes, 'Una storia di due codici', *A fil di spada, il duello dalle origini agli ori olimpici*, ed. Alda Spotti (Rome, 2005), pp. 53–4.

[8] Hughes, *Politics of the Sword,* p. 8. On honour groups and reflexive notions of horizontal honour, see Frank Henderson Stewart, *Honor* (Chicago, 1994), pp. 54–71.

[9] The two most important writers on German duelling in this period agree that the notion of chivalry was critical to the duelling ethic in the nineteenth century, although they differ substantially in their emphasis: Ute Frevert, *Men of Honour: A Social and Cultural History of the Duel* (Cambridge, 1995); Kevin McAleer, *Dueling: the Cult of Honor in Fin-de-siècle*

the nineteenth century, Baron Chateauvillard's *Essai sur le duel* of 1836, makes no mention of either chivalry or knighthood. The same is true for what many consider to be the basic reference of modern English and American duelling, the Irish *Code Duello* of 1777. Likewise, as the chivalric cultural revival gained ground in England during the Victorian period, the duelling ethic did not just weaken, but disappeared entirely after the 1840s.[10] These differences reveal how definitions of chivalry could differ, and also how Italian elites privileged certain virile and combative aspects of the knightly tradition, with less attention paid to gallantry, protection of the weak, or even gentility towards women.

This essay thus examines the integral identity of duelling and a particular form of chivalry in nineteenth-century Italy, and seeks to understand its power and its provenance. Specifically it argues that the duelling ethic became inextricably linked to medieval images of chivalric honour during the struggle for Italian independence and unification. Moreover, during the Risorgimento the duelling ritual itself came to play a symbolic political role that fed on and reinforced narratives of the defence of Italian honour during the medieval period, such as the Battle of Legnano and the Sicilian Vespers. As patriotic elites sought to find pan-Italian principles to legitimise their status and to patch over the deep-seated political tensions that had attended a conflicted process of unification, chivalry came to the fore as a positive model for Italy's politically active and socially mobile classes. Yet for all the ready references to the Middle Ages, chivalry was, temporally speaking, a boundary-bending concept that allowed for creative anachronism as it helped create a new class of 'gentlemen' who came to unify and then run the new country.

That Gelli's conception of chivalry – so clearly vaunted in the title of his code – was connected to medieval knighthood seems abundantly clear from his own personalised bookplates, which adorned the volumes in his well-known library dedicated to fencing and duelling (figure 6.1).[11] The image abounds with knights in armour, most of whom are on horseback with lances and plumed helmets. Gelli might well have felt an affinity for these paladins since he himself had done rather well out of his chivalric enterprises: he had been made a knight by King Umberto I in the late 1880s and then an officer in the Order of the Crown of Italy in 1890.[12] This was a

Germany (Princeton, 1994). An excellent contemporary example can be seen in the second edition (1891) of Gustav Hergsell's *Duell-Codex*, published in Vienna, Pest and Leipzig. The cover depicts a kneeling armoured knight, helmet to the side, offering his sword in service to a young woman (possibly a generic image of Germania or, more probably, Germanic honour) who crowns him with an oak-leaf wreath. In the background two knights joust before a medieval audience. For a somewhat different description, see McAleer, *Dueling*, p. 209.

10 Anthony Simpson, 'Dandelions and the Field of Honor: Dueling, the Middle Classes, and the Law in Nineteenth-century England', *Criminal Justice History* 9 (1988), pp. 106–7; Robert B. Shoemaker, 'The Taming of the Duel: Masculinity, Honour and Ritual Violence in London, 1660–1800', *The Historical Journal* 45 (2002), pp. 542–5; Donna Andrew, 'The Code of Honour and its Critics: The Opposition to Dueling in England', *Social History* 5 (1980), pp. 409–34.

11 Gelli's bookplate is actually a modified frontispiece from a Renaissance book of poetry by Girolamo Benivieni, published in 1522 in Venice.

12 His appointment is listed in the *Gazzetta Ufficiale del Regno d'Italia* for 21 June 1890,

Figure 6.1 Bookplate from Gelli's copy of Pasquale Cicirelli, *Riflessioni sul duello* (Reggio di Calabria: Lipari e Basile, 1873). With permission of the Centrale Bibliotheek KU Leuven, Tabularium; indexed BRES, R4A304.

considerable achievement for the son of a coppersmith who had left the army as a young lieutenant after only a few years of active service. However, the iconographic connection of knighthood and duelling in Italy can be seen as early as 1858, when Teodoro Pateras, a republican patriot, sought to 'gather together, as much as possible, the so called *laws of chivalry*'.[13] The cover of Pateras' early duelling code

p. 2. His obituary in 1935 listed him as a *commendatore* and member of the Order of St Maurizio, but official recognition of the honour is elusive. *Il Telegrafo*, 17 December 1935, p. 6. By 1895, he was listed in an Italian equivalent of *Who's Who* as having been inducted into the Order of the Liberator of Venezuela. Angelo de Gubernatis, *Piccolo dizionario dei contemporanei italiani* (Rome, 1895), p. 442.

[13] Teodoro Pateras, *Dei doveri del secondo nel duello* (Locarno, 1858). One notes the Swiss provenance of the book: a result, one might assume, of Pateras, a Mazzinian-style republican commemorated for participating in the defence of the Roman republic, being in exile at the time.

Figure 6.2 Teodoro Pateras, *Dei doveri del secondo nel duello* (Locarno: Tip. Cantonale, 1858). With permission of the Biblioteca Nazionale Centrale di Roma; indexed Levi Duello I.1.I.13.

vaunted no fewer than four knightly helmets and bristled with lances, swords and axes, albeit with four duelling pistols half-hidden on the bottom edge (figure 6.2). A similar image appeared on the cover of Oreste Ristori's 1872 *On Duels: Chivalrous Rules for Acting Faithfully in a Duel* (figure 6.3).[14]

However, it was the cover of one of Italy's most prestigious codes, written by the aforementioned General Achille Angelini, that really pulled out all the stops (figure 6.4).[15] Here the general's illustrator went beyond the symbols of helmet and lance to portray a peacock-plumed knight on horseback, complete with his own herald, whose trumpet proudly sports the she-wolf on the ensign of Rome, thus tying the capital city to a host of Savoyard crosses, the blazon of the royal ruling

[14] Oreste Ristori, *Dei duelli: regole cavalleresche per agire lealmente in duello* (Torino, 1872).

[15] Achille Angelini, *Codice cavalleresco Italiano* (Rome, 1888).

DEI

DUELLI

REGOLE CAVALLERESCHE

PER AGIRE LEALMENTE IN DUELLO

PEL NOBILE

ORESTE RISTORI

GIÀ MAESTRO DI SCHERMA

NELLA R. SCUOLA MILITARE DI CAVALLERIA IN MODENA.

TORINO

TIPOGRAFIA E LITOGRAFIA FOA

1872.

Figure 6.3 Oreste Ristori's *On Duels: Chivalrous Rules for Acting Faithfully in a Duel* (Torino: Tip. Foa, 1872). With permission of the Biblioteca Nazionale Centrale di Roma; indexed Levi Duello I.I.I.4.

family. The latter symbols cleverly underline the pan-Italian nature of chivalry while subtly suggesting royal, if not state, approval. Such iconography directly linked Italy's 'gentlemen' to medieval attributes of knighthood – such as courage, loyalty and gallantry – while simultaneously recalling aristocratic rituals of individual combat that reinforced the duel as the touchstone of elite status. A different and somewhat bizarre approach can be seen on the cover of Ernesto Salafia Maggio's *Codice cavalleresco nazionale*, which was published in Palermo in 1895. His cover (figure 6.5) sported a bare-breasted *Italia* wearing a judge's cap, her torso twisted to titillating advantage as her right hand grasps a massive two-handed medieval sword that was quite distinct from the sabres and rapiers generally used in contemporary duels. The blade carries the inscription 'don't use me without reason', a clear caveat that chivalric combat should not be entered into lightly and a handy evocation (along with the legal headgear) of duelling's long pedigree and its original role as a trial by ordeal in the Middle Ages.

Figure 6.4 Achille Angelini, *Codice cavalleresco Italiano* (Rome: Eredi Vercellini, 1888). Author's private collection.

Yet compared to Angelini's mounted knight, Salafia Maggio's cover is a pastiche of creative anachronism. Under the protection of the massive medieval weapon (and, on the other side, the healing symbolism of a *caduceus*), there lies a motley pile of law books and duelling weapons, including a rapier, a flintlock pistol, and another two-handed sword that is also very obviously a crucifix. Here the image is deliberately ambiguous. Is Salafia Maggio trying to suggest that his national code will finally cut through what had become a mess of competing chivalrous legislation? Or, more likely, does the image argue that both the law (as designated by the book *Lex*) and the church fall before the feet of Italian honour? Less obscure is the strength and energy of *Italia* herself, whose swashbuckling leather belt hangs just low enough to demonstrate her fertile female midriff while simultaneously creating an aura of virile combat. The whole enterprise succeeds in capturing the essential icons of Italy's need for national honour (while appealing to the sexual tastes and

Figure 6.5 Ernesto Salafia Maggio, *Codice cavalleresco nazionale* (Palermo: Sandron, 1895). With permission of the Biblioteca Nazionale Centrale di Roma; indexed Levi Duello H.8.I.11.

market motivators of Italian males), but always under the auspices of medieval tradition.[16]

Similar medieval/modern combinations would appeal to Italy's fencing masters, who formed a pan-Italian framework for the actual practice of the duelling ritual. Not only were ninety-three per cent of all recorded duels fought with either swords or sabres (the latter accounting for the vast majority), but over half (fourteen) of Italy's twenty-four duelling codes published between 1859 and 1914 were written by fencing masters.[17] Eventually, the National Fencing Academy in Naples would

[16] Another example would come as late as 1928, when General Giuseppe Ettorre adorned the cover of his book (which was trying to reconcile the duelling tradition and fascism) with a medieval knight framed by two Renaissance rapiers. Giuseppe Ettorre, *Questioni d'onore* (Milan, 1928).

[17] On weapons used in duels, see Hughes, *Politics of the Sword*, p. 89. For a complete list

formalise this special relationship between fencing and chivalry by creating a Permanent Court of Honour to adjudicate disputes among its members. In terms of iconography, one should consider the 1864 fencing manual (figure 6.6) of Cesare Alberto Blengini, who wrote a duelling code as well.[18] The foreground is dominated by two Italian officers proudly holding sabres, with a variety of swords (including a Roman *gladius*) at their feet. However, in the background – both figuratively and temporally – two armoured knights engage in open combat under the flying ensign of the royal house of Savoy. Thus the monarchy and modern Italian fencing both

Figure 6.6 Cesare Alberto Blengini di san Grato, *Trattato della moderna scherma Italiana* (Bologna: Fava & Garagnani, 1864). With permission of the Biblioteca Nazionale Centrale di Roma; indexed Levi Duello I.4.I bis,8.

of the duelling codes between these dates, see Hughes, 'Una storia di due codici', pp. 51–6.

[18] Cesare Alberto Blengini di san Grato, *Trattato della moderna scherma Italiana* (Bologna, 1864). For his code, see *Duello e sue norme principali per effetuarlo* (Padua, 1868).

find their roots in a mystic past of chivalrous glory, as one stalwart paladin calmly waits to receive the charge of his mounted counterpart. Medieval images could be more subtle – such as the knightly spurs adorning Costantino Cacchione's *Scherma e codice per duello* of 1895 – or they could be cleverly amalgamated with other symbols, as demonstrated by a 1902 postcard from Italy's official fencing academy in Rome, in which a lance, helmet, shield and heraldic trumpet are obvious, although the presence of a swashbuckling musketeer provides an extra layer of tradition, if not anachronism (figure 6.7).[19]

Figure 6.7 Postcard from the Accademia Nazionale della Scherma, 1902. Author's private collection.

[19] The postcard was generously given to me by Dott. Claudio Mancini, whose expertise on fencing and duelling in Italy has been of enormous help in my work. Similar eclectic devices also adorned Masaniello Parise's *Trattato teorico-pratico della scherma* (Rome, 1884).

*

In seeking to understand the clear connection between chivalry and duelling in post-unification Italy, one might first ask if its roots were not Renaissance rather than medieval. After all, the modern code of honour, which adopted the rituals of the duel for its enforcement, is generally thought to have evolved in Italy during the Renaissance and from there gradually spread to the rest of Europe.[20] With the rise of the duel itself, Italy also saw a veritable explosion of books and pamphlets which purported to justify, explicate and teach the proper defence of one's honour. Print capitalism found this *scienza cavalleresca* or 'science of chivalry' to be a tasty topic, and during the sixteenth century Italian presses cranked out forty-six new duelling manuals released in 110 different editions.[21] This massive edifice of paper was reinforced by steel, as Italians refined the rapier out of the broadsword and developed scientific fencing techniques to go with it. Italy during the Renaissance became famous for its fencing masters, such as Sanseverino, Lovino, Pompeo, Bonetti and Fabrizio, as well as for instruction manuals by Marozzo, Agrippa, Saviolo and Capo Ferro.[22] Indeed, many of the techniques still taught in fencing schools across Italy after unification would have been created on the peninsula during the sixteenth century. With theory, practice and ritual rising out of the Renaissance, one might expect that references to such a glorious past would have punctuated the images and allusions of the duel as it came to dominate the lives of Italy's elites.

But such was not the case. One searches the post-unification duelling codes in vain for references to the many Renaissance tracts regarding the *scienza cavalleresca*. It may be that the elites had simply lost track of that tradition. For a variety of reasons, the duel had virtually disappeared in much of Italy by the middle of the eighteenth century, and – according to Erspamer – the lexicon of the *scienza* had become mired

[20] Steven C. Hughes, 'Soldiers and Gentlemen: The Rise of the Duel in Renaissance Italy', *Journal of Medieval Military History* 5 (2007), pp. 99–152. See also François Billaçois, *The Duel: Its Rise and Fall in Early Modern France* (New Haven, 1990), pp. 18–20; Robert Schneider, 'Swordplay and Statemaking: Aspects of the Campaign against the Duel in Early Modern France', *Statemaking and Social Movements*, ed. Charles Bright and Susan Harding (Ann Arbor, 1984), p. 269; Henri Morel, 'La fin du duel judiciaire en France et la naissance du point d'honneur', *Revue historique du droit français et étranger* 42 (1964), pp. 633–4; Micheline Cuénin, *Le Duel sous l'ancien regime* (Paris, 1982), p. 24; Markku Peltonen, *The Duel in Early Modern England: Civility, Politeness and Honour* (Cambridge, 2003), pp. 4–64; Claude Chauchadis, *La loi du duel: Le code du point d'honneur dans l'Espagne des XVI e XVIIe siècle* (Toulouse, 1997); Marco Cavina, *Il duello giudiziario per punto d'onore: genesi, apogeo e crisi nell'elaborazione dottrinale italiana (sec. XIV-XVI)* (Torino, 2003); Marco Cavina, *Il sangue d'onore: storia del duello* (Rome, 2005).

[21] Francesco Erspamer, *La biblioteca di Don Ferrante: duello e onore nella cultura del Cinquecento* (Rome, 1982), pp. 58–61.

[22] Sydney Anglo, 'How to Kill a Man at Your Ease', *Chivalry in the Renaissance* (Woodbridge, 1990), pp. 6–9. For France, see Pascal Brioist, Hervé Drévillon and Pierre Serna, *Croiser le fer: violence et culture de l'épée dans la France moderne, XVIe-XVIIIe siècle* (Paris, 2002), pp. 63–70. On Italian fencing teachers in England, see Iacopo Gelli, *Duelli celebri* (Milan, 1928), pp. 54–8. For a general treatment of masters and manuals, see Sydney Anglo, *The Martial Arts of Renaissance Europe* (New Haven, 2000), pp. 7–90.

'in a state of profound decadence'.[23] This lack of interest had led to a drastic decline in the value of the old treatises on honour, which one contemporary, Apostolo Zeno, noted had 'fallen so decidedly into disfavor' that they had 'become trash of the bookcases and useless clutter in the shops'.[24] Even when the author Alessandro Manzoni recognised the previous importance of the tradition in his *I promessi sposi* – set in the 1620s and arguably the most important Italian novel of the Risorgimento period – he attached it to Don Valeriano (later Don Ferrante), a vapid creature of no ethical worth who offered legitimacy to an imperious and wrong-headed code. Perhaps even more telling was the fact that when Lombard patriots – some of them of noble birth – began to fight political duels against Austrian officers in the name of Italian independence in the 1850s, they had to resort to Chateauvillard's *Essai sur le duel* from France in order to figure out the details.

Thus the paucity of direct Renaissance connections to the chivalric ethic could have been the effect of ignorance. As mentioned, the many sixteenth-century treatises regarding chivalry had gone out of fashion a hundred years earlier. However, one has to consider another more blatantly political motive, albeit perhaps an unconscious one, which is that during the Risorgimento, the Renaissance – as a period of history – had become associated with Italy's loss of independence to foreign powers. The internecine fighting and (literally) Machiavellian manoeuvres of the major city states had opened the doors first to the French and then to the Spanish, resulting in a series of 'Italian Wars' that ended with Habsburg control over a good deal of the peninsula. It is significant perhaps that the great 'discoverer' and proponent of Renaissance Italians as the 'first-born among the sons of modern Europe' in 1860 was Jacob Burckhardt, a Swiss rather than an Italian. Instead, Italian patriots in particular viewed the period as one of political decline, in which the republics had given way to ever more princely autocrats, and foreigners had installed heavy-handed, stifling regimes.[25] Perceived mediocrity, supposed national indolence, obvious military weakness and a certain lack of virile spirit seemed to easily find their way back to Machiavelli's laments in the last chapter of *The Prince,* as Italians failed to rally against the 'barbarian' invasions.[26] Following the Restoration in 1815, those Renaissance 'invaders' or their descendants were still dominating large parts of Italy – and as an Italian identity evolved, its political and cultural affinities would not be with the Renaissance.

Enter the Middle Ages: comfortably distant, reassuringly obscure, and covering a long-enough period to offer a variety of positive referents. Interest in the medieval period also matched the Romantic sensibilities of the day, and Sir Walter Scott's novels, loaded with duels and chivalry alike, were enormously popular in Italy.

[23] On the decline, see Hughes, *Soldiers*, pp. 139–47.

[24] Erspamer, *La biblioteca*, pp. 18–20.

[25] Adrian Lyttelton, 'Creating a National Past: History, Myth and Image in the Risorgimento', *Making and Remaking Italy: The Cultivation of National Identity around the Risorgimento*, ed. Albert Russell Ascoli and Krystyna von Henneberg (New York, 2001), pp. 45, 60.

[26] On the pervasiveness and importance of these negative identifiers in nineteenth-century Italy, see Silvana Patriarca, 'Indolence and Regeneration: Tropes and Tensions of Risorgimento Patriotism', *The American Historical Review* 110 (2005), pp. 380–408.

Such was the taste for these topics that Gaetano Melzi in 1838 created a specialised bibliography of more than eight hundred chivalric novels and poems that had been printed earlier in Italy – mostly from the sixteenth century, which had had its own predilection for medieval knightly tales, as best illustrated by the epic works of Ariosto and Tasso.[27]

Renato Bordone has argued that Italy in the nineteenth century experienced a true 'historical infatuation for the medieval period' that would prove widespread and polyvalent in its cultural and political manifestations.[28] This fascination had long Italian roots back into Vico's postulation of the 'heroic' Middle Ages as a primitive wellspring of European civilisation, and more concretely in Antonio Muratori's extensive investigations into medieval source materials. However, according to Bordone, Italy's taste for medieval motifs was enhanced by the pan-European literary currents of Romanticism, with an emphasis on the mysterious, the dramatic and the 'irregular' as a fecund field of genuine inspiration and invention, as opposed to the more restricted repertoire of neoclassicism. More specifically, Anglo-Saxon (as the Italians like to say) influences – from Macpherson's *Ossian* to 'sublime' Gothic garden styles that vaunted medieval rather than classical ruins – proliferated throughout Italy during the latter part of the eighteenth century. Combined with the aforementioned impact of Sir Walter Scott's novels and post-revolutionary soul-searching, these forces overcame much of the opposition of the neoclassicists and *illuministi* to 'medieval barbarism' and, by the middle of the Restoration period, had created an aesthetic matrix of literary and plastic arts that privileged the Middle Ages and reached through all levels of Italian society.

> Much more than before – in that now the medieval period appears familiar to a large number of spectators – set design and costumes become in fact a vehicle for the spread of a definite iconography, providing shape to the evocations of the written romance. Theater, illustrations, and historical painting – just like neo-medieval architecture – thus offer an illusion of objectivity, truly rendering the Middle Ages 'contemporary' to the desires of identification of the public.[29]

That matrix – perhaps best symbolised by the fact that over ten (more than half) of Verdi's operas vaunted medieval settings – offered a common locus and a focus for self-identity as Italians came to grips with the political issues of the day.[30]

That medieval references should eventually serve as the aesthetic stalking horse of much Risorgimento propaganda only made sense since – according to Bordone – their ubiquity and popularity assured a primed popular audience. However, as

27 Gaetano Melzi, *Bibliografia dei romanzi e poemi cavallereschi italiani* (Milan, 1838).

28 Bordone, 'Il medioevo nell'immaginario dell'Ottocento italiano', *Bulletino dell'Istituto storico italiano per il Medioevo* 100 (1995–96), p. 110.

29 Ibid., p. 137.

30 According to Bordone, Verdi offered 'a faithful mirror of the impulses of public taste'. He counts eleven Verdi operas that evoke the Middle Ages, but he includes *I due Foscari*, *Il Trovatore* and *Rigoletto*, which one might consider Renaissance settings, and leaves out *Aroldo*, *Jerusalem* and *Falstaff* (the latter being very much on the border). Ibid., pp. 142–3.

demonstrated by Adrian Lyttelton, the relationship between the Middle Ages and Italian patriotism proved more historically conditioned than simple mass appeal.[31] Rather, as patriotic Italians searched for a national past, ancient Rome was either too local or too universal, while the Renaissance could not be used as it had marked the end of 'Italian' liberty. In contrast, positive *exempla* of political freedom and even successful cooperative struggles against foreign interlopers could be found in the history of the independent urban communes which spanned much of the medieval period. The critical ur-text in this regard was J. C. L. De Sismondi's *Histoire des républiques italiennes du Moyen Âge,* published in sixteen volumes between 1807 and 1818, which offered a mass of detail and analysis regarding the communes, but was thoroughly leavened with a liberal view of municipal and personal freedom as a touchstone of political success. Thus it offered the first 'unifying narrative' of the Italian city states which, according to Lyttelton, 'stimulated Italian pride by demonstrating that the medieval republics of Italy had led the way in the revival of European civilization and the growth of political liberty'.[32] That such was De Sismondi's intention for 'ill-fated Italy' was made clear in the introduction to a one-volume version of his *magnum opus*, published simultaneously in French and English in 1832, with the title *A History of the Italian Republics, Being a View of the Rise, Progress, and Fall of Italian Freedom*.

> I thus found the opportunity of reproducing, in the two languages of freemen, the memory of what Italy was the first to achieve for the greatest of blessings, – the memory of the impulse and example which she gave, and which all others but followed, – and at the same time, the memory of those crimes of her oppressors which have robbed her of the advantages with which she has endowed the rest of the human race. It seemed to me that the more rapid my recital of the starting up of Italy from her slumber, – of her struggles, her misfortunes, and her glories, – the stronger would be the impression, and the greater the facility with which I could seize, in the history of Italian freedom, that unity of interest which escapes in the simultaneous existence of a hundred independent states.[33]

Small wonder that many Italians found De Sismondi to their liking, as he flattered their past in both European and universal terms, while at the same time bringing to the fore a series of incidents that acted as chivalric analogues to contemporary concerns of independence and, eventually, unity.

How so chivalric? As De Sismondi vaunted the enterprise, creativity and liberty of the communal city states, the underlying *basso continuo* of his account was the constant armed struggle against domestic tyranny and foreign oppression – both of which resonated with current politics. While the general slant of his narrative was anti-aristocratic, he nevertheless elucidated the heroic high points that best demonstrated the will and the courage of the Italians in pursuit of their freedom:

31 Lyttelton, 'Creating a National Past'.
32 Ibid., p. 42.
33 From the preface of the 1855 edition (New York).

the foundation of the Lombard League at Pontina (1167); the subsequent battle of Legnano against the Empire (1176); and the Sicilian Vespers, in which the Sicilians rose up against the French in 1282. All of these became fodder for artistic production – as much for their obvious dramatic qualities as for their possible political import – but in nineteenth-century hands they also involved chivalric images of bonding oaths, knightly battles and the armed defence of honour.

Plate 2 Amos Cassioli, *La battaglia di Legnano*, 1860–70. Galleria d'Arte Moderna di Palazzo Pitti, Florence.

This is readily apparent in visual representations of the battle of Legnano, such as those by Massimo D'Azeglio (1831) and Amos Cassioli (1860–70), in which the Lombard allies staunchly defend the medieval war cart – or *Carroccio* – against the German knights of Emperor Barbarossa (for Cassioli, see plate 2). Reputedly adorned with a relic of the warrior archbishop Ariberto, who had stood up against Emperor Henry III in the previous century, the *Carroccio* provided a palladium of protection, a platform of defence and a symbol of the allies' (and more specifically Milan's) honour. According to tradition, the *Carroccio* was guarded by the Knights of Death who had sworn to die in its defence, and it was against this bulwark of honour that Barbarossa's cavalry supposedly broke their impetus and opened the way for his defeat and subsequent withdrawal from Italy. Barbarossa could thus be easily counted as a stand-in for current Germanic 'oppression' under the Habsburgs – a connection perhaps most concretely demonstrated by the painter and patriot D'Azeglio, when he later reportedly pushed for a historical reconstruction of the *Carroccio* in Milan to attend the troops of General Giovanni Durando as they marched off to fight the Austrians in the spring of 1848.[34] Significantly, it was

[34] Bordone, *Il medioevo nell'immaginario*, p. 112. See also p. 109 for a list of secondary works elaborating on Barbarossa's image in Italy during the nineteenth century.

membership of the Knights of Death that served as a pivotal point in Verdi's convoluted telling of star-crossed lovers and patriotic duty in his opera *La battaglia di Legnano,* written during the revolutions of 1848, and whose protagonist's last words were 'Italy is saved'.[35]

Plate 3 Francesco Hayez, *I vespri siciliani*, 1846. Galleria Nazionale d'Arte Moderna e Contemporanea, Rome. Creative Commons licence.

An equally popular topic of medieval honour and its chivalric defence – again brought to the fore by De Sismondi – came from the Sicilian Vespers of 1282. Shrouded in diplomatic intrigue and sufficiently vague in its particulars, the Sicilian revolt against French occupation offered an open tableau for romantic and patriotic treatments (the most tortured of which was undoubtedly Verdi's opera of 1855). The story – of how the rape, fondling and insult of a woman by a Frenchman on Easter Monday outside Palermo set off a 'national' revolt – contained all the elements for a chivalric defence of female honour that easily extended the comparison to the island itself. Weaponry became an important part of the tale, for in its most popular version – captured in two dramatic paintings by Francesco Hayez in 1822 and 1846 – a French soldier had used the new government's ban on weapons to rummage in the bosom of a young noble woman, who had fainted in the arms of her husband and whose brother immediately killed the foreign offender with his own sword (plate 3). At that dramatic moment, the local church bells began to ring for Vespers and

35 Likewise, the Knights of Death – identified by a skull and crossbones on their chests – featured prominently in Cassioli's representation of the battle, see plate 2.

the populace 'spontaneously' rose up to massacre some four thousand Frenchmen across Sicily. Family ties, the right to carry a sword, foreign insolence, martial prowess and outraged female modesty all came together in a patriotic package that could be presented – according to Lyttelton – as 'the first successful struggle for national liberation'.[36]

Plate 4 1903 poster for the four-hundredth anniversary of the *Disfida di Barletta*. Creative Commons licence.

However, the most direct example of Italian invocation of the chivalric code of combat stretched the boundaries of the late Middle Ages, and moved a medieval mounted mêlée into the early sixteenth century. This was the famous *Disfida di Barletta*, or Challenge of Barletta, which recalled the valiant action of thirteen Italian knights at Barletta in 1503 in response to French insults regarding their courage and ability. It became the subject of one of the most popular novels of the Risorgimento period, once again by D'Azeglio, as well as an 1886 opera, *Ettore Fieramosca*

[36] Lyttelton, 'Creating a National Past', p. 52.

by Achille Lucidi.[37] The French, according to D'Azeglio's account, had accused the Italians of being terrible soldiers whose only real skills were trickery and treason.[38] Thus, in the novel, a French knight, La Motte, complained to a Spanish counterpart: 'During the five years that I have traversed Italy I have learned to know them [...] and I assure you that the deceptions of the Italians kept us busy more than their swords. The only warfare they know is that which ignores the French [conception of] loyalty.'[39] This was an old insult felt acutely by many Italians, and it had not been assuaged in any way by the consistent and successful intervention of Austrian troops on the peninsula after the recent revolutions in Naples, Piedmont and the Papal States. In *Fieramosca,* D'Azeglio managed to project this inferiority complex back into historical fiction, and the resounding defeat of thirteen French knights by an equal number of Italian knights served to advertise the chivalric duel as a means of manifesting current Italian courage, prowess and honesty (plate 4). Indeed, Luigi Settembrini described how this worked among his fellow patriots: 'We all trembled to read D'Azeglio's *Ettore Fieramosca*; the artist represented in different ways the champion of Italy, and all who loved weaponry exulted in having swords and daggers, the blades of which had on them inscribed the day and hour of the duel of Barletta.'[40] D'Azeglio had thus created on an epic and historic scale an example of Italian knights defending their collective honour, and his romantic treatment found its way into the hearts of Italy's young elites. If the code of chivalry promoted national sentiment, the poet of patriotism championed the duelling ethic.

D'Azeglio's evocation of a successful medieval mêleé, albeit in a Renaissance setting, fed into a growing tendency not just to tolerate or accept chivalric combat, but to promote its precepts as a positive force in Italian society. This resonated with a general manifestation of the concepts of chivalry and honour as a cornerstone of Italian nationalist thought in the first half of the century. The importance of such ideas is deftly revealed by Alberto Banti in a ground-breaking book aimed at discerning the cultural and literary fonts of Italian identity and unity.[41] Rejecting both economic and social causes of the unification movement as secondary, Banti maintains that early Italian nationalists were inspired primarily by the literature they read. Carefully examining the memoirs of thirty-three important figures of the Risorgimento, Banti argues that they commonly attributed the discovery of their 'Italianess' to a canon of texts, produced between 1803 and 1848, which included poems, plays, histories and operas, by such familiar names as Foscolo, Berchet, Leopardi, Pellico, Cuoco, Guerrazzi, D'Azeglio, Rossini, Donizetti, Bellini and Verdi. These works offered a shared set of formative images or tropes that led to the 'creation of a mythology, of a symbology, of a historical reconstruction of the Italian nation which had in itself an exceptional communicative force'.[42] At the base of this

[37] One might later add three films, the name of an Italian submarine, and a commemorative postage stamp in 2003.

[38] Lyttelton, 'Creating a National Past', p. 96.

[39] Massimo D'Azeglio, *Ettore Fieramosca o la disfida di Barletta* (Torino, 1842), p. 24.

[40] Luigi Settembrini, *Ricordanze della mia vita*, ed. Adolfo Omodeo (Bari, 1934), p. 41.

[41] Alberto Banti, *La nazione del Risorgimento* (Torino, 2000).

[42] Ibid., p. 30.

mythology he found three pre-political and pre-existing totemic matrixes, 'family-ties, sanctity, and honour', which allowed for easy reference and recognition of new national concepts. The sentiment of patriotism was thus built on a framework of familiar feelings and assumptions that already permeated Italian society, and many of those texts looked back to the medieval period.

Naturally, with regard to the duel, honour was the most important of these national concerns, and Banti demonstrates how the image of honour was constant in the works of the canon.

> Liberty, independence, and a national state are all fundamental objectives for the patriots of the Risorgimento with Mazzini taking the lead. But alongside these values there appeared another which was more profound and troubled: the need to defend honour – honour offended in the violation of the land, honour in the violation of people's dignity, honour offended in the violation of the purity of women.[43]

Within this matrix Banti sees the chivalric duel as a symbolic means of manifesting or reasserting Italy's military valour. Even more important, however, was the chivalrous image of defending the purity of Italy's women, which abounded in the novels and plays he studied. This image was easily transferred into defending the honour of *Italia* as a woman, which, as he effectively demonstrates, was a common poetic and pictorial means of reifying the new nation.[44] Given all of this cultural baggage, he sees the many duels portrayed in the canonical texts as expanding the individual notion of honour to represent instead the communal honour of Italians, and as leading to a 'nationalization of honor'.[45] In fact, many of the duels in the canon tended to take place in the remote past, and specifically in the Middle Ages, and they recalled a world of grand and selfless gestures highly attractive to romantic tastes. Celebrating the duelling heroes of yesteryear, they helped to reinforce an ideal chivalric stereotype which could then be linked to the ideal of Italian regeneration, thus making duelling ever more acceptable or even laudable.

The best practical example of this was the role chivalry played in the most famous duel of the early Risorgimento, which was between Gabrielle Pepe, a Neapolitan colonel in exile, and the French author/diplomat Alphonse de Lamartine. In 1825, Lamartine published a poem in memory of Lord Byron containing a number of lines highly insulting to Italians. Weak, obsequious, fawning and treacherous, they had betrayed the majesty and courage of their Roman past and now fought only from behind in the dark.[46] 'Italy,' he maintained, was 'a fallen monument, where there lives only an echo; dust of the past, moved by sterile winds; a land where the descendants no longer carry the blood of their ancestors.'[47] Such slurs, which

43 Ibid., p. 93.

44 Ibid., pp. 67, 84–5, 140–1, 183.

45 Ibid., pp. 105, 147.

46 'Où le fer avili ne frappe que dans l'ombre.' The entire offending stanza is quoted in Giovanni Jannone, *Il duello Pepe-Lamartine su documenti inediti* (Terni, 1912), pp. 13–14.

47 'Dernier chant du pèlegrinage d'Harold.' The quotation is in Gabriele Pepe, *Epistolario*,

managed to combine images of decadence, cowardice and bastardy, were bound to create an enormous uproar among Italy's literati, especially in Florence, which had become a safe haven for liberal exiles after the revolutions of 1821. It also happened to be the city to which Lamartine had been assigned as part of the French royal legation, just a month before his damaging diatribe was released in Italy in November 1825. Yet Lamartine was not expecting any trouble over the poem.[48] Nevertheless, he quickly found it in the form of Pepe, a soldier and writer who had sought refuge in Tuscany after having served two harsh years of prison, imposed by the restored Bourbon regime in Naples for his participation in the recent revolution.

Numerous authors had hoped to provoke Lamartine in print, but the Tuscan censors had successfully managed to suppress all such reaction in the hope of avoiding a diplomatic flap with the French. Pepe had cleverly managed to circumvent their surveillance by slipping a back-handed barb against Lamartine as being both weak and cowardly into an otherwise innocuous analytical article, or *Cenno*, on Dante. Lamartine twice requested in writing an 'explanation' of Pepe's prose, and subtly offered a literary equivocation that might have allowed them both to escape with honour intact.[49] Pepe, however, had no intention of avoiding an encounter. He politely responded on both occasions that gentlemen, especially writers, did not provide explanations on demand and that his words stood for themselves. Lamartine then asked for a personal meeting. Pepe received him at home, and his description of the event, written some weeks later to his brother, reveals reams about his use of chivalry as a foil of patriotism.

> He came on February thirteenth: I received him with all possible courtesy, just as our written correspondence had been genteel and courteous. I tell you this because, knowing full well that the dart fired by my *Cenno* would lead to an affair of arms, I wanted to use and exaggerate the forms of chivalry. I was dealing with a Frenchman who had depicted the Italians as assassins capable only of treacherously using a dagger in the night. It was thus necessary to demonstrate with facts that the Italians are more chivalrous than the French. Moreover, the Florentines, who shared my estimation of events, were carefully watching to see in what ways I would carry out the part of Champion of Italy. And since we Neapolitans, because of past military events, do not have a good reputation, I was simultaneously stimulated by both Italian and patriotic [for his birthplace Naples] feelings. And I said, since I find myself in the dance, I should conduct myself with no less nobility than courage.[50]

Here then was a chance to prove the Italians as chivalrous as the French, to counter the image, which had haunted Italy since the seventeenth century, of the perfidious stiletto in the shadows, and finally to redeem the martial valour of his countrymen

ed. Alberto Pasquale De Lisio (Naples, 1980), vol. 1, p. 390, n. 1.

48 Jannone, *Il duello*, p. 11.

49 Lamartine asked in his note if Pepe's criticism had been levelled at his poem or his person – the assumption being that, if the former, it could be excused.

50 Letter to Raffaele Pepe: Pepe, *Epistolario*, i, p. 400.

in the face of past defeats and desertions. Courtesy combined with bravery could assure both personal and national respect.

Consequently, Pepe went out of his way to be polite and accommodating to Lamartine, all the while offering no hope of pacification. During their meeting, he decorously avoided offering any mitigating explanation for his words against Lamartine, who now had no choice but to challenge him to a fight. They did not fix an exact date, however, because Lamartine was still recovering from a riding accident and did not have full use of his right foot. According to Pepe, gallantry demanded that he should not take advantage of his opponent's weakened condition. This was only the first of a series of chivalrous gestures by Pepe which became part of the official story in Italy. For instance, he did not wish to compromise any of his Italian compatriots with the Tuscan government, which had a reputation for being hard on participants in a duel, and so he offered to accept any second that Lamartine might suggest. He thus placed his security in the hands of strangers, with the assertion that he knew the French well enough not to expect any high-handedness: a perfect blend of chivalry and bravery. Likewise, when Pepe was 'invited' to appear before the Tuscan police, who hoped to prevent an encounter, he feared that he might be deported and, worse, that it might be interpreted as a means of escaping his obligations. He thus hurriedly arranged with Lamartine to carry out the duel before meeting with the police. Having little time to prepare, the seconds presented the participants with swords which were not of equal length, and Pepe gallantly rejected a selection by lot and took up the shorter weapon. After all, he was the senior duellist who had previously served in the French and Neapolitan armies for over twenty years. When the duel ensued, Pepe soon stabbed Lamartine in the arm and then rushed to bind the bleeding wound with his own handkerchief: an act of brotherly concern for his fellow writer. The veracity of all these details is unclear; Lamartine's account, written years later, is significantly different. It omits the shorter sword and the handkerchief, and even suggests that he allowed himself to be wounded when he could have killed Pepe, because he knew that such a fatal outcome would only have led to further duels with other Italians seeking revenge.[51] But it does not matter; Pepe's description quickly became the Italian version and was soon celebrated as a sublime act of courage, esprit and chivalric manners.

Equally important was the reaction of the authorities. Apprised of the duel, which they had so assiduously attempted to deter, the police immediately put Pepe under house arrest. However, public opinion was so clearly on the Neapolitan's side that they soon had to reconsider. And such pressure came not only from the Italians. Many diplomats and foreign dignitaries had been especially impressed by Pepe's attention to the niceties of chivalry, and openly communicated their general support to the government.[52] In particular, the French ambassador, the Marquis de la Maisonfort, pleaded with Tuscany's foreign minister, Count Fossombroni, that the duel was primarily the responsibility of his subordinate, Lamartine, and that Pepe had acted the perfect gentleman in response. He even went so far as to say that

51 This from his autobiography, which is quoted at length in Jannone, *Il duello*, pp. 56–7.

52 Pepe, *Epistolario*, p. 402.

he would throw himself at the feet of the grand duke to plead for Pepe's immunity.[53] Lamartine's own wife apparently did approach the grand duke and, having reported that her husband's wound was not grave, she asked that Pepe be forgiven. Such requests, combined with the general reaction of the city, had their effect; the chief of police, Puccini, visited Pepe at home on the same day as the duel, complimented him on his part in the affair, and assured him that no further action would be forthcoming against him. Rumours even circulated that the grand duke was not at all displeased by the results of the encounter.[54]

If official reaction was positive, the popular response was overwhelming. Both participants were lionised for their bravery, a celebratory dinner was arranged on their mutual behalf, and Lamartine was honoured at the opera by the toast of Florentine society.[55] Pepe in particular became a hero of the first order, and Ranieri reported that he was 'the most venerated, the most adored of the exiles' to whom 'all the Italians, all the foreigners who were in Florence knelt down'.[56] Similar enthusiasm emanated from the rest of Italy. Indeed, the participants gained such fame as gentlemen that it put a polish on their other achievements, however grand. Pepe in particular took on an almost saintly aura – hence the numerous references to those who felt they should fall on their knees before him. And who was this icon of national valour? An ex-army colonel of common birth, scraping by as a writer far from home, who had taken on with pen and sword an aristocratic poet of talent and prestige acting in the service of the king of France. Nothing could better advertise the chivalric duel as an instrument of parity in the shifting social and political sands of post-Napoleonic Italy.

It would be hard to overestimate the importance and impact of Pepe's example for duelling in Restoration Italy. It had, in many ways, been a 'perfect' duel. Above all, it had been a public event from start to finish, with Lamartine's poetic attack being countered by Pepe's literary retort, leading to a duel broadcast throughout the peninsula. The evidence of insult was easily available in print for all to see, and the injury had transcended personal rancour to reach questions of national character. More to the point, chivalry had been at the core of the drama, with Pepe deliberately working to prove himself 'more chivalrous' than the Frenchman, although both participants carried out their prescribed 'knightly' roles correctly. Thus Carlo Poerio, a fellow revolutionary and poet, having attended a celebratory lunch given by Lamartine in Pepe's honour, reported in all seriousness 'that the laws of the Knights of the Round Table were religiously observed'.[57]

On a more practical note, the affair had clearly announced that a duel carried out correctly for the right reasons would enjoy legal immunity from prosecution, and such protection had carried the seal of an international community of elites.

[53] Such was the report from Fossombroni to the Tuscan ambassador in Paris, which is quoted in Jannone, *Il duello*, p. 59.

[54] See Jannone, *Il duello*, p. 61, especially n. 2; Pepe, *Epistolario*, pp. 397–402.

[55] Jannone, *Il duello*, p. 67.

[56] Quoted in Alma Serena Lucianelli, 'Il viaggio in Italia', *Ranieri Inedito: Le notti di un eremita & Zibaldone scientifico e letterario* (Naples, 1994), p. 98.

[57] Quoted in Jannone, *Il duello*, p. 62.

Equally significantly, Pepe had created a paradigm which could allow almost any duel between an Italian and a foreigner to be read as an analogue of national struggle, as long as the combat was appropriately chivalrous in its execution. For instance, in March of 1833, when a tiff during Mardi Gras between a group of Imperial officers and a Milanese engineer led to a duel that left one of the officers dead, it was interpreted as a political event as much as a personal one, leading to the arrest of a number of liberal sympathisers.[58] Thus, the chivalric action of a few could be seen as inculcating a masculine sense of self into the entire nation, and that algorithm of patriotic honour became all the more important when the mass efforts of revolution and war, which had been variously vaunted as regenerative tools in the 1840s, came a cropper in the failures of 1848 and 1849.

The practical results of those failures for the culture of chivalry appeared clearly in the 1850s, commonly called the Risorgimento's 'decade of preparation', as the duel became a self-conscious means of continuing the national struggle.[59] This was particularly the case in Lombardy, as Giovanni Visconti Venosta (brother of one of united Italy's most successful foreign ministers) recalled in his memoirs:

> The thought of duels kept our youthful fantasies burning. Duelling with Austrian officers seemed a patriotic duty; it was individual combat substituted for the war we were unable to fight; and it was certainly a means of keeping alive that continual tension of soul and that moral battle which were our force.[60]

As part of that battle, Visconti Venosta and other young elites conspired to use the duel to pointedly political purposes. The stage was set when, in the wake of the bitter clashes of 1848–49, the Milanesi came to ostracise the Austrians in a more or less coordinated plan of silent but effective protest. Socially isolated in general, and specifically shunned by the high society with which they naturally identified, Austrian officers often resorted to hot words and hasty actions as tensions mounted. For their part, Milan's elite youth always acted correctly, but made sure that no insult went unanswered and that each *vertenza* (or chivalric affair) was pushed to its logical conclusion. Moreover, at the end of each duel, the Italians were polite to a fault, but they refused any form of comradely reconciliation that might be misconstrued as social acceptance.[61]

This deliberate use of the duel as a weapon of propaganda and provocation was not restricted to Austrian officers. It was also employed against Italians who might fraternise with the enemy. This became particularly important after the emperor, in the hope of being able to win back the affections of the populace, sent his brother, Archduke Maximilian, to become governor of Lombardy/Venetia in 1857. Glib,

58 Iacopo Gelli, *Duelli Mortali del Secolo XIX* (Milan, 1899), pp. 55–64.

59 Steven Hughes, 'Men of Steel', *Men and Violence*, ed. Pieter Spierenburg (Columbus, 1998), pp. 69–70.

60 Giovanni Visconti Venosta, *Ricordi di gioventù: cose vedute o sapute, 1847–1860* (Milan, 1906), p. 337.

61 Raffalele Barbiera, *Il salotto di contessa Maffei* (Milan, 1919), pp. 178–80.

intelligent and well meaning, the archduke exerted his considerable charms on Milan's upper echelons, while offering a number of important reforms, including a political amnesty. There was consequently real fear that he might be able, in Visconti Venosta's words, 'to open a breach in the rigid and disciplined patriotism which had hitherto held fast'. In order to forestall any such threat to the region's Risorgimento élan, something *chiassoso* (or clamorous) was necessary, so Visconti Venosta and his well-heeled compatriots hit upon a scheme one evening over cigars to force a duel on anyone willing to socialise at the court of the archduke. 'The idea was accepted with enthusiasm; this bravado seemed beautiful to us, and in fact it indicated the temperature of our heads and of the times in which we lived. That evening we separated with our heads hot with schemes and duels.'[62] They soon carried out their plot, and forced the Marchese Luigi d'Adda into a duel over his shared passion with the archduke for equestrian exercise. D'Adda was also well known in Milan, and the notoriety of such an affair would serve as a proper example to the rest. In fact, given the power of the chivalric compulsion to duel, d'Adda actually helped avoid police interference and – along with the man who challenged him, Alfonso Carcano – slipped out of a performance at La Scala, jumped into two waiting carriages, and traded innocuous pistol shots just over the Piedmontese border. The duel soon became the talk of the town, but the police were unable to prosecute because the principals all agreed to deny any knowledge of the event.[63]

Such almost *pro forma* duels between patriots and officers served as a practical training ground for the proliferation of the duelling ethic among Italy's future elites. Indeed, the names in these accounts are something of a *Who's Who* of the Lombard elites who soon came to share power in the young country of Italy, and their experiences in the 1850s would inform attitudes toward honour and the duel after the Austrians were long gone. Engulfed in images of the duel on stage and in print, often within a glorified medieval context, Risorgimento elites had embraced a notion of chivalry that would be crucial in identifying and affirming the new ruling class of Italy. The duel thus owed much of its vivacity and continuity to the fact that it provided a variety of political and social functions inherent to the arrival of a liberal, constitutional regime on the peninsula. Free speech, parliamentary debate and relatively relaxed press laws created new forms of interchange with which Italians had little social or legal experience. In this new public sphere, the code of chivalry offered a means of adjudicating those disputes that might result from the often acrimonious exchanges between journalists and politicians. Within Italy's evolving social structure, the duel acted as a touchstone of 'gentlemanly' status, not only standing as the final arbiter of honour, but also proving that a man had the 'right stuff' in terms of education, sensibility and courage. Thus the practice aided in the creation, legitimisation and empowerment of a new elite: an elite that self-consciously set itself apart from the rest of society by using exclusive chivalric concepts of honour and its defence. If duelling had been useful in creating the new

[62] Visconti Venosta, *Ricordi*, p. 396.
[63] Ibid., p. 404.

Italy, it was equally important in creating the new Italians, or at least those who felt they counted in society.

The chivalric ethos that emerged around the duel found additional support as the house of Savoy came to head up the unification movement after 1848, and eventually installed itself – despite the plans and pleas of the Mazzinian republicans – as a constitutional monarchy over the new country of Italy in 1861. Marco Minghetti had already described Victor Emmanuel in 1848 as being a knight of the Middle Ages, who was determined 'to not put down his sword as long as a single Austrian remained in Italy', and the Savoyard dynasty brought with it a long and illustrious

Figure 6.8 Postcard of the *Moschettieri del Duce*, n.d. Author's private collection.

tradition of feudal titles and honours.[64] As Italian society sorted itself out during the decades after unification, and as various elites jockeyed for position in a liberal parliamentary regime, there was a notorious clamour for chivalric decorations (such as *commendatore* or *cavaliere*) from the crown, and they ranked highly among the popular favours traded by the regime for political support.[65] Appropriately, Victor Emmanuel was famous for his assertion that he could never refuse either a knighthood or a cigar to a gentleman, and he must have grasped the popularity of such an attitude among the *ceto civile,* or civil class, hungry for honour.[66]

However, the chivalric ethic ran deeper than that. Proponents of the duel in Italy argued that the *codice cavalleresco* was critical in the creation of a new nobility, beyond birth, not just of talent but also of temperament. It was this same image that prompted Italy's most prestigious intellectual, Benedetto Croce, to characterise Italy's ruling elites as 'a spiritual aristocracy of upright and loyal gentlemen', who would provide 'a permanent source of moral and political education'.[67] As demonstrated above, the attending icon of this spiritual aristocracy was the medieval knight, whose symbolic devices were seen in both fencing and duelling manuals. Such iconography directly linked Italy's *gentiluomini* to ancient attributes of knighthood – courage, loyalty and gallantry – while simultaneously recalling ancient rituals of individual combat that reinforced the duel as the touchstone of elite status. Yet in the end this was a very limited notion of medieval chivalry, and one that focused primarily on defending one's honour according to rules and precepts that had actually been created during the Renaissance. Virile combat, *sang-froid* and punctilious sensibility clearly dominated over any Christian concept of duty to the downtrodden or protection of the weak. But such anachronisms did not bother the purveyors of the Italian duelling codes. They were happy to look back at the Middle Ages through the romantic novels and operas of the Restoration and find there a palimpsest upon which they could write their own assertions of nobility, as tied to both patriotism and easily-bruised masculinity. And they would hold their own until after the First World War, when a new 'aristocracy of the trenches' would come to the fore and fascism would eventually substitute the people's dagger-cum-bayonet as Italy's iconic weapon of honour, in the hand of one of Mussolini's *Moschettieri* or honour guards (figure 6.8).

64 Minghetti, quoted in Banti, *La nazione*, p. 188.

65 Nasalli Rocca, *Memorie di un prefetto* (Rome, 1946), p. 183. See also Silvio Lanaro, *L'Italia nuova: Identità e sviluppo. 1861–1988* (Torino, 1988), pp. 38–9.

66 Piero Del Negro, *Esercito, stato, società: saggi di storia militare* (Bologna, 1979), p. 149; Niccola Marselli, *La vita del reggimento osservazioni e recordi* (Rome, 1984), p. 153.

67 Croce quoted in Lucy Riall, *Sicily and the Unification of Italy* (Oxford, 1998), p. 9.

7

The German Crusade: The Battles of Tannenberg, 1410 and 1914

Stefan Goebel

Germany's greatest victory in the First World War happened to take place not far from an ancient battlefield where, in 1410, an allied army of Lithuanian and Polish forces had defeated the knights of the Teutonic Order near the villages of Tannenberg (Stębarg) and Grunwald (Grünfelde). This historical coincidence gave rise to one of the most powerful German myths of the war: the Tannenberg myth. The name of 'Tannenberg' that was granted to the battle fought between 27 and 30 August 1914 was a deliberate evocation of the medieval clash of 1410. Initially, the press named the operation after the encounters at Gilgenburg (Dąbrówno) and Ortelsburg (Szczytno), but eventually Tannenberg gained acceptance. The triumph in the east (which resulted in Russian losses of 120,000) caused great excitement as it came at a time of bitter disappointments in the west. Yet, without sustained efforts to recall the events of August 1914, Tannenberg would not have taken on mystic proportions as a celebration of a historic victory within the framework of military defeat in the First World War. Two focal points for rehearsals of the Tannenberg story evolved: first, the project of the erection of a Tannenberg monument, and second, the apotheosis of Field Marshal Paul von Beneckendorff und von Hindenburg, commander of the victorious Eighth Army in East Prussia. This essay explores the ways in which the architects of remembrance intended to contain oblivion by fusing two layers of memory.[1] The elision of the existential memory of death in war with the cultural memory of the distant past was meant to accommodate the human toll of the war in a vision of historical continuity – continuity between the past, present and future. The story of the battle of Tannenberg in 1914 is an integral part of the process of 'medievalising' the memory of the Great War. In Germany (but also in other European nations), there were many people

[1] For an introduction to theories of cultural memory, see Jan Assmann, *Cultural Memory and Early Civilization: Writing, Remembrance, and Political Imagination* (Cambridge, 2012); Aleida Assmann, *Cultural Memory and Western Civilization: Functions, Media, Archives* (Cambridge, 2011); Stefan Goebel, 'Cultural Memory and the Great War: Medievalism and Classicism in British and German War Memorials', *Proceedings of the British Academy* 160 (2012), pp. 135–58.

whose epochal consciousness was premised on continuity, people who refused to see history as irretrievably past. Looking to a misty past in order to understand the war-torn present, they enveloped recollections of the First World War in an imagery derived from interpretations of native, pre-industrial history, particularly the Middle Ages. Medieval military history provided rich, protean sources of images, tropes and narrative motifs for people to give meaning to the legacy of the Great War. An accessible mode of war commemoration that ennobled the fallen and gave comfort to the bereaved, the building blocks of medievalism had been assembled during the nineteenth century. The very term 'medievalism', dating from the mid nineteenth century, is indicative of the historical consciousness of that epoch. In the period between the Napoleonic wars and the outbreak of the Great War, the idealisation of the Middle Ages had pointed to dissatisfaction with the aesthetic, moral and social condition of contemporary society and a desire to return to (or at least to remember) the imagined harmony or purposefulness of the remote past.[2] What had essentially been a discourse of national identity in the era of industrialisation was later transformed into a discourse of remembrance in an age of industrialised slaughter.[3] While the Tannenberg myth was the most prominent medievalist narrative after 1914–18, it should not be equated with *the* German memory of the Great War. The war did not generate one large-scale national community of remembrance, but rather facilitated the emergence of different commemorative *milieux* and narratives.

The Great War left its mark on the surviving bulwarks built by the Teutonic Order. In 1916, at the time of the second anniversary of the 1914 battle of Tannenberg, an initiative was formed with the support of the provincial governor to restore – or to 'heal' – the damage inflicted on the late-fourteenth-century Neidenburg Castle in 1914. It was to be launched as a national site of Tannenberg worship:

> Five hundred years ago, it [Neidenburg Castle] saw the wild bands of the Polish King Władysław II Jagiełło and the Lithuanian Prince Witowd in front of her walls; at the time of the Great Elector [Frederick William], it repelled the invasion of the Tartars; two years ago, it looked down again on a struggle

[2] The literature on nineteenth-century medievalism is vast. Particularly important is the journal *Studies in Medievalism*, ed. Leslie J. Workman, 1 (1979). See also *Die Deutschen and ihr Mittelalter: Themen and Funktionen moderner Geschichtsbilder vom Mittelalter*, ed. Gerd Althoff (Darmstadt, 1992); *Italia e Germania: Immagini, modelli, miti fra due popoli nell'Ottocento: il Medioevo*, ed. Reinhard Elze and Pierangelo Schiera (Berlin and Bologna, 1988). Medievalism in the first half of the twentieth century has received less attention. However, see Otto Gerhard Oexle, 'Das Mittelalter and das Unbehagen an der Moderne: Mittelalterbeschwörungen in der Weimarer Republik und danach', in *Spannungen und Widersprüche: Gedenkschrift für František Graus*, ed. Susanna Burghartz *et al.* (Sigmaringen, 1992), pp. 125–53; Megan Cassidy-Welch and Anne E. Lester, 'Memory and Interpretation: New Approaches to the Study of the Crusades', *Journal of Medieval History* 40 (2014), pp. 225–36.

[3] For a more detailed discussion, see Stefan Goebel, *The Great War and Medieval Memory: War, Remembrance and Medievalism in Britain and Germany, 1914–1940* (Cambridge, 2007).

of nations, and defied the Russian shells with her iron-solid walls. Let us turn it into a national memorial of the entire German *Volk* for Tannenberg![4]

The plan, which did not come to fruition, was absolutely in line with nineteenth-century ideas about Germany's medieval heritage. The crumbling castle of Marienburg, the former residence of the grand master of the Teutonic Order, had been reconstructed between 1817 and 1830.[5] A second phase of rebuilding had begun under the Kaiser's patronage in 1882. The war years interrupted the restoration work and gave the project a new significance. The idea of mending the decaying towers of the *Plauenbollwerk* (an extension to Marienburg Castle erected under Heinrich von Plauen in the aftermath of the first battle of Tannenberg) in honour of famous generals of the World War soon emerged. The reconstruction of the central tower as a Hindenburg shrine was at the core of the project.[6] In September 1927, shortly before the eightieth birthday of the war hero and, since 1925, Reich President, the Reich Minister of the Interior gave the requested subsidy of 50,000 marks for the undertaking, which was nothing but a monumental celebration of German defiance in an age of destruction.[7]

September 1927 also saw the unveiling of a new building of triumphal monumentality at the site of the Tannenberg epic near Hohenstein. Eight massive clinker towers and high walls fenced in an octagonal arena that was to be used for rallies. The whole structure was reminiscent of medieval castles. *The Times* noted that 'there is a medieval flavour in the very name of Tannenberg, and it is hardly surprising that something resembling a medieval fortress, covering fifteen acres, should have been erected even now in the centre of an ancient battle zone of East Prussia'.[8] The memorial's architecture was a hybrid of art history. The towers connoted prehistoric stone circles; the fortress-like structure reminded observers of the castles of the Teutonic Order, or the Castel del Monte in Puglia in southern Italy built by Frederick II in 1240; and the simple but elegant design revealed the influences of modernism.[9] Yet the diverse functions of the memorial added to its peculiarity: the Tannenberg memorial served as a monument, mausoleum, museum and meeting place. The towers accommodated youth hostels, military-historical exhibitions, an archive,

4 Berlin, Bundesarchiv [hereafter BArch], R 8034 II/7690, fol. 110, 'Tannenberg-Gedächtnishalle auf der Neidenburg', *Deutsche Tageszeitung*, 412, 13 August 1916; see also Ibid., fol. 106, 'Tannenberger Gedächtnis', *Deutsche Tageszeitung*, 326, 28 June 1916.

5 Hartmut Boockmann, *Die Marienburg im 19. Jahrhundert* (Frankfurt am Main, 1982), p. 36.

6 BArch, R 43 I/834, fol. 62, Regierungspräsident Marienwerder to Reichskanzler, 7 July 1927.

7 BArch, R 43 I/834, fol. 164, Reichminister des Innern to Staatssekretär in der Reichskanzlei, 30 September 1927.

8 'Tannenberg and an Indiscretion', *The Times*, 20 September 1927, p. 15.

9 Jürgen Tietz, *Das Tannenberg-Nationaldenkmal: Architektur, Geschichte, Kontext* (Berlin, 1999), pp. 75–84; Heike Fischer, 'Tannenberg-Denkmal und Hindenburgkult: Hintergründe eines Mythos', *Unglücklich das Land, das Helden nötig hat: Leiden und Sterben in den Kriegsdenkmälern des Ersten und Zweiten Weltkrieges*, ed. Michael Hütt *et al.* (Marburg, 1990), p. 31; Meinhold Lurz, *Kriegerdenkmäler in Deutschland, IV: Weimarer Republik* (Heidelberg, 1985), pp. 202–7.

Figure 7.1 The Tannenberg memorial around 1927. Underneath the metal cross in the centre was a grave of twenty unknown soldiers from the Eastern Front. Source: *Tannenberg: Deutsches Schicksal – Deutsche Aufgabe*, ed. Kuratorium für das Reichsehrenmal Tannenberg (Oldenburg [1939]), fig. 2.

and commemorative rooms in honour of soldiers and generals; all functions were subject to frequent review.[10] In a sense, Tannenberg can thus be better described as a permanently evolving memory workshop rather than a monument set in stone.

In the centre of the arena, underneath a huge metal cross, there was a grave holding the remains of twenty unidentified German soldiers from the Russian front. Tannenberg thus illustrates a German transformation of the Anglo-French institution of the Unknown Soldier, who originally represented the recovery and restoration of the individual, but now was turned into a symbol of the *völkisch* community of the dead. In doing so, the designers anticipated the concept of *Totenburgen*, 'fortresses of the dead', housing mass graves of soldiers, an idea developed in the 1920s and 1930s. A commentary of 1935 explained the ideology behind the construction of mass graves: 'the individual grave has been subordinated to the idea of community. It is the greater and lasting. Seen over decades and centuries – once the name will have been blown away and faded away – it will merely be crucial to know that those, who have been laid to eternal rest here, were Germans and soldiers.'[11]

The people and social groups behind the Tannenberg memorial scheme referred to it as 'the national memorial'. Although a structure of national attention and importance, it was not made an official Reich memorial (*Reichsehrenmal*) during the Weimar Republic. The memorial never stood a chance of fulfilling the basic

[10] Tietz, *Tannenberg*, pp. 54, 127–44.

[11] 'Die Bauten des Volksbundes in ihrer geschichtlichen und kulturellen Bedeutung', *Kriegsgräberfürsorge* 15:2 (1935), p. 20.

requirement of widespread acceptance; it was too exclusive and polarising. Tannenberg was contested terrain, and the memorial enshrined the myth of the 'Eastern Front experience' for a nationalist audience. An examination of the participants in the unveiling ceremony on 18 September 1927 is revealing. The Generals Hindenburg, Ludendorff and Mackensen made grand entrances, cheered by the members of the assembled right-wing groups. The Social-Democratic veterans' league, the Reichsbanner Black-Red-Gold, deliberately stayed away from the spectacle, in which the colours of Imperial Germany (black, white and red) were expected to dominate.[12] The Social-Democratic state government of Prussia, though hosting the ceremony on its territory, pursued the same policy of conspicuous absence. The federal government that had been formed recently by centre-right parties, including the German National People's Party, was represented by Reich Chancellor Wilhelm Marx of the Centre Party and some of his cabinet ministers.[13] The event of 1927 was an ostentatious display of nationalist sentiment and arguably something of a prelude to future Nazi ceremonies at Tannenberg.[14]

The democratic politicians of the Weimar Republic had hoped to create a Reich memorial that would unite the German people in remembrance, but the project did not get off the ground until after the Nazis' accession to power. On 2 October 1935, Adolf Hitler personally proclaimed the Tannenberg memorial in East Prussia a Reich memorial. At the time of its eventual elevation to Reich memorial status, the memorial makers could look back on more than fifteen years of planning and building. Veterans had first expressed their wish to see a Tannenberg monument established during a review to mark the fifth anniversary of the battle of 1914. Five years later, in June 1924, a working committee comprising the heads of the associations of German officers and of East Prussian veterans was brought into being. Hindenburg accepted the position of honorary chairman. Somewhat remarkably, early moves seem to indicate a long-term though shaky plan. As early as 31 August 1924, the foundation stone was laid in a ceremony on the battlefield, whereas the architectural competition, won by the brothers Walter and Johannes Krüger, did not take place until the following year. The entire venture was a leap in the dark since the finances were low.

The ceremonial opening of the shell of the unfinished monument in September 1927, amid a blaze of publicity, was a bold move. Over the following years, building work continued and was nearing completion by the time Hitler, the 'artist-politician', ordered extensive alterations to the original plan.[15] The rebuilding of the Tannenberg

[12] Benjamin Ziemann, *Contested Commemorations: Republican War Veterans and Weimar Political Culture* (Cambridge, 2013), pp. 180, 191.

[13] BArch, R 43 I/834, fol. 15, note by the Staatssekretär in der Reichskanzlei, 19 March 1927; Ibid., fols 82–93, Reichsminister des Innern to Preußischer Ministerpräsident, 3 August 1927; see also Lurz, *Kriegerdenkmäler*, iv, p. 208.

[14] Wolfgang Wippermann, 'Die Geschichte des "Reichsehrenmals Tannenberg": Ein historisches Lehrstück', *Niemandsland* 1:2 (1987), p. 63; Hans-Ulrich Thamer, 'Nationalsozialismus und Denkmalskult', *Historische Denkmäler: Vergangenheit im Dienste der Gegenwart?*, ed. Thomas-Morus-Adademie (Bergisch-Gladbach, 1994), p. 18; Tietz, *Tannenberg*, pp. 51, 86.

[15] Lurz, *Kriegerdenkmäler, IV*, p. 206; Lurz, *Kriegerdenkmäler in Deutschland, V: Drittes Reich* (Heidelberg, 1986), p. 46.

memorial reveals in exemplary fashion the ability of the Nazis to recycle and reinvent existing *lieux de mémoire* for their own purposes. The communal grave of the twenty unknown soldiers was removed from the centre of the arena and one of the towers was rebuilt to create space for a crypt in which the bodies of the deceased Hindenburg and his wife were entombed in October 1935.[16] Tannenberg was thus relaunched as the mausoleum of the recently-deceased hero of the battle of 1914, Hindenburg. The unknown dead were subsumed into the cult of military leadership. Already deprived of their individuality, they were now subjected to the oligarchy of commemoration. At Tannenberg, the notion of elite heroism superseded the idea of equality of sacrifice which had been intrinsic to the genuine Unknown Warrior in London. The Tannenberg memorial was reconstructed to eternalise just one single name: Hindenburg.[17]

For the Nazis, Hindenburg's ceremonial burial on the site of the historic battle was the ideal crown for the memorial project. Cunningly, the Nazis coupled two interlinked but not identical myths – those of Tannenberg and Hindenburg. Hindenburg had emerged as a legend from the war following the successful repelling of the Russian invasion into East Prussia in August and September 1914. Overnight, the victor of Tannenberg became a household name in Germany. The cult of the general gathered momentum during the war, and by 1918 he had grown into a 'living memorial' in his own right, a fact which helped him to win the German presidential election of 1925. Hindenburg seemed the embodiment of the war in general, and the Russian front in particular. Throughout the Reich, streets, places, schools, et cetera were named after him as testimony to his significance in the memory of the war.[18]

When the Reich President attained the age of eighty, the Hindenburg Donation was introduced. This benevolent fund for the welfare of ex-servicemen and the surviving dependants of soldiers killed in the war paralleled, in a certain sense, the Haig Poppy Appeal in Britain. Yet the German charity sold objects which encouraged the personality cult surrounding Hindenburg, such as Hindenburg stamps, Hindenburg postcards, a Hindenburg memorial volume and other Hindenburg kitsch.[19] No other hero of the war, either at home or abroad, could equal him in popular fame and adoration. War memorials and 'war landmarks' (that is, wooden objects into which people hammered iron nails in public ceremonies) developed

16 Fischer, 'Tannenberg-Denkmal', pp. 30, 38f.; Tietz, *Tannenberg*, pp. 85–154.

17 Gert Buchheit, *Das Reichsehrenmal Tannenberg: Seine Entstehung, seine endgültige Gestaltung und seine Einzelkunstwerke* (Munich, 1936), p. 9.

18 See Wolfram Pyta, *Hindenburg: Herrschaft zwischen Hohenzollern und Hitler* (Munich, 2007); Anna von der Goltz, *Hindenburg: Power, Myth, and the Rise of the Nazis* (Oxford, 2009); Jesko von Hoegen, *Der Held von Tannenberg: Genese und Funktion des Hindenburg-Mythos (1914–1934)* (Cologne, 2007); Detlef Lehnert, 'Die geschichtlichen Schattenbilder von "Tannenberg": Vom Hindenburg-Mythos im Ersten Weltkrieg zum ersatzmonarchischen Identifikationssymbol in der Weimarer Republik', *Medien und Krieg – Krieg in den Medien*, ed. Kurt Imhof and Peter Schulz (Zürich, 1995), pp. 37–71.

19 BArch, R 601/1100, 'Hindenburg-Spende: Allgemeines', 1927–36, esp. fols 161, 249. For a fine example of wartime Hindenburg kitsch, see Jay Winter, *Sites of Memory, Sites of Mourning: The Great War in European Cultural History* (Cambridge, 1995), p. 83.

into the principal foci of the public cult of Hindenburg. Berlin's colossal iron-nail figure of the general as a modern-day Roland, inaugurated on the first anniversary of the battle of Tannenberg, led the way.[20] Smaller communities followed suit.[21] The war landmark of Havelberg, Brandenburg, articulated the malleability of the medieval chivalric lens and celebrated Hindenburg as a Teutonic Knight triumphing over the beast, in the tradition of older representations of St George. In Graudenz (Grudziądz), West Prussia, too, Hindenburg appeared as a Teutonic crusader, 'as a symbol of northern German colonisation'.[22] At the unveiling ceremony, local girls sold miniature shields of Teutonic Knights carved out of wood by soldiers wounded at Tannenberg.[23]

In the aftermath of the war, the popularity of this imagery abated somewhat. In an age of the 'democratisation' of remembrance, a general, however popular, could not represent the ordinary fallen soldier in the local communities. Of course, one can name notable exceptions like the war memorial of Bad Reinerz (Duszniki Zdrój), Lower Silesia, which figured 'Reich President v[on] Hindenburg in the garb of the Order of [Teutonic] Knights with sword and shield'.[24] Hindenburg's long pedigree seemed to justify the drawing of analogies between the general and the Teutonic Knights. Hindenburg was supposedly following in the footsteps of one of his forebears, who had taken part in the 'bold, faith and culture disseminating Crusades' of the Teutonic Order, as we learn from a book entitled *Hindenburg Memorial for the German People* (1922).[25]

The aged Reich President died on 2 August 1934. Hindenburg's mortal remains were transferred to the Tannenberg memorial. The carefully choreographed funeral provided the occasion to rehearse the legend of the war hero and to fuse it with the Nazis' version of the Tannenberg myth. Wrapped in the habit of the Order of St John, Hindenburg's dead body lay in state at the memorial.[26] The costume signified that the German crusading fervour was directed towards north-eastern Europe. For Nazi ideologists, the endeavours of the Teutonic Knights perfectly exemplified the necessity of German territorial expansion into eastern Europe at the expense of

20 Stefan Goebel, 'Exhibitions', *Capital Cities at War: Paris, London, Berlin 1914–1919, II: A Cultural History*, ed. Jay Winter and Jean-Louis Robert (Cambridge, 2007), pp. 152–8.

21 'Die Enthüllung des Neuköllner Roland', *Neue Preußische Zeitung* [*Kreuz-Zeitung*], 442, 31 August 1915; 'Die Nagelung des "Ritters von Neukölln"', *Neue Preußische Zeitung* [*Kreuz-Zeitung*], 466, 13 September 1915; see Gerhard Schneider, *In Eiserner Zeit: Kriegswahrzeichen im Ersten Weltkrieg. Ein Katalog* (Schwalbach, 2013), pp. 144–5.

22 Otto Weltzien, 'Kriegsnagelungen in Niederdeutschland', *Niedersachsen* 22:3 (1916), p. 39; Warburg-Haus, Hamburg, Bildindex 100/10, Postcard Havelberg, n.d.

23 'Der Eiserne Hindenburg: Nagelungsfeiern in Berlin und Graudenz', *Berliner Illustrierte Zeitung* 24 (1915), p. 503.

24 BArch, R 32/351, fol. 131, Stadtbaumt Bad Reinerz to Reichskunstwart, 14 December 1930.

25 Paul Lindenberg, 'Beim Armee-Oberkommando Hindenburgs während der Schlacht bei Tannenberg', *Hindenburg-Denkmal für das deutsche Volk: Eine Ehrengabe zum 75. Geburtstage des Generalfeldmarschalls*, ed. Paul Lindenberg (Berlin, 1922), p. 119.

26 Volker Ackermann, *Nationale Totenfeiern in Deutschland: Von Wilhelm I. bis Franz Josef Strauß: Eine Studie zur politischen Semiotik* (Stuttgart, 1990), p. 116.

Figure 7.2 Hitler speaks at Hindenburg's funeral at the Tannenberg memorial on 7 August 1934. Source: *Tannenberg: Deutsches Schicksal – Deutsche Aufgabe*, ed. Kuratorium für das Reichsehrenmal Tannenberg (Oldenburg [1939]), pp. 225–6.

Slavic *Untermenschen*. A book on the making of the new Reich memorial published in 1939 resolved that:

> The name of Tannenberg is a symbol of the centuries-lasting battle of Germanness in the east for national self-assertion. Here, on old-Germanic soil of settlement, did the Order of Teutonic Knights lay the foundation stone of its work of German state formation and German culture, which following generations time after time had to defend against alien force. [...] Only this settlement and culture work, which for ever will be part of the historic record, has created the imperative precondition for a German Reich of world-wide recognition by giving the German people the indispensable basis for its *Lebensraum* [living-space].[27]

It is worth contrasting this statement with the unveiling volume of 1927:

> For the conquest of Prussia, the Teutonic Order had gathered Saxon, Swabian, Thuringian, and Franconian lords who were soon followed by a corresponding influx of burghers and peasants. The ancient *Pruzzen* [Prussians] were either extinguished or absorbed by the predominance of the settlers. Here tribal

[27] Hans Pfundtner, 'Vorwort', *Tannenberg: Deutsches Schicksal – Deutsche Aufgabe*, ed. Kuratorium für das Reichsehrenmal Tannenberg (Oldenburg [1939]), p. 7.

peculiarities ceased to exist. Here were simply German land and German people.[28]

While both commentaries are pointedly aggressive and annexationist in tone, one can discern subtle differences between the two accounts. In 1927, the east was seen as a territory which could be manipulated and colonised (even allowing some mixture of races), whereas in 1939 it appeared to be an eternal combat zone of racial struggle. Historical scholarship has highlighted the ahistorical tendencies behind the use of historical arguments in Nazi ideology. Historical phenomena were decontextualised and lumped together as racial clashes. The alleged 'drive to the east' (*Drang nach Osten*) of the Teutonic Order in particular – a notion of historical determinism advanced by historians during the nineteenth century – gave the Nazis ideological ammunition. But in contrast to the earlier writings of nationalist scholars, the Nazis regarded the Teutonic crusaders as racial warriors in pursuit of *Lebensraum*, 'living-space', rather than *Kulturträger*, upholders and apostles of a superior culture colonising the east.[29]

The Tannenberg memorial was intended to give tangible expression to Germany's ethnic or cultural aspirations in eastern Europe. The agitation surrounding the planning and inauguration of the monument would not have fallen on fertile ground if previous decades had not established categories for viewing the east and its history. Nineteenth-century historical research into the Teutonic Order certainly helped to shape the agenda. But above all, commemorative politics and signifying practices of the Wilhelmine era had a bearing on later developments. In 1902, Wilhelm II delivered an infamous speech at the restored castle of Marienburg (Malbork), West Prussia – the seat of the grand master of the Teutonic Order between 1309 and 1457 – in which he defended German imperial interests and warned of the Polish danger in the east. The performative framework of the speech is illuminating. The Kaiser received a delegation of the surviving branch of the Teutonic Order from Vienna. Some fifty years earlier, a similar invitation to Marienburg had scandalised the Austrian knights. For the historic reunion, Wilhelm and the Prussian aristocrats dressed in the habit of the Order of St John (Knights of St John had also accompanied the Kaiser to Jerusalem in 1898). To complete the pageant, the Prussian guards were also in medieval dress in order to suggest continuity between the medieval crusaders and Imperial Germany.[30]

Nationalist Poles launched a commemorative counter-attack in the same year by organising a celebration of the victory of Grunwald – the name under which the battle of 1410 is known in Poland – in Austrian Galicia. To mark the five-hundredth

[28] *Festschrift zur Einweihung des Tannenberg-Denkmals am 18. September 1927* (Königsberg [1927]), pp. 25f.

[29] Wolfgang Wippermann, *Der Ordensstaat als Ideologie: Das Bild des Deutschen Ordens in der deutschen Geschichtsschreibung und Publizistik* (Berlin, 1979), pp. 218f., 253; see also Gerd Althoff, 'Die Beurteilung der mittelalterlichen Ostpolitik als Paradigma für zeitgebundene Geschichtsbewertung', *Die Deutschen und ihr Mittelalter*, p. 161.

[30] Boockmann, *Marienburg*, pp. 38ff.

anniversary of the battle in 1910, Great Polish agitators unveiled about sixty Grunwald memorials throughout Galicia, notably an impressive, twenty-four metre high equestrian statue of Władysław II Jagiełło, king of Poland and champion of Grunwald, in Kraków.[31]

Figure 7.3 The *Hochmeisterstein* dedicated to Ulrich von Jungingen in 1902. The inscription read: 'Here died Grand Master Ulrich von Jungingen a hero's death on 15 July 1410 in the struggle for German character, German right'. Source: *Tannenberg: Deutsches Schicksal – Deutsche Aufgabe*, ed. Kuratorium für das Reichsehrenmal Tannenberg (Oldenburg [1939]), pp. 184–5.

German agitators had not lapsed into silence, either. In 1901/02, one of the most prominent of the right-wing 'Patriotic Leagues', the *Deutscher Ostmarkenverein* (founded in 1894 to campaign for further German settlement in the eastern provinces), pressed the provincial officials to set up a boulder in memory of the unfortunate Ulrich von Jungingen. The memorial celebrated the grand master of the

31 Sven Ekdahl, 'Die Grunwald-Denkmäler in Polen: Politischer Kontext und nationale Funktion', *Nordost-Archiv*, new series 6 (1997), pp. 76f., 80; Christoph Mick, '"Den Vorvätern zum Ruhm – den Brüdern zur Ermutigung": Variationen zum Thema Grunwald/Tannenberg', *Zeitenblicke* 3:1 (2004), <http://zeitenblicke.historicum.net/2004/01/mick/index.html>, accessed 28 February 2014.

Teutonic Knights as a proto-German nationalist: 'Here died Grand Master Ulrich von Jungingen a hero's death on 15 July 1410 in the struggle for German character, German right', reads the inscription.[32] (Legend has it that Hindenburg fitted in a visit to Jungingen's memorial stone when commanding the Eighth Army in summer 1914, thus suggesting that history had been reversed and the medieval defeat revenged.[33])

In anticipation of the Polish celebrations in 1910, German firebrands intended to reconstruct the Atonement Chapel built by Heinrich von Plauen, the saviour of Marienburg from the Polish-Lithuanian advance and grand master of the order between 1410 and 1414. The head of the provincial administration of East Prussia strongly advised the Berlin government against supporting the initiative. He reasoned that the reconstruction of the chapel would provide plenty of ammunition for Polish propaganda and hence increase the tensions that already existed between the Prussian state and its Polish subjects.[34]

The politics of intersecting and competing memories in the decade before the First World War had prepared the ground for the monumental assertion of an inevitable historic German surge into the east at Tannenberg. A second factor that helped to shape German perceptions of the east was the memory of the 'Eastern Front experience' of the First World War. Having repelled the Russian invasion of East Prussia in summer and autumn 1914, the German army pushed deep into enemy territory in the following year. In the north-west of Russia, *Ober Ost* (*Oberbefehlshaber Ost*), a quasi-independent military state, was established under the Supreme Commander in the East, Hindenburg, assisted by his energetic chief of staff, Ludendorff. *Ober Ost* was more of a vision – a cultural-military utopia – than a bureaucratic experiment or programme; it opened up new spaces of thinking and created 'a German imperialist "mindscape" of the East'.[35]

A key element of the mental conquest of eastern Europe was the juxtaposition of German *Kultur* and native *Unkultur*. In their occupation zone, the German soldiers encountered an insistent but incomprehensible 'mess of history', a situation incompatible with western concepts of historical sense and order. They faced a primitive society in which a bewildering array of traces of the past coexisted, detached from all historical contexts. This unfamiliar chaos seemed to call for help from the German genius for organisation; this was the message *Ober Ost*'s sophisticated propaganda machinery drummed into the heads of the soldiers and the indigenous people alike. In practice, German officials got down to cataloguing, exhibiting and preserving local art-historical treasures. The invaders would play the role of 'custodians of

32 *Tannenberg: Deutsches Schicksal – Deutsche Aufgabe*, ed. Kuratorium für das Reichsehrenmal Tannenberg (Oldenburg [1939]), pp. 184f.; see Wippermann, 'Geschichte des Reichsehrenmals', p. 62. On the *Deutscher Ostmarkenverein*, see Wippermann, *Ordensstaat*, pp. 185–97.

33 Lindenberg, 'Beim Armee-Oberkommando', p. 124.

34 Berlin, Geheimes Staatsarchiv Preußischer Kulturbesitz [hereafter GStAPK], I. HA Rep. 77 Tit. 151 Nr. 15 Fasz. 48 (M), fols 3–4, Oberpräsident der Provinz Ostpreußen to Minister des Innern und Minister für Landwirtschaft, Domänen und Forsten, 14 December 1908.

35 Vejas Gabriel Liulevicius, *War Land on the Eastern Front: Culture, National Identity, and German Occupation in World War I* (Cambridge, 2000), p. 151.

history for native populations, using German Work to interpret and define the area's past'.[36] In the end, the German reckoning was frustrated by the resistance of the native people, who insisted on a national identity of their own. The military planners now rejected their positive approach to the east and gave way to radically racist notions of a dangerous 'dirty East of dirty populations' that had to be 'cleared and cleaned'.[37]

The radicalisation of the language of propaganda about the German cultural mission in the east is not necessarily reflected in subsequent representations of the war. In fact, spreading culture or securing 'living-space' was one (but not the dominant) theme of war remembrance. In effect, when the Nazis appropriated the Tannenberg memorial they singled out a sub-narrative of the 'Eastern Front experience' (that of Germanic 'living-space') for official use; a narrative which had evolved alongside others in the Weimar Republic. Two alternative narratives which emphasised either cultural mission *and* territorial defence, or solely national defence, emerged.

The Teutonic Order Infantry Regiment No. 152 was less traditional than its name implied, as it was founded only in 1897. The war gave the regiment and its members the opportunity to make a name for themselves as 'the new knights of the order'. At the unveiling of the regimental memorial in Marienburg in 1925, the guard of honour was appropriately dressed in the costume of a Teutonic Knight. The account of the battle(s) of Tannenberg printed in the regiment's book of remembrance (which also includes a list of the names of its fallen soldiers) is ambiguous. In places, the essays draw parallels between the cultural mission of the order and the achievements of the regiment: 'They [the soldiers] have matched them [the knights] and their brave leader, the great champion of Germanness, Ulrich von Jungingen, by suffering a heroic death while fighting gloriously under the sign of the black cross against a white background.'[38] Other passages, however, stress the defensive nature of the hostilities:

> A young regiment – still without military glory – the Teutonic Order Regiment 152 went out for the defence of the native soil. As once 500 years before the Teutonic Order had formed a living rampart against the Slavic invasions, so did the descendants, whom the supreme commander had, with that proud name, entrusted the record of great history, defend the German *Heimat* against the superior Slavic force.[39]

The same ambiguity manifested itself in a second memorial of the Teutonic Order Infantry Regiment, unveiled in 1929, which was integrated into the Tannenberg site. The commemorative plaque showed a Teutonic Knight parrying an attack with his

[36] Ibid., p. 129.

[37] Ibid., pp. 219f., 272. See also Rudy Koshar, *Germany's Transient Pasts: Preservation and National Memory in the Twentieth Century* (Chapel Hill, 1998), pp. 92ff.

[38] *Das Deutsch Ordens-Infanterie-Regiment Nr. 152 im Weltkriege*, ed. Karl Strecker (Berlin, 1933), pp. 11, 30.

[39] Ibid., p. 9.

large shield and starting a counter-offensive with his sword raised to strike. The posture was understood to portray both the ideal of iron defence and the 'ruthless spirit of the offensive'.[40] What is striking here is the absence of any reference to 'chivalry' or *Ritterlichkeit*. Chivalry as an imagined code of conduct played a prominent role in medievalist representations of the Great War in Britain, but this discourse was without parallel in Germany. Here images of knights and their metal armour connoted iron endurance and military virtues.[41]

Surprisingly, the Social Democratic Party (SPD) saw Germany's war against Russia initially as a defensive *and* missionary measure, too – though for different reasons. The Social Democrats had for a long time despised the autocratic and reactionary regime of the tsar. Already the founding fathers of the party had harboured thoughts of waging a revolutionary war against tsarist despotism.[42] In 1914, in a situation where the arch-enemy seemed to have gone on the offensive, the SPD readily joined the national camp and gave its consent for the loans that financed the war effort.[43] Until the split of the party in spring 1917, national defence against tsarist Russia was held up as a moral imperative. Despite the fact that, towards the end of the war, the party dissociated itself from the German war effort – and especially from the declared annexationism of the Right – the Social Democrats could not close their minds to the notion of a war of defence in the east. After all, had not Russian troops devastated East Prussia in 1914–15?

In November 1926, a Prussian government official suggested to the Prussian Minister of the Interior that the 'memory of the liberation of the German Eastern Marches [*Ostmark*] from the enemy can lay claim to be of especial extensive and outstanding significance'.[44] The argument carried conviction. The state government reconsidered its former negative attitude towards the projected Tannenberg memorial and granted its permission to organise fund-raising campaigns such as lotteries. Up to this time, the Social Democrats had obstructed the project on the grounds of the priority of the welfare of the surviving war victims over the cult of the fallen soldier.[45]

The memory of the Russian invasion of East Prussia fired popular imagination

40 Ibid., p. 76.

41 Stefan Goebel, 'Chivalrous Knights versus Iron Warriors: Representations of the Battle of *Matériel* and Slaughter in Britain and Germany, 1914–1940', *Picture This: World War I Posters and Visual Culture*, ed. Pearl James (Lincoln, NE, 2009), pp. 79–110.

42 Reinhard Rürup, 'Der "Geist von 1914" in Deutschland: Kriegsbegeisterung und Ideologisierung des Krieges im Ersten Weltkrieg', *Ansichten vom Krieg: Vergleichende Studien zum Ersten Weltkrieg in Literatur und Gesellschaft*, ed. Bernd Hüppauf (Königstein, 1984), pp. 9f., 15; see also Lehnert, 'Geschichtlichen Schattenbilder', p. 47; Nicholas Stargardt, *The German Idea of Militarism: Radical and Socialist Critics, 1866–1914* (Cambridge, 1994), pp. 59–67.

43 Wolfgang Kruse, *Krieg und nationale Integration: Eine Neuinterpretation des sozialdemokratischen Burgfriedensschlusses 1914/15* (Essen, 1993), pp. 71–4.

44 GStAPK, I. HA Rep. 77, Tit. 1215 Nr. 3d Beiakten, Preußischer Staatskommissar für die Regelung der Wohlfahrtspflege to Preußischer Minister des Innern, 20 November 1926.

45 See Lurz, *Kriegerdenkmäler*, iii, p. 180; Michael Jeismann and Rolf Westheider, 'Wofür stirbt der Bürger? Nationaler Totenkult und Staatsbürgertum in Deutschland und Frankreich seit der Französischen Revolution', *Der politische Totenkult: Kriegerdenkmäler in der Moderne*, ed. Reinhart Koselleck and Michael Jeismann (Munich, 1994), p. 36.

in the inter-war period. Tannenberg was cited to refute the so-called 'war-guilt lie' enacted in article 231 of the Treaty of Versailles. All political parties were in agreement about fundamental opposition to the 'dictate of Versailles'. German politicians demanded in particular the revision of the new boundaries in the east and the repeal of the controversial war-guilt clause.[46] The Tannenberg memorial proved the ideal setting for agitation against the 'dictate'. In September 1927, Reich President von Hindenburg shocked the international public by declaring that Germany had entered the war as a 'means of self-assertion against a world full of enemies. *Pure* in heart we set off to the defence of the fatherland, and with *clean* hands the German army carried the sword. Germany is prepared to prove this before impartial judges at any time!'[47] This passage from his speech was recorded verbatim on a bronze plaque later erected at the Tannenberg site.[48]

The Armistice silenced the guns, but the verbal gunfire never ceased in the east in the inter-war years. The conclusion of a second Locarno Treaty for eastern Europe was out of the question. The memory of the battles of 1410 and 1914 was used to remobilise the German people against the Slavic and especially the Polish 'threat'. Plebiscite memorials sprang up in addition to war memorials. In Allenstein, it took the form of an abstract stone circle. In Marienburg, the memorial – with the castle in sight – featured a Teutonic Knight. The inscription in Marienburg said: 'This land/ remains German!/ 11 July 1920'.[49] In July 1920, a plebiscite was held in parts of West and East Prussia on the region's territorial status. However, most of the provinces of Posen and West Prussia had been allocated to Poland in the Treaty of Versailles. Embittered Germans turned towards the Tannenberg memorial for symbolic compensation. The memorial committee cleverly linked the two battles of Tannenberg to the border issue:

> German! Do you think of Tannenberg? On the fields of Tannenberg, the knights of the Teutonic Order succumbed to the onslaught by the superior Slavic force in the middle ages. 500 years later, German heroic courage and leader genius stopped the further advance of the colossal Russian military masses, which, after flooding East Prussia, wanted to deal the deathblow to Germany. For this reason, Tannenberg is the fate in the east, perhaps German fate in general. Today, people are fighting on there at the plough and the forge, also for you, the Germans in the Reich: alien subversives, memories of referenda mean that Tannenberg shall not fall into oblivion.[50]

[46] Ulrich Heinemann, *Die verdrängte Niederlage: Politische Öffentlichkeit und Kriegsschuldfrage in der Weimarer Republik* (Göttingen, 1983), esp. pp. 236, 254.

[47] BArch, R 43 I/834, fols 162–3, 'Ansprache des Herrn Reichspräsidenten bei der Einweihung des Tannenberg-Denkmals', 18 September 1927 [orig. emphasis].

[48] See the illustration in Buchheit, *Reichsehrenmal*, p. 57.

[49] *Das 1. Masurische Infanterie-Regiment Nr. 146 1897–1919*, ed. Vereinigung ehemaliger Offiziere des Regiments (Berlin, 1929), fig. 36; *Deutsch Ordens-Infanterie-Regiment Nr. 152*, fig. i.

[50] BArch, R 43 I/834, fol. 33, Tannenberg-Nationaldenkmal-Verein e.V., 'Aufruf!' [c. 1927]; see also Ibid., fol. 60, 'Helft das Tannenberg-Nationaldenkmal bauen!' [c. July 1927].

The memorial of Tannenberg was intended to broadcast German determination to resist and fight Polish expansionism. To judge by international reactions, the memorial's founders succeeded in getting the message across. As was the case twenty years before, nationalist Poles embarked on anti-monuments. In 1931, a nephew of Marshal Piłsudski unveiled a Grunwald monument at Uzdowo (Usdau), launched in symbolic retaliation for the building of the Tannenberg memorial on East Prussian soil. Polish cultural memory was mobilised in an effort to reassert the historical legitimacy of the post-Versailles Polish state.

The resurgence of Grunwald nationalism in Poland led to commemorative frictions with now-independent Lithuania, which also claimed the legacy of the battle of 1410 (named Žalgiris in Lithuanian). In 1932 Kaunas, the capital city, saw the dedication of a magnificent statue of Vytautas the Great, a cousin of the Polish king Jagiełło. The iconography was unambiguous. The memorial depicted four symbolic figures, easily identifiable as a Pole, a Russian, a Tartar and a Teutonic Knight, surrendering to the Lithuanian grand prince. The final act of the commemorative struggle over Tannenberg-Grunwald-Žalgiris in the inter-war years was played out before the eyes of the world in 1939. At the World's Fair in New York, an equestrian statue of Jagiełło holding aloft two crossed swords adorned the Polish pavilion, while the Lithuanian contribution featured a bronze sculpture of Vytautas. Later in the same year, Hitler's *Wehrmacht* occupied Poland and demolished the large figure of Jagiełło in Kraków, originally erected in 1910.[51]

The Tannenberg memorial did not escape the attention of the former enemies in the west, either. 'According to one of the architects, the fortress-like character of the building is meant to symbolize the position of East Prussia as a German outpost surrounded by Slavs,' reported *The Times* about the unveiling.[52] To most viewers in 1927, it was clear that the architecture of Tannenberg was supposed to recall the castles built by the Teutonic Order in the region. Yet later, during the Third Reich, the architects Walter and Johannes Krüger emphatically rejected allusions to Teutonic fortresses.[53] Instead, the Krügers insisted on the formative influence of Germanic stone circles. Their clients did not share the architects' point of view. The unveiling brochure explicitly linked the design of the façades to the example of the brick buildings of the Teutonic Order.[54]

The Teutonic castles mirrored splendidly the renewed feeling of encirclement and the spirit of defensiveness. Their architecture set a precedent for memorial designs and offered an ideal framework for various remembrance activities. Guidebooks to the battlefield directed the travellers towards the castles of the Teutonic

51 Sven Ekdahl, 'Tannenberg – Grunwald – Žalgiris: Eine mittelalterliche Schlacht im Spiegel deutscher, polnischer und litauischer Denkmäler', *Zeitschrift für Geschichtswissenschaft* 50 (2002), pp. 108ff.

52 'Tannenberg Memorial: Fortresslike Monument', *The Times*, 19 September 1927, p. 11.

53 Walter Krüger and Johannes Krüger, 'Bauliche Gedanken um das Reichsehrenmal Tannenberg und seine Einfügung in die Landschaft', *Tannenberg: Deutsches Schicksal – Deutsche Aufgabe*, ed. Kuratorium für das Reichsehrenmal Tannenberg (Oldenburg [1939]), p. 230; see Tietz, *Tannenberg*, p. 75.

54 *Festschrift zur Einweihung*, pp. 38ff.

Order.[55] Ex-servicemen used the castles as a location for commemorative services. The 1st Masurian Infantry Regiment No. 146, for instance, erected its memorial in Allenstein Castle:

> No nicer site could have been chosen for the memorial: with a view of the magnificent castle of the order, a stronghold of Germanness against alien arrogance. [...] At the foot of the garrison church, which had been built to foster the spirit which let the soldiers go to their death with the old German song of refuge and strength [*Schutz – und Trutzlied*] in their hearts: 'A mighty fortress is our God' [*Ein feste Burg ist unser Gott*].[56]

The commemoration of the war in the east was articulated around a complex historical geography. The Tannenberg story did not go unchallenged. The efflorescence of variant encodings of the war on the Eastern Front testifies to the robustness of local and regional traditions. It shows that different people with different sets of values could draw different lessons from history. However, alternative narratives were rarely formulated as counter-narratives.

Chance and convenience rather than opposition to the Tannenberg myth were crucial factors in the making of the memorial fountain of Lippstadt, Westphalia. It depicted Bernhard II of Lippe, founder of the city in 1168, hailed as the very epitome of Victorian values: 'a lauded hero, a devoted sovereign, a happy father, a man of strong faith in God'.[57] Initiated and completed in peacetime, the opening of the fountain was originally scheduled for August 1914 but was then postponed until after the expected military victory. With the outbreak of hostilities, the life of Bernhard took on an unexpected topicality. As Bishop of Selonia, Livland, Bernhard had done missionary work in the Baltic region. His reputation as a 'warrior of God' invited comparisons with the German soldiers fighting at the Russian front.[58] Hence, after the war, it seemed opportune to turn the fountain into a war memorial, the secular monument into a sacred one.

Bernhard II of Lippe had been a follower of one of the most enigmatic characters of German history: Henry the Lion, duke of Saxony and Bavaria in the late twelfth century. Henry the Lion attracted scathing criticism but also effusive praise from nineteenth- and twentieth-century academics, poets and politicians.[59] His admirers

[55] Robert Traba, 'Kriegssyndrom in Ostpreußen: Ein Beitrag zum kollektiven Bewußtsein der Weimarer Zeit', *Krieg und Literatur* 3:4 (1997–98), p. 408.

[56] Vereinigung ehemaliger Offiziere, *1. Masurische Infanterie-Regiment Nr. 146*, p. 314. The song 'Ein feste Burg', which is based on *Psalm* 46, was written by Martin Luther around 1528. On the song and Protestant identity during the war, see Stefan Laube, *Fest, Religion und Erinnerung: Konfessionelles Gedächtnis in Bayern von 1804 bis 1917* (Munich, 1999), pp. 382f., 389.

[57] Münster, Staatsarchiv Münster, OP 5626, fol. 2; C. Laumanns, *Der Gründer Lippstadts: Bernhard II. Edler Herr zur Lippe* (Lippstadt, 1914), p. 71.

[58] Arnold Vogt, *Den Lebenden zur Mahnung: Denkmäler und Gedenktstätten: Zur Traditionspflege und historischen Identität vom 19. Jahrhundert bis zur Gegenwart* (Hanover, 1993), pp. 130ff.; Martin Bach, *Studien zur Geschichte des deutschen Kriegerdenkmals in Westfalen und Lippe* (Frankfurt am Main, 1985), pp. 290f., 294.

[59] Johannes Fried, 'Der Löwe als Objekt: Was Literaten, Historiker und Politiker aus

regarded him as a pioneer of German expansion into eastern Europe, his critics as a traitor to the Reich and the Holy Roman Emperor. Henry the Lion had made the city of Brunswick the centre of his duchy; his putative tomb (redesigned by the architects Krüger for the Nazis in 1937) is situated in the cathedral church.

A figure of the Saxon duke was the natural choice for the war landmark of Brunswick, presented to the public in December 1915. The statue's grave facial expression, Roland-style deportment and large shield conveyed stoicism and defensiveness, rather than thirst for imperial adventure. This impression is confirmed by the picture of Henry's endeavours presented by the cathedral preacher at the dedication. He characterised the medieval ruler as a model protector of Germanness against Slavic aggression. In his dedication speech, the reverend suggested that:

> Following the path which the great duke had shown, a good deal of the energy of the German people has turned eastward. And when we think of the enemies all around in the north and west and south, who have been united with Slavdom in hatred against us, and when we remember that they all have been unable to do anything against us during sixteen months of war, then our soul fills with humble gratitude to God, our Lord.[60]

The paranoia about the Slavic threat took on new dimensions after the war. The territorial losses due to the Treaty of Versailles fanned the flames of loathing for the eastern neighbours. First and foremost, the populace of Silesia suffered the consequences of the peace treaty. According to the outcome of a referendum in March 1921, Upper Silesia remained mostly German, but the industrial centre became Polish. Plans for a Reich memorial on Silesian ground had every prospect of succeeding. A Silesian initiative, backed by the local branch of the Centre Party, demanded that the national memorial be established on Mount Zobten, Lower Silesia – that 'outpost [...] of Germanness' surrounded by hostile Slavs.[61] Their advertising campaign juxtaposed German cultural achievements with the aggressive instincts of the Mongolians, Slavs, Hussites and others. A turning point in history, they argued, had occurred when Germans colonised Silesia in the thirteenth century: 'Silesia was German again as in prehistoric times and it remained so till the present, defying all surging waves of the later combat-ready Slavdom.'[62] Such hatred was, of course, not universal, and not every Silesian agent of remembrance presented history in black and white. In Namslau (Namysłów), Lower Silesia, the war memorial in the form of

Heinrich dem Löwen machten', *Historische Zeitschrift* 262 (1996), pp. 673–93; Stefanie Barbara Berg, *Heldenbilder und Gegensätze: Friedrich Barbarossa und Heinrich der Löwe im Urteil des 19. und 20. Jahrhunderts* (Münster, 1994).

[60] As cited in Wulf Otte, 'Heinrich der Löwe – in Eisen', *Braunschweigisches Landesmuseum: Informationen und Berichte* 3 (1987), p. 37; see also Gerhard Schneider, 'Nageln in Niedersachsen im Ersten Weltkrieg', *Niedersächsisches Jahrbuch für Landesgeschichte* 76 (2004), pp. 262–3.

[61] BArch, R 43 I/716, fol. 79, Schlesisches Komitee für das Reichsehrenmal to Reichskanzler, 10 June 1930; ibid., fol. 81, Theo Johannes Mann, 'Reichsehrenmal Zobtenberg' [c.1930].

[62] Ibid., fol. 81, Theo Johannes Mann, 'Reichsehrenmal Zobtenberg' [c.1930].

an 'old watch-tower' was placed at 'a historic spot [...], where the Slavic settlement had stood out of which the city developed'.[63]

Medievalism in the remembrance of the Great War had two constituents: first, resonances of historically remote incidents, and secondly, repercussions of recent events. Historical romance (grounded on the nation's cultural memory as it had evolved in the nineteenth century) and human trauma (ingrained in the existential memory of wartime sacrifice) formed a narrative symbiosis. The process of joining the existential memory of death in modern war and the cultural memory of a distant past together in public was intended to vindicate memory down the ages. The dialectic of imagining historical continuity and lamenting human catastrophe was at the core of medievalist diction in war remembrance.

Ultimately, it was the Second World War that severed the link between cultural and existential memory, between the remote past and the traumatic present. In the aftermath of the second great post-war transition in the twentieth century, it became infinitely more difficult to locate the present within a coherent temporal order.[64] The very notion of historical meaning appeared problematic after the horrors of genocidal war, the mass bombing of civilians and the uprooting of millions of refugees. By and large, no significant upsurge of medievalism in commemorative culture took place after 1945.

Even though the Allies were determined to eradicate the culture of Prussian militarism, numerous streets and squares named 'Tannenberg' or 'Hindenburg' were left untouched by their measures. Ironically, it was the American military administration that choreographed the most significant restatement of the medievalist theme in post-war Germany: the interment of Hindenburg's body in St Elizabeth Church at Marburg in August 1946. With the Red Army hard on their heels, the *Wehrmacht* had blown up the Tannenberg memorial in January 1945, but not before removing from the vault the coffins of Hindenburg and his wife for safe keeping. An odyssey had begun which finally ended in a church originally built by the Teutonic Order – much to the annoyance of the Social-Democratic interim government of Hesse. They warned the occupation authorities of a potential revival of the Hindenburg myth. But the Americans had their way.

In the event, the Social Democrats' concerns were unfounded. In the course of time, the grave of the last of the Teutonic Knights, surrounded by the heraldic arms of his historic predecessors, sank into obscurity.[65] The collapse of the Reich in May 1945 marked not a single turning point, but the beginning of a period of transition in commemorative culture. In 1945, medievalism was not yet dead, but it was certainly fading away.

[63] BArch, R 32/350, fol. 180, Magistrat Namslau to Reichskunstwart, 28 November 1930.

[64] Jay Winter, 'Commemorating War, 1914–1945', *The Cambridge History of War, vol. IV: War and the Modern World*, ed. Roger Chickering, Dennis Showalter and Hans van de Ven (Cambridge, 2012), pp. 310–26.

[65] Ingrid Krüger-Bulcke, 'Der Hohenzollern-Hindenburg-Zwischenfall in Marburg 1947: Wiederaufleben nationalistischer Strömungen oder Sturm im Wasserglas?', *Hessisches Jahrbuch für Landesgeschichte* 39 (1989), pp. 311–52; Fischer, 'Tannenberg-Denkmal', pp. 46ff.

8

'Hark ye back to the age of valour': Re-enacting Chivalry from the Eglinton Tournament to Kill Streak[1]

Paul Pickering

'The first rule of Fight Club is that you don't talk about Fight Club.' But talking about it is half the fun!

Fight Club (1999 screenplay) quoted in 'Medieval Combat Organizations' <http://www.romanempire.net/romepage/Links/FightingLinks.htm>

'I wouldn't ask too much of her,' I ventured. 'You can't repeat the past.' 'Can't repeat the past?' he cried incredulously. 'Why of course you can!' He looked around him wildly, as if the past were lurking here in the shadow of his house, just out of reach of his hand.

F. Scott Fitzgerald, *The Great Gatsby* (1925)

This 'Tournament' was a grand moving picture of the history of the valourous days of Europe.

John Richardson, *The Eglinton Tournament* (1843)

Ivanhoe was Sir Walter Scott's only historical novel set in England. It is ironic therefore that it is the work for which the archetypal Scot is best remembered. Published in 1820, the book was an instant success, going quickly through numerous editions and remaining in print ever since. Rivalling Malory's chronicle of the Arthurian legend that was published in the fifteenth century, *Ivanhoe* reached an immense audience. Moreover, almost before the ink had dried on the first copy off the press, it had spawned a plethora of songs, poems and popular dramas. Indeed, criticising his fellow dramatists, Thomas Moncrieff complained that all that was required was 'paste, shears, and a Scottish novel'.[2] Other measures of *Ivanhoe*'s

1 N.B. All websites cited in this chapter were correct at the time of writing; subsequently, some online content may have moved or changed. The quotation is from *The Canberra Times*, 18 May 1992.

2 W. T. Moncrieff, *Ivanhoe! Or, The Jewess: A Chivalric Play in Three Acts* (London,

capacious impact are not hard to come by. At the opposite end of the British world in Sydney, New South Wales, for example, the patrons of Mr McQueen's Room at King's Wharf celebrated St Andrew's Day in 1820 with a fine supper and 'many appropriate toasts', followed by dancing to the tune of 'Sir Walter Scott's Ivanhoe'.[3] It seems that cultural production travelled speedily, despite what has been called the tyranny of distance.[4] The novel was widely available in Sydney's bookshops, and as late as 1836 the 'Liberal Public of Australia' were entertained at the Theatre Royal by performances of Thomas Dibden's 'Splendid Historical DRAMA', *Ivanhoe; Or, The Jew's Daughter*, replete with 'New Dresses, Decorations, &c. in a Style superior to any thing ever yet attempted in this Colony'.[5] The advertisement drew particular attention to Act I, which featured a 'GRAND TOURNAMENT' involving 'several Knights arraying in COMPLETE ARMOUR'. Patrons were promised 'Several Trials of Skill with Mace and Shield – Faulchion and Shield Lance – Broadsword and Shield, Dirk &c.'[6]

Representations of *Ivanhoe* on stage and screen (large and small) continued well into the twentieth century, the most recent being a six-episode BBC mini-series broadcast in 1997 (advertised as an 'heroic tale of courage, honour and romance').[7] The first feature film was completed in 1913, relatively early in the history of the genre. Although the film was shot on location in England, it was produced by a US company and distributed by Universal Pictures. The director was Irish-born Herbert Brenon, who had adapted the screenplay from Scott's novel (and a play by Walter and Frederick Melvile). King Baggot, an American who was undoubtedly one of the most famous actors of the day, portrayed Ivanhoe. Perhaps the most memorable rendition for the screen, however, was another US production filmed in Britain. Released in 1952, the eponymous MGM film (scripted – although uncredited – by the well-known left-wing activist Marguerite Roberts) starred Robert Taylor as Ivanhoe and a young Elizabeth Taylor, in one of her most alluring performances,

1820), frontispiece. Other plays included A. Bunn, *Ivanhoe; or, The Jew of York: A New Grand Chivalric Play* (Birmingham, 1820); Thomas Dibden, *Ivanhoe; or, The Jew's Daughter: A Melo Dramatic Romance, in Three Acts* (London, 1820); Mr Farley, *Ivanhoe; or, The Knight Templar: Adapted from the Novel of that Name* (London, 1820); George Sloan, *The Hebrew: A Drama, In Five Acts* (London, 1820). The plays are in the collection of the Huntington Library in California, USA. See also Mark Girouard, *The Return to Camelot: Chivalry and the English Gentleman* (New Haven and London, 1981), p. 90; H. Philip Bolton, *Scott Dramatized* (London, 1992), pp. 345–6 provides a comprehensive list.

[3] *The Sydney Gazette*, 2 December 1820.

[4] This phrase was coined by Geoffrey Blainey and is now widely invoked to emphasise the distance between New South Wales and Britain. See Geoffrey Blainey, *The Tyranny of Distance: How Distance Shaped Australia's History* (Melbourne, 1966).

[5] *The Sydney Gazette*, 28 April 1836.

[6] Ibid.

[7] See <http://www.imdb.com/title/tt0118354>. Reviewing the series, John O'Connor commented: 'Here we have realistic chilly locations in Scotland and the Northumberland region of England. The costumes and everything else have been whipped up with an eye to authenticity. And there are enough bloody sword fights and nasty stabbings to strike envy into the heart of any American action flick.' *The New York Times*, 18 April 1997.

as Rebecca. Both films were box office hits, the latter setting a new record for MGM releases.[8]

The longevity of the story is in keeping with its initial impact. Ignoring Scott's extensive earlier writings, the irascible Thomas Carlyle, for example, went so far as to credit *Ivanhoe* with reigniting the practice of writing history itself. Scott had published a lengthy and erudite essay on chivalry in 1818, predating *Ivanhoe* by more than a year, but it was the novel that had a profound effect on the popular imagination.[9] In fact, for many commentators then and now, Scott single-handedly initiated the medieval revival that gripped the Anglophone world.[10]

Scott's fascination with the age of chivalry saw him satirised as Mr Chainmail in T. L. Peacock's deliciously wicked novel, *Crotchet Castle*, published in 1831. Chainmail, Peacock tells us, 'believes that the best state of society was that of the twelfth century, when nothing was going forward but fighting, feasting and praying'. Scott/Chainmail, Peacock suggests, was also something of a re-enactor. 'He has a large hall,' he writes, 'adorned with rusty pikes, shields, helmets, swords, and tattered banners, and furnished with yew-tree chairs, and long, old, worm-eaten oak tables, where he dines with all his household, after the fashion of his favorite age.'[11] Whatever the truth of Peacock's imaginings, Scott undoubtedly helped to inspire what was arguably the first modern secular, civilian and unofficial re-enactment – the famous tournament of August 1839 organised by Archibald Montgomerie, thirteenth earl of Eglinton.[12] The words secular, civilian and unofficial are crucial here. Re-enactments had, of course, been at the core of religious observance for centuries. For Christians, the Passion of the Christ is perhaps the best-known example; among Shia Muslims the tragedy of Karbala, depicting the murder in 680 of the Prophet's grandson, Hussein ibn Ali, has a somewhat comparable prominence as an annual ritual re-enactment.[13] In contrast, the Eglinton tournament was not connected to the church.

[8] See <http://www.imdb.com>. For Roberts, see her obituary in the *Los Angeles Times*, 17 March 1989. See also Kevin Harty, 'The Arthurian Legends on Film: An Overview', *Cinema Arthuriana* (New York, 1991), pp. 3–28; Kevin Harty, *The Reel Middle Ages* (Jefferson, 1999).

[9] Sir Walter Scott, *Essays on Chivalry, Romance and The Drama* (Edinburgh, 1834).

[10] See Alice Chandler, 'Sir Walter Scott and the Medieval Revival', *Nineteenth-Century Fiction*, 19:4 (1965), pp. 315–32, esp. 315. Chandler makes the point that the commonplace crediting of Scott is only half right. Elsewhere she notes that in some respects the revival was well under way before Scott was born. See Alice Chandler, 'Chivalry and Romance in Scott's Medieval Novels', *Studies in Romanticism* 14:2 (1975), p. 187. See also Jerome Mitchell, *Scott, Chaucer, and Medieval Romance: A Study of Sir Walter Scott's Indebtedness to the Literature of the Middle Ages* (Kentucky, 2014).

[11] T. L. Peacock, *Crotchet Castle* (1831), *Novels of Thomas Love Peacock* (London, 1967), p. 288.

[12] Ian Anstruther, *The Knight and the Umbrella* (London, 1963), lists several earlier tournaments from the eighteenth and nineteenth centuries held in Europe, Scandinavia and the USA. See Appendix 1, pp. 246–8. See also Howard Giles, 'A Brief History of Re-enactment', <www.eventplan.co.uk>. Rollin Osterweis, *Romanticism and Nationalism in the Old South* (New Haven, 1949) provides a splendid description of a tournament held in Fauquier Springs, Virginia, in 1845, which pitted 'Brian de Boris-Guilbert' against 'Ta-ta-ra, ta-ta-ra – Wilfred of Ivanhoe', pp. 3–5, 98–9.

[13] P. J. Calkowski, *Ritual and Drama in Iran* (New York, 1979), pp. 95–120.

It is also important to separate Eglinton's secular enterprise from the well-worn tradition of official military re-enactment that had flourished at least since the days of the celebration of the victories of Rome's legions. This practice was established in Britain hundreds of years before Eglinton drew up his plans. For example, on a well-known May Day visit to Shooters Hill in Greenwich in 1516, Henry VIII had witnessed a re-enactment of a medieval archery contest by the bowmen of the King's guard. The event featured 'Robyn Hood' and a two-hundred-strong band of green-clad coadjutors. The rotund Henry did not fire any arrows, but he did participate in the re-enactment later in the day by eating venison with the merry outlaws at a feast in a mock Great Hall erected in nearby woodland.[14] Three centuries later, as Iain McCalman has shown, the renowned artist and scenographer Jacques De Loutherbourg composed a number of his famous paintings of British battles when viewing re-enactments. This is not surprising. After all, it was the time when, rather than lead his armed forces, George III headed up legions of spectators at re-enactments of British triumphs at sea and on land.[15]

Nor was Eglinton's joust part of the long tradition of official civic pageantry in Britain (including that associated with monarchy).[16] At every coronation dinner from 1170 up to and including 1821, for example, a panoplied knight, known as the King's Champion, rode into the lavish banquet in Westminster Hall, threw down the gauntlet and invited anyone to challenge the new king's right to rule. Despite the growing public fascination with all things medieval, the practice was discontinued at the coronation of William IV in 1831; cost triumphed over sentiment.[17] A civic ritual that has survived far longer is the Lord Mayor's Show in London. The original Charter of 1189 prescribes an annual procession of the Lord Mayor to the Royal Courts of Justice; by the sixteenth century it had become a source of popular entertainment. Today the 'Show' involves approximately six thousand processors and features an ornate coach dating from 1757 (except in 2012, when a broken wheel meant that a Land Rover was pressed into service), highly stylised robes, exaggerated mustachios and martial accoutrements such as muskets and pikes.[18]

Eglinton neither sought nor received official sanction for his attempt to reclaim a lost past. In other words, he undertook what was essentially a freelance initiative. The story of the tournament and revel is well known and requires only a cursory rehearsal here. It took place over several days at the end of August 1839, at Eglinton

[14] See *Mirror of Literature, Amusement and Instruction* 2 (1843), p. 58; Agnes Strickland, *Memoirs of the Queens of Henry VIII* (Philadelphia, 1853), p. 85; Ronald Hutton, *Rise and Fall of Merry England: The Ritual Year 1400–1700* (Oxford, 1994).

[15] Iain McCalman, 'Loutherbourg's Simulations: Reenactment and Realism in Late Georgian Britain', *Historical Reenactment: From Realism to the Affective Turn*, ed. Iain McCalman and Paul Pickering (Basingstoke, 2010), pp. 200–17.

[16] See *inter alia* David Bergeron, *English Civic Pageantry 1558–1642* (Columbia, 1971).

[17] The discontinuance of the banquet in Westminster was one of many factors that inspired Eglinton. See Girouard, *Return to Camelot*, p. 92; Mary S. Millar, 'Montgomerie, Archibald William, thirteenth earl of Eglinton and first earl of Winton (1812–1861)', *Oxford Dictionary of National Biography* (Oxford, 2004), <http://www.oxforddnb.com/view/article/19057>.

[18] *The Guardian*, 28 October 2013.

Castle in Ayrshire in the south-west of Scotland. The earl had anticipated approximately 4,000 spectators; in the event his venture drew a vast crowd estimated at between 60,000 and 150,000. The participants included approximately forty knights – described as the flower of Britain's aristocracy – amongst several hundred others (women and men) portraying associated personages: men-at arms, halberdiers, chamberlains, retainers, pages, ladies-in-waiting and even the odd harlequin. A well-known actor took the part of the jester. Eglinton had requested spectators to dress for the occasion and many – perhaps two-thirds – did. A tartan bonnet was a particularly popular choice.[19]

Unfortunately for the earl, his guests and his onlookers, persistent rain turned the field of battle into a quagmire. Careful rehearsals in London's Regent's Park (themselves attracting large crowds) had not fitted the re-enactors for a deluge. Many chevaliers became more firmly stuck in the ensuing swamp than in the ancient past, rust posing more of a threat than an opponent's lance. Indeed, the abiding image of the event – described by Charles Mackay as full of 'frivolous and scarcely picturesque unrealities' – was of the marquis of Londonderry holding a lance in one hand and in the other that 'most unromantic of modern implements', the umbrella.[20]

The vast gathering, notwithstanding the weather, was an indication of the extent to which Eglinton, following Scott, had captured the nation's attention. However, the overwhelming majority of commentary in the press was suffused with sarcasm. Given that the tourney's *dramatis personae* included a number of leading Tories, including Londonderry ('King of the Lists') and Eglinton himself, it is not surprising that the Whig-Liberal prints took every opportunity for derision. [21] The weather only added to the scope for splenetic wit: 'Perhaps you will suppose that the knights at least were waterproof,' noted one correspondent, 'but remember the interstices of the armour, and then believe that no-one had cause to envy them.' He continued: 'In the midst of all this confusion, by way of crowning calamity, it was discovered that the rain had penetrated the temporary buildings erected for the banquet and ball, and that neither banquet nor ball could take place':

> Oh! Ye Undines! Ye sprits of water! ye aqueous influences! Ye imbriferous demons! malignantly have ye intruded upon a day sacred to the Genius of Chivalry, and devoted it to catarrhs and rheumatism.[22]

For radicals, the tournament was an irresponsible endorsement of violence (at a time when they were being accused of 'sputterings of conflagration') and an obscene demonstration of profligacy. 'We have heard of an Eglinton Tournament at the small cost of an hundred thousand pounds,' fumed the editor of the Glasgow *Chartist Circular*, 'while thousands of weavers worked fifteen hours a day, and went

19 *The Morning Post*, 3 September 1839.

20 *The Morning Post*, 3 September 1839; Charles Mackay, *Through the Long Day: or, Memories of a Literary Life During Half a Century* (London, 1887), p. 73. See also Anstruther, *The Knight and the Umbrella*.

21 Alex Tyrrell, 'The Earl of Eglinton, Scottish Conservatism and the National Association for the Vindication of Scottish Rights', *Historical Journal* 53 (2010), pp. 87–107.

22 *The Morning Post*, 3 September 1839.

supperless to bed.'[23] The *Northern Liberator*, on the other hand, regarded the antics of the 'Knights of the Windmill' as 'ridiculous mummery'.[24]

Like *Ivanhoe*, Eglinton's joust was soon converted to the stage, including a splendid piece of counter-theatre: a 'satirical sequel' in which 'Clown and Pantaloon rush into mortal combat so grotesque and fantastical as to excite roars of laughter'.[25] Like *Ivanhoe,* too, the tourney excited interest further afield in the British world. The sarcastic tone travelled with the reports. The *Sydney Morning Herald*, for example, reported that the event had passed off without injury; indeed, that on the first pass in the lists Eglinton and his opponent had missed. Most missed. The radical-inclined *Colonist* reported under the rubric 'Playing at Old Times'.[26]

Nearly two hundred years later, re-enactment is undoubtedly one of the fastest-growing forms of public history. *Inter alia* it is possible to explore the practice through numerous categories of investigation, such as entertainment, expiation, commercialism, methodology, realism and affect.[27] It is also possible to divide re-enactors into sub-groups along an authenticity axis of sorts: from hobbyists (weekend enthusiasts sometimes called FARBs – Fast And Researchless Buying of the costumes etc.) to 'hard-core' practitioners (sometimes called pejoratively 'authenticity Nazis'). Most re-enactors probably fall somewhere in between.[28] They are concerned that tunics, hats and weapons match the period being re-enacted, but are not insistent that the leather used in the manufacture of their slippers has been softened with urine in the manner of their subject. More likely they shop than soak (and assume that the manufacturer has also forgone the urine). Most of the above distinctions and definitions need not detain us here. At the risk of offending many, for my purposes I will more often than not refer to re-enactors generically.

Among students of re-enactment, the Eglinton tournament does not enjoy the prominence that I have afforded it here. On the contrary, most commentators associate the modern practice of re-enactment with the United States and, more specifically, with the Civil War.[29] According to Simon During, for example, it was in the aftermath of America's fratricidal conflict that modern re-enactment '*really* began'.[30] Notwithstanding the fact that the celebration of the fiftieth anniversary of the Battle of Gettysburg in 1913 famously included a re-enactment of Pickett's ill-fated charge, for many commentators the practice did not '*really*' commence until the centennial commemorations of the Civil War in the early 1960s. Certainly there are legions of Civil War re-enactors in America who can lay claim not only to what was reputedly the largest re-enactment ever staged (on the 135th anniversary of Gettysburg in 1998,

[23] *The Northern Star*, 21 September 1839; *The Chartist Circular*, 12 October 1839; Thomas Carlyle, *Chartism* (1840), *Thomas Carlyle: Selected Works* (London, 1980), p. 151.

[24] *The Northern Liberator*, 7 September 1839.

[25] *The Caledonian Mercury*, 30 December 1839.

[26] *The Sydney Morning Herald*, 6 January 1840; *The Colonist*, 19 January 1839.

[27] Vanessa Agnew, 'History's Affective Turn: Historical Reenactment and its Work in the Present', *Rethinking History* 11:3 (2007), pp. 299–312; McCalman and Pickering, *Historical Reenactment, passim.*

[28] Giles, 'A Brief History'.

[29] Robert Lee Hadden, *Reliving the Civil War* (Mechanicsburg, 1999), pp. 1–35.

[30] McCalman and Pickering, *Historical Reenactment*, p. 197.

in which anywhere between 15,000 and 20,000 re-enactors participated), but also to the largest number of individual re-enactment societies.[31] It has been estimated that anywhere between 30,000 and 50,000 Americans trudge around on weekends and public holidays clad in grey or blue. As Toby Horowitz puts it in a splendid account of his experience among re-enactors, *Confederates in the Attic*, it is an important expression of a developing national obsession.[32]

But in terms of both location and periodisation, Rebs and Yankees are by no means the only re-enactors at play. Re-enactment societies exist in at least thirty-five countries in all corners of the globe. There are close to one hundred societies active in Britain and more than twenty in Australia. However, there is also a plethora of re-enactment societies located variously in Russia, Belarus, Poland, Greece, Finland, South Africa, Germany, Austria, Portugal, Romania, Brazil, Argentina, Taiwan, South Korea, Israel, Lithuania and Ireland. And the list goes on. Many societies have branches in multiple locations. Nova Roma, for example, is a re-enactment society devoted to reliving Roman history, which has branches ('legions') in Canada, Brazil, Mexico, Argentina, Italy, France, Spain, Portugal, Britain, Germany, Hungary, Romania, Finland and Sweden, as well as in the US.[33] Taken together, we are surely talking of millions of people engaged in re-enactment on a regular basis. Histrenact, the umbrella organisation of re-enactment societies in Britain, reports over one million distinct users of its website.[34]

Like Eglinton's re-enactment, the preponderance of the activity undertaken revolves around conflict, but again the American Civil War does not predominate. In fact, the range of combat re-enactments is capacious: from the Peloponnesian Wars to the Maori wars in New Zealand; from the Wars of the Roses to the Norman invasion; from the Spanish-American War to the exploits of the Robber Knights of Gelderland. A precise head count is all but impossible to compile, but the strong impression that emerges from an exhaustive exploration of the labyrinthine World Wide Web is that re-enactments of the Second World War, including some disturbing playing at the nefarious activities of the *Waffen SS*, are the most common. The reasons for this are worthy of an essay in and of themselves, but that is another story for another day.

Numerically, however, re-enactments of the Middle Ages (military and civilian) are not far behind those devoted to the Second World War. Medieval enthusiasts can be found on all continents: from the Red Čuvara grada Zagreba in Croatia to Skt. Martin Kompagniet in Denmark; from Varmesjord Combate Vikingo in Chile to Pendragón Grupo Medieval in Colombia; from the Shire of Adamastor on the Eastern Cape of South Africa to the Ancient Arts Fellowship in the Australian

[31] Giles, 'A Brief History'. There is no national umbrella organisation, but there are numerous regional organisations that bring together dozens of individual societies. See <http://www.pacwr.org> for the Pacific Area Civil War Re-enactors Association, which brings together nine individual societies in a relatively small area.

[32] Toby Horowitz, *Confederates in the Attic: Dispatches From the Unfinished Civil War* (New York, 1998); Giles, 'A Brief History'.

[33] See <http://www.novaroma.org>.

[34] See <www.histrenact.co.uk>.

Figure 8.1 Re-enactment of the Battle of Tewkesbury, England, 2009. Photograph: Antony Stanley.

Capital Territory.[35] Indeed, the number of knights active globally in 2014 was sufficient to populate two separate 'World Championships' (held in Spain and Croatia respectively). These events brought together competitors from well over twenty countries for full-contact medieval combat. The largest of these international tournaments, the 'Battle of the Nations', has been held annually since 2009 and boasts an audience of 'dozens of thousands of tourists' as well as extensive media coverage.[36] Not surprisingly, then, the largest transnational re-enactment organisation (focusing on any era), the Society for Creative Anachronism (SCA), is dedicated to 'researching and re-creating the skills of pre-17th-century Europe'.[37]

Across the globe, the SCA comprises over thirty thousand members (or

[35] See, for example <http:www.cuvari.hr>; <http://www.sktmartinkompagniet.dk>; <https://es-la.facebook.com/varmesjord>; <https://es-la.facebook.com/PendragonMedieval>; <http://www.adamastorshire.co.za>; <http://www.aaf.org.au>.

[36] See <http://www.battleofthenations.ua>; <http://battleheritage.co.uk/event/imcf-world-championship-castillo-de-belmonte>. I am grateful to Rhys Williams for drawing my attention to the recent championships.

[37] See <http://www.sca.org>.

'SCA-dians', as they affectionately refer to each other), based in nineteen 'kingdoms', who conduct more than one thousand events a year. Among SCA-dians, Eglinton is explicitly identified as the progenitor. According to their official history, the Society was inspired by a '19th-century recreation of medieval life called the "Last Tournament", which is elsewhere identified as Eglanton's [*sic*] audacious episode'.[38] Despite the spelling error, the line to Eglinton is thus rendered in their history as unbroken. Effectively thirty thousand souls regularly follow in his footsteps to find their own mud. But what they are doing? Or, more correctly, what do they think they are doing? And why? Are their answers the same as the earl's? Using the SCA as a starting point, the remainder of this essay will explore modern medievalism – the profile and motivations of its multifarious practitioners and promoters – and set it into the broader context of a chivalric revival, possibly beyond anything Scott or Eglinton could have imagined.

The SCA is not only the most extensive international network of re-enactment societies, but it is also one of the oldest, having been founded in 1966 at Berkeley in California. The society is the brainchild of Diana Paxson (now known as 'Countess Diana the Listmaker') who, at the time, was a literature major at Berkeley. According to her own account, the catalyst that resulted in the foundation of the SCA was seeing members of a local sci-fi appreciation club (David Thewlis – now 'Duke Siegfried von Holflichskeit' – and Ken de Maiffe – now 'Duke Fulk de Wyvern') playing with plywood swords and shields in a field. As she puts it, 'it occurred to me that other fans and students of the Middle Ages would love to see what it was really like, and I got the bright idea of throwing a tournament in my back yard'.[39] Could Eglinton have put it any better?

Paxson's insouciant reference to the potential of re-enactment to provide affective knowledge – 'what it was really like' – takes us to the heart of the recent debates among historians about the usefulness or otherwise of re-enacting the past in the pursuit of historical understanding. For some, such as the well-known ethnographic historian Greg Denning, the practice is little more than 'the present in funny clothes'.[40] Others recognise that turning our collective backs on what is effectively a democratised form of engaging with history (which is also evident in period films, historical fiction, museums, interpretative heritage sites, theme parks and computer games) takes historians further along the road to irrelevance in the public discourse about the past. What is known as 'immersive' or 'experiential' learning has insinuated itself into classrooms, leaving books penned in the academy to gather dust on library shelves.[41] Under various headings – such as 'extreme history' and 'living history' – some historians (*not* including me, I hasten to add) have begun dressing

[38] William R. Keyes (Wilhelm von Schlüssel), *The History of the Kingdom of the West: The Origins of the SCA*, <www.westkingdom.org>.

[39] See <http://www.diana-paxson.com/about>. Note that the others claim that it was their idea.

[40] Greg Denning, *Mr Bligh's Bad Language* (Cambridge, 1992), pp. 4–5.

[41] See Paul Pickering, 'No Witnesses. No Leads. No Problems. The Reenactment of Crime and Rebellion', *Historical Reenactment*, ed. McCalman and Pickering, pp. 109–33.

up in Denning's 'funny clothes' to meet this challenge by exploring the proposition that we can learn about the past by doing it.[42]

Unlike the sceptics and nay-sayers skulking in university corridors, there are legions of re-enactors who believe that they produce knowledge. Varmesjord Combate Vikingo, for example, describe themselves as a 'group of historians' who use 'special sources' to strive for the 'most historically accurate' re-enactments possible.[43] At the extreme edge of the authenticity spectrum in medieval re-enactment are the Guardians of Zagreb. In pursuit of the 'highest level of historical correctness', they adopt '*persona revicta* [*sic*]', 'set in one precisely specified temporal, spatial, historical and social' era, that of the Knights Hospitallers.[44] 'By constant studying,' they argue, they 'keep increasing the level of historical correctness.'[45] To take another example, the Company of Chivalry, formed in the West Country of England in 1988, boast that they are now the 'only fully-trained Medieval Siege Engine crew' in Britain, having perfected the art of firing four different apparatuses themselves. In their public statements these societies do not explicitly claim that it is affect-cum-experience that produces knowledge, although it is implicit in the fact that they are 'living history' as the core of their historical enquiry – they are doing it. For others, the value of affect-cum-experience is more explicitly asserted. The nuances of the language are important. Canberra's Ancient Arts Fellowship comes close to making the claim aloud. They insist that their 'main aim' is to 'spread knowledge of history throughout the community':

> We create costume, jewelry, armour and accessories according to documented period styles. We shoot traditional bows and feast on food that William the Conqueror would have eaten.[46]

Similarly, the Stork's Beak School of Historical Swordplay in Edinburgh promises instruction in the 'European tradition of martial arts'. 'And,' they continue, 'you may pick up some history [and] philosophy' ('and fitness').[47] Much the same is true of the Harlech Knights. Since its foundation in 1984 the society has sought to 'extend the knowledge and appreciation of local history and heritage' through re-enactment, although, admittedly, they introduce a note of caution: they 'recreate life and combat as it *may* have been in 13th Century England and Wales [emphasis mine]'.[48] Howard Giles (himself a re-enactment aficionado) puts the case with more conviction: re-enactment offers people their 'best opportunity to see, smell, touch and feel

42 See McCalman and Pickering, eds, *Historical Reenactment*; Agnew, 'History's Affective Turn'; Alex Cook, 'The Use and Abuse of Historical Reenactment: Thoughts on Recent Trends in Public History', *Criticism* 46:3 (2004), pp. 487–96.

43 See <https://es-la.facebook.com/varmesjord>.

44 Apparently, their pursuit of accuracy does not run to Latin.

45 See <www.cuvari.hr>.

46 See <www.aaf.org.au>. The AAF has been creating, shooting and feasting in Australia's national capital for over twenty years – 'living history', as one member put it. See *The Canberra Times*, 18 May 1992.

47 See <www.storksbeak.co.uk>.

48 See <www.clash-of-steel.co.uk/links/view/38>.

and generally experience the essential essence of past eras'. The members of the SCA entertain no doubts. In line with Paxson's original conception, they '*experience* tournaments, royal courts, feasts, and dancing [emphasis mine]'. Similarly, tournaments organised by the Battle of the Nations, an organisation with branches in more than thirty countries, take place under the watchful eye of an 'Authenticity Committee'. 'This is HISTORICAL and MEDIEVAL battle,' insists the Serbian representative, 'not fantasy role-playing.' The promotional material proclaimed by the Australian branch asks: 'Where were you when history was made?'[49]

Of course, accuracy was also high on Eglinton's agenda for his pageant. 'I wished to see myself, and show others,' he told a crowd in Irvine, 'the sports of chivalry as much as the customs of our time would permit.'[50] However, for most modern medieval re-enactors, affective knowledge via the pursuit of exactitude is not the only, or even the most important, part of the attraction. From observation it is clear that most re-enactors (even the 'authenticity Nazis') are having a rollicking good time. At Ancient Arts Fellowship gatherings, for example, there is nothing like a 'good bash-em-up'. Giles, presumably referring to himself, agrees: 'most primarily do it for enjoyment'.[51] In an article in an online fanzine, Brian Price, principal of the Academy of European Medieval Martial Arts, does a fairly good job of translating Eglinton into a modern idiom:

> The techniques, and the exciting combats that ensue, are cool. The armour and weapons are cool. The medieval stuff even down to the pointy shoes and goofy hats, is cool.[52]

For some, the physicality of combat and the prospect of ultimate victory, with its attendant risks, is what matters. It is the pursuit of undiluted affect. The World Championships, for example, are designed to sort out the 'Best of the Best'; after all,

[49] See <http://www.sca.org>; Giles, 'A Brief History'; <http://botn.info/en>; <http://www.battleofthenations.ua>.

[50] John Richardson, *The Eglinton Tournament* (London, 1843), p. 2; *The Morning Post*, 1 November 1839. The comparison with David Garrick's play, *Cymon*, is instructive here. Although it debuted in the 1760s, a newer version written after Garrick's death was performed as an opera in the 1790s, eclipsing the original, at least in terms of sensationalism. The latter concluded with a 'Grand Procession of the Hundred Knights of Chivalry, and the representation of an Ancient Tournament', but the aim was to create an extravaganza, not a faithful re-enactment. Alongside the chevaliers were 'Indians, Turks, Scythians, a dwarf, a giant, Hymen, piping fauns, bands of cupids etc.' See *Cymon: A Dramatic Romance. Written Originally by David Garrick, Esq.* (London, 1792); Harry Pericon and Frederick Bergman, *The Plays of David Garrick* (Carbondale, 1980), p. 325; John A. Parkinson, 'Cymon', *The New Grove Dictionary of Opera*, ed. Stanley Sadie, <http://www.oxfordmusiconline.com.virtual.anu.edu.au/subscriber/article/grove/music/0901166>. I am grateful to David Worrall for this reference.

[51] See <http://www.aaf.org.au>. In a multiple-choice survey of SCA members, conducted in 2010, 30.9% nominated 'fun' and 25.7% were looking for friendship as one of their motivations for participating. See <http://www.sca.org/scacensus2010>.

[52] Brian R. Price, 'Chivalry and the Modern Practice of the Medieval Martial Arts', *Journal of Western Martial Art*, Vol. 2000, 10/00, n.p. <www.ejmas.com>. He is being deliberately flippant. Price is a controversial figure in the area of medieval and martial studies.

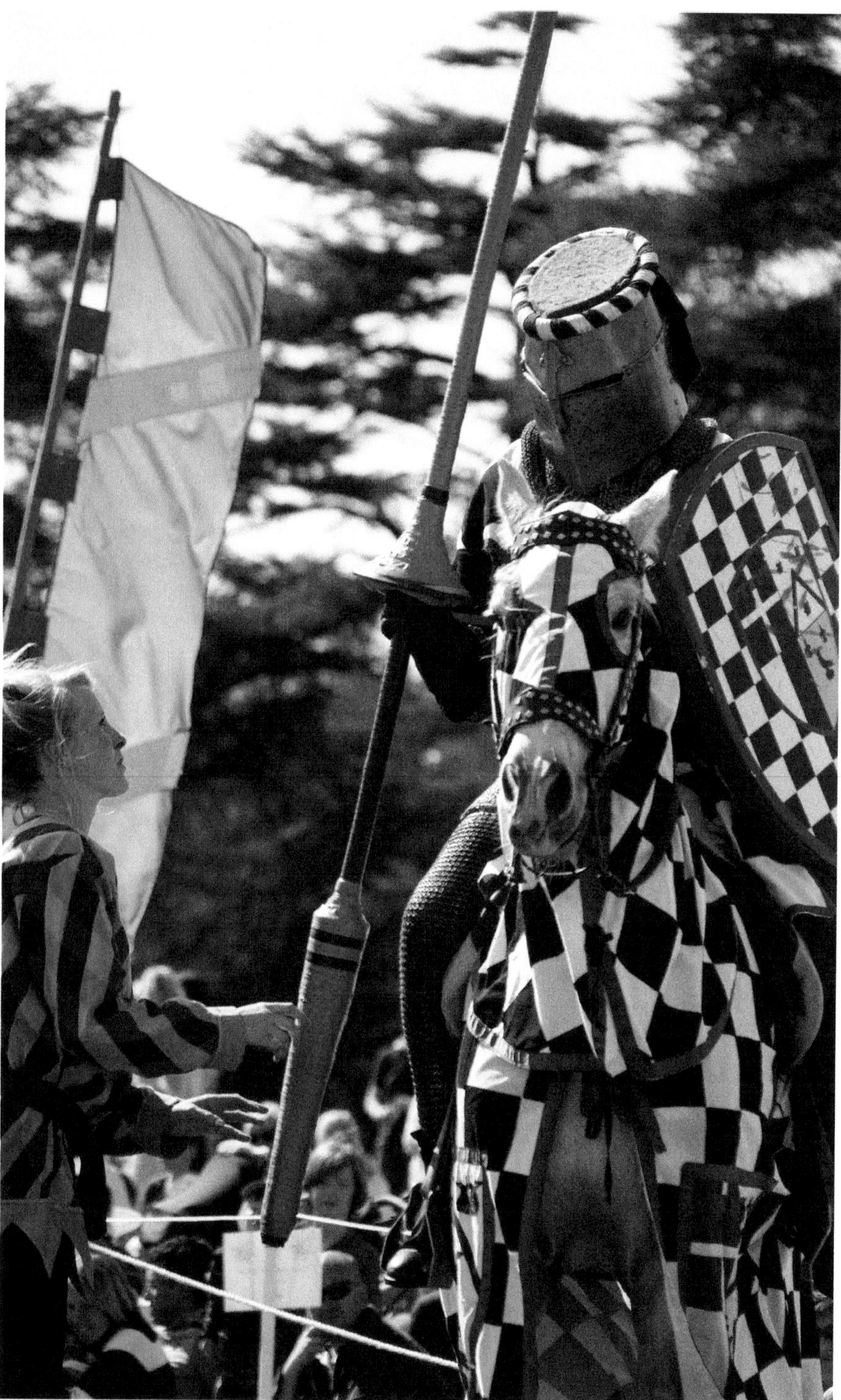

Plate 5 Jousting in Oxford, England, 2013. Photograph: Peter Lusabia (Demotix).

when a full-contact 'bash-em-up' involves swinging authentic weapons fuelled by testosterone, the risk of serious injury is ever present. As the 'Battle of the Nations' organisers note, the introduction of rules proscribing slashing at the face, groin, neck, feet and back of the knees has limited 'misunderstandings' and reduced the number of injuries and 'dangerous situations' to 'an acceptable minimum'.[53] Here the 'medieval' in medieval re-enactment is surely incidental; the Middle Ages were conveniently violent.

At the same time, the clang of chainmail is often drowned out by the ring of the cash register. Many re-enactment groups supply fee-for-service activities for schools and provide paid extras for films and documentaries as a sideline. For others, re-enacting is simply part of a commercial enterprise. The 'transformation' of Warwick Castle, one of England's great heritage sites, into 'Merlin: the Dragon Tower' represents the commercialisation of cultural tourism at its nadir or *reductio ad absurdum* or both. In a magnificent castle dating from the twelfth century, visitors are offered 'an interactive experience' inspired by a 'BBC family drama': 'Stepping back into the Arthurian legend,' the publicity boasts, 'you can join Merlin in his quest to aid Arthur and fulfil his destiny.' 'Magic is Alive! Experience the excitement of Merlin's world first hand.'[54] Among the troop of attendant re-enactors, a William the Conqueror is nowhere to be found.[55] Re-enactment has claimed other significant historical sites. The medieval combat World Championships, for example, have been, *inter alia*, staged at the fifteenth-century Castillo de Belmonte in Spain and the fourteenth-century Khotyn Fortress in western Ukraine. The former (well known for its role as a location in Samuel Bronston's 1961 epic production *El Cid*) now even offers special rates for medieval combat tournaments and hosts a domestic league of armoured re-enactors.[56]

Medieval re-enactment has also spawned historically dubious but popular tourist attractions in bespoke premises. At Kryal Castle in central Victoria, Australia, for example, patrons are offered 'Red Hot Deals' on accommodation and conference facilities in a 'new land of Medieval adventure!' replete with a dungeon, a dragon and 'heroic knights': 'Experience the thundering drama of the joust as brave knights and their magnificent mounts face each other in the Castle Arena.'[57] As a result, the castle's knights have become international celebrities on the re-enactment circuit. A jouster since 1966, 'Sir' Justin Holland has plied his trade world-over, winning numerous awards – including the 'Ultimate Knight in Shining Armour' trophy for

53 See <http://www.battleofthenations.ua>.

54 See <http://www.warwick-castle.com/explore/merlin-the-dragon-tower.aspx>.

55 William the Conqueror built the original wooden structure on the site in 1068; it was rebuilt in stone in the twelfth century. As a significant marker of England's heritage, the castle became a 'tourist' attraction in the nineteenth century. Merlin Entertainments purchased it in 1978.

56 See <http://castillodebelmonte.com>.

57 See <http://kryalcastle.com>; <http://ausmed.arts.uwa.edu.au>. This is all innocent enough, but for the fact that the proprietors claim to 'shed light on the dark ages' for students. The redevelopment of the castle in 2012–13 was supported by substantial tourism grants from the Commonwealth and State Governments. See *Hansard*, House of Representatives, 19 March 2013, p. 2685; *Courier*, 7 December 2012.

rescuing a 'real-life damsel in distress'. Philip Leitch, another of the castle's knights, is an ex-special forces soldier and expert martial artist who is also known for his role in the History Channel's reality television show, *Full Metal Jousting*.[58] Similarly, at Château Laroche on the banks of the Little Miami River in Loveland, Ohio, clients can hold weddings and receptions; day visitors can picnic, examine an extensive collection of medieval weapons and chat to the Knights of the Golden Trail who guard the castle.[59]

Of course, the practice of re-enacting has itself spawned a massive service industry (as it did for the Eglintonians). As noted, many re-enactors make their own paraphernalia as an essential part of the historical adventure, but for many

Figure 8.2 Butterick Costume Sewing Pattern 3552, 'History Series'.
Photograph: Timothy Pickering.

58 See <http://kryalcastle.com.au/attractions/castle-knights>. Kryal has links to the Australian Re-enactment Association and the SCA. See <http://www.ausleisure.com.au>.

59 See <http://www.lovelandcastle.com>.

others a credit card is the ticket to the past. There is a vast number of traders open for business. The prosaically named 'Re-enactment Supplies', to take one example, is an online store specialising in medieval equipment for shoppers worldwide. Here a budding re-enactor can purchase everything from a medieval dining set for £34.99 and a pair of fourteenth- or fifteenth-century leather ankle boots for £49.99, to a 'Knight Starter Kit' reduced from £1,499 to a bargain basement price of £899.99.[60] This is indeed a giveaway when compared to the estimated cost of fitting out one Eglinton knight in a suit of armour: £105 in 1839 (£7,300 in today's terms). Eglinton spent a personal fortune, estimated at £40,000 (just over £3 million in 2013 terms), on staging his escapade.[61] Whereas the earl drew upon a relatively small number of couturiers, the number of re-enactment suppliers today is impossible to estimate: Info.com points to ten search engines, each of which expands exponentially with one click. The success of the tourist attractions is easier to gauge. Warwick Castle, voted one of the top ten tourist attractions in Britain in 2010, has had an estimated twenty million patrons since it went into private ownership in 1978.[62] According to one estimate, Kryal Castle is worth AUD$10 million.[63]

It is easy to be cynical about dubious pedagogy, machismo and crass commodification. Similarly, medievalism can be dismissed as nothing more than escapism. Scott's timing was perfect. *Ivanhoe* appeared at a moment when the certainty of a society based on church and state, and patronage and deference, was under direct challenge. After all, in the year before the book's publication the nation had been convulsed by the massacre of Peterloo, when a contingent of cavalry – aristocrats on horseback, to borrow E. P. Thompson's memorable characterisation – charged into a peaceful demonstration in favour of democratic reform, slashing women, men and children as they went.[64] Eglinton's tournament was also held at a moment of acute political crisis. As the 'flower' of the British aristocracy waded through the mud in south-west Scotland, legions of working people, animated by an abrasive class-consciousness, marched through Britain's industrial cities and towns bearing torches and demanding a place in the political nation.[65] The sound of this none-too-subtle

[60] See <www.info.com/ReenactmentEquipment>; <www.re-enactmentsupplies.co.uk>. See Anstruther, *The Knight and the Umbrella*, p. 159. I have converted prices using a real-price commodity index. See <http://www.measuringworth.com/calculators/ukcompare>. There are, of course, dedicated and highly-trained craftsmen who also produce work for re-enactors without an explicit commercial purpose in mind.

[61] The earl's outlay is estimated by Ian Anstruther, *The Knight and the Umbrella*, p. 234 based on an average of reports in the press. Again, I have converted this using a real-price commodity index. See <http://www.measuringworth.com/calculators/ukcompare>.

[62] 'Warwick Castle', *New Histories*, Vol. 1, Issue 3 (2010), <http://newhistories.group.shef.ac.uk/wordpress/wordpress284>; *The Daily Mail*, 26 April 2012.

[63] 'Vile Kryal? Not when it comes to flogging Victoria to the world', *The Sydney Morning Herald*, 15 May 2012.

[64] Donald Read, *Peterloo: The Massacre and its Background* (Manchester, 1958); E. P. Thompson, *The Making of the English Working Class* (London, 1978).

[65] See, *inter alia*, Dorothy Thompson, *The Chartists* (London, 1984); Malcolm Chase, *Chartism: A New History* (Manchester, 2007).

threat of violence in the streets of Glasgow must have surely reverberated within the walls of Eglinton Castle.

In a more general sense, the episodes were set against a backdrop of profound social and economic change. The first half of the nineteenth century was the 'Age of Great Cities', when hundreds of thousands of labouring people were thrown together in fetid, overcrowded agglomerations where they literally lived in excrement and where their average age of death had declined to seventeen.[66] For polite society this was almost too much to contemplate. Many fled to new suburban dwellings where the prevailing winds carried the incessant smoke from a forest of factory chimneys in the other direction. Others sought refuge in the bucolic life of a lost age. As Alice Chandler, paraphrasing Wylie Sypher, put it, during the industrial revolution dreaming of the Middle Ages was the 'quickest way out of Manchester'.[67] Standing in the shadow of Blake's 'Dark Satanic Mills', the Dark Ages did not seem all that dark.

Eglinton was undoubtedly an escapist. 'I hear the clang of armour and the shrill blast of the trumpet calling me back to the tented field,' he mused. 'I awake from my dream of chivalry to find myself in a [...] most unromantic age.'[68] Eglinton's desire to escape to a different time in history is echoed by the experiences of re-enactors today. An article on the website of the National Association of Re-enactment Societies in Britain makes the earl's point at greater length. Re-enactors, the author notes, 'put aside their everyday lives as they immerse themselves in the re-enactment world'. 'With this outlet from hum-drum life,' the article continues, 'the re-enactor has a unique freedom to roam the centuries [...] unconstrained by the present.'[69] A guide for budding members of the SCA makes much the same point: 'Society members create a persona, the person who they would like to have been had they lived in the Middle Ages. Some SCA members have chosen only a name. Others have fully developed personas and can talk to you in detail about their medieval "lives".'[70] The members of the Most Noble Order of the Rouse Clan were 'bored in Baltimore' so they started dressing up – 'becoming someone new (or olde)', and having 'a blast while doing it'.[71]

[66] Paul Pickering, *Chartism and the Chartists in Manchester and Salford* (Basingstoke, 1995), chapter 1.

[67] Chandler, 'Chivalry and Romance', p. 185. For the founders of the SCA, this was the key to understanding Eglinton and Scott. According to their official history, 'with a head full of the novels of Sir Walter Scott', Eglinton 'decided to dramatize the values of the Middle Ages, which were Scott's and his own answer to the problems of the industrial revolution'. Keyes, <www.westkingdom.com>.

[68] *The Morning Post*, 1 November 1839. See also Pamela O'Neill, 'Historical Reconstruction or Imaginative Recreation? The Nineteenth-Century Approach to the Early Medieval', *antiTHESIS* 4 (2005), pp. 1–8.

[69] 'Re-enactment. What's that then?' <www.nares.org.uk>.

[70] 'Forward Into the Past', <http://www.sca.org>. See also Adina Hamilton, 'A New Sort of Castle in the Air: Medievalist Communities in Contemporary Australia', *Medievalism and the Gothic in Australian Culture*, ed. Stephanie Trigg (Melbourne, 2006), pp. 205–22.

[71] See <www.orderoftherouseclan.org>. Erica May, a member of the Hundred Swords, a 'battle gaming group' comprising students of the Australian National University, put it thus: 'It's just a nice opportunity to dress up – you don't normally get to dress up in costumes.' *Canberra City News*, 29 August 2013.

Both Scott and Eglinton, however, escaped to the medieval period because it represented an age of lost values. They were not alone. As Edmund Burke had lamented famously in 1790 when reflecting on the French revolution, 'the age of chivalry is gone':

> Never, never more shall we behold that generous loyalty to rank and sex, that proud submission, that dignified obedience, that subordination of the heart, which kept alive, even in servitude itself, the spirit of an exalted freedom.[72]

Even for those diametrically opposed to Eglinton in their politics, the loss of chivalry would exacerbate the current malaise. As Richard Oastler, a firebrand radical, wrote in a furious public letter to the 'nobles' of Nottingham, published two months ahead of the tournament: 'What insane un-English notions can have subdued your old English feelings? What malignant spirit can have banished from your hearts every spark of native chivalry?'[73] A similar appeal to lost values is almost ubiquitous among modern medieval re-enactors: indeed, it is far and away its most often intoned justification for their choice of era. I have so far not encountered a re-enactor who has quoted Burke back at me, but his jeremiad for the death of chivalry at the hands of 'sophisters, economists, and calculators' is surely perfectly suited to our age of economic rationalism.

Which are the values that appeal to re-enactors? Most could have been adapted directly from the pages of *Ivanhoe*. 'Chivalry! – why, maiden,' he told Rebecca in a well-known passage, 'it is the nurse of pure and high affection – the stay of the oppressed, the redresser of grievances, the curb of the power of the tyrant.'[74] For Eglinton it was 'courtesy and high feeling which were the principal features of the knightly character', which 'now only existed on the page of history, or the legends of romance.'[75] There is no shortage of behavioural codes penned by latter-day Scotts, most of which are variations on a predictable theme. The Order of Good Knights, formed in 1999 in Vancouver, Canada, for example, devote themselves to 'striving towards the Good – defending the weak and innocent, upholding loyalty, truth and honour.'[76] Dunraven Keep's code is truth, honour, justice, valour, prowess, loyalty, largesse, courtesy, noblesse and humility.[77] For Brian Price, spokesman for the Academy of European Medieval Martial Arts, 'Chivalry is a distillation of universal values to which most human beings subscribe: prowess (strength), courage, loyalty, humility, largesse (generosity), faith, honesty, and fidelity.' 'Additionally,' he

72 Edmund Burke, *Reflections on the French Revolution*, in *Collected Works of Edmund Burke*, Vol. XXIV, Part 3 (New York, 1909–14).

73 *Champion and Weekly Herald*, 2 June 1839. For Oastler, see Cecil Driver, *Tory Radical: The Life of Richard Oastler* (Oxford, 1946).

74 W. Scott, *Ivanhoe* (1819), edited and introduced by Graham Tulloch (London, 2000), p. 249. As Tulloch has noted, Scott's response to Peterloo was to stoutly defend the authorities, p. xi.

75 *The Morning Post*, 1 November 1839.

76 See <www.goodknights.org>. The creed of the Swords of Chivalry, founded in 1993 in Hertfordshire, England, is the 'Arthurian ideals of honour and chivalry'. See <http://www.swordsofchivalry.co.uk/aboutus.htm>.

77 See <www.21stcenturychivalry.com>.

continues, 'a knightly combatant has duties to defend those who are themselves defenceless be it physical, social or political.'[78] The Knights of Castleton invite visitors to their website to 'bear witness' to the code they uphold, which comprises an all too familiar list in a *faux* period idiom: 'Justice! Hold thyself to honesty and integrity', 'Mercy! Deal not in revenge', 'Nobility! Uphold thyself in good and honourable behavior' and so on.[79] By far the most eloquent manifesto is offered by The Knights of the Olde Code – but, as one of their leading members admitted to me, they cribbed it from the 1996 fantasy film *DragonHeart* ('to protect and serve'): 'A Knight is sworn to valor, his heart knows only virtue, his blade defends the helpless, his might upholds the weak, his word speaks only truth, his wrath undoes the wicked.'[80]

Equally important is the widespread insistence among re-enactors that these values are relevant today and worth fighting for. This was true of Eglinton. In the face of the derision he endured, he insisted that he had 'at least, done something towards the revival of chivalry'.[81] The earl's admirers agreed wholeheartedly. In a lavishly illustrated account of the tournament published in 1843, John Richardson argued that the tourney 'was a living representation of the manners, modes, fashions, and thoughts of those who played in their times, the great parts in the theatre of the world, and whose example it would be well for the present generation if, in many instances, it were more respected and imitated'. It was nothing less than a 'practical lesson' for 'the present race of nobility of England' of 'pristine dignity and ancient virtues'. Eglinton deserved all the credit, Richardson enthused: 'His Lordship' has 'read a great moral lesson.'[82] A brief survey illustrates the extent to which modern re-enactors agree. The plagiarising DragonHeartists, for example, are members of a self-described 'International Network bringing forth into the Modern World the Values & Ideals of Chivalry & Knighthood'.[83] Vancouver's Order of Good Knights, to take another example, announce that they are 'united by the common goal of reviving the ancient ideals of knighthood'.[84] Similarly, the Knights of Castleton in Oklahoma want to inspire 'the young and young at heart to take hold of the flame of knighthood' and 'live in this modern world with the virtues of chivalry in mind'.[85] *Modern Medievalism*, an Australian-based blog, operates under the banner: 'Applying old-world solutions to new-world problems.' The Knights of the Order of the Marshall are bent on bringing 'some of history's finer moments back into the real world of today (many consider these [values] to be archaic and dated, we disagree)'; the Order of the Golden Unicorn, re-enactors from Texas, believe that their values are 'needed now more than ever'. Similarly, the Knights

78 Price, 'Chivalry and the Modern Practice of the Medieval Martial Arts'.

79 See <www.facebook.com/notes/the-knights-of-castleton/official-code-of-chivalry>.

80 See <www.facebook.com/pages/Knights-Of-The-Olde-Code>. Email communication from Calla von Loggerenberg, 5 January 2014. Patrick Johnson and Charles Pogue, *DragonHeart* (1996), <http://www.imdb.com/title/tt0116136>.

81 Richardson, *Eglinton Tournament*, p. 2

82 Ibid., p. 145.

83 See <http://www.medievalfantasiesco.com/KnightsoftheOldeCode.htm>.

84 See <www.goodknights.org>.

85 See <www.facebook.com/KnightsofCastleton>.

of the Golden Trail have been 'reactivated to save society'; in Mexico Lady Lisste, Queen Commander Magnanimous of the local medieval re-enactment society, is committed to defending 'those who cannot or will not help themselves! Keep the spirit of chivalry alive!! Its what a real knights does [*sic*].'[86]

Nonetheless, wrenching the values of a long-ago age – or any other age – into the modern world is inherently problematic. Not surprisingly, some modern medieval re-enactors are selective about the values that they choose to portray. As one put it: 'We try to recreate the best of medieval times [...] and leave out the worst things.'[87] Despite the best efforts of those bent on turning a blind eye, the Middle Ages were, for example, inherently unequal. As Alice Chandler notes, in *Ivanhoe* chivalry is the 'property of the chosen few'; the masses give loyalty 'without hope of reward'.[88] For an organisation such as the Guardians of Zagreb, replicating a strict hierarchical structure in their organisation is essential to the pursuit of historical knowledge, but for many this approach is unsustainable.[89] What we see instead is either an uneasy compromise or a deliberate self-contradiction. On this point an examination of the SCA *Guide* is instructive. On the one hand, it states that the Society is 'open to any person who shares the Society's interest in medieval re-creation and re-enactment', but, at the same time, the code is replete with rules instantiating inequality:

> Medieval society was highly structured with a system of ranks: kings, dukes, barons and lords. The SCA has a similar system of hierarchy. It is often difficult for a newcomer to tell if the person with whom he is conversing is 'Somebody Important.' If you are in doubt, be courteous and polite, and address the person as 'my lord' or 'my lady.'[90]

In essence, then, the SCA is more equal as an organisation than was the era they are exploring, and this is how, at least in part, members come to terms with the inequality of the medieval period.

Although there is little argument about the nature of medieval society, some medieval re-enactors claim as a virtue the fact that their societies provide opportunities for ennoblement (presumably without compromising the pursuit of understanding). Moreover, some latter-day re-enactors argue that the possibility of assuming new personas is quintessentially egalitarian. 'In many cases re-enactors will tell you that they do not actually know what are the "real-life" occupations of their fellow participants,' writes the author of the National Association of Re-enactment Societies' pitch. 'On a personal level, this is one of the great attractions of re-enactment; that an individual's worth is measured by their skills and abilities rather than their wealth, class or occupation.'[91] Similarly, Amy Farrell (known as Dame Armsmere D'Ravenglass), a prominent medieval re-enactor, insists: 'Unlike

86 See <modernmedievalism.blogspot.com/>; <http://www.orderofthegoldenunicorn.freeservers.com>; <http://www.medievalfantasiesco.com/>.

87 *The Canberra Times*, 24 June 1995.

88 Chandler, 'Chivalry and Romance', p. 193.

89 See <www.cuvari.hr>.

90 'Forward Into the Past', <http://www.sca.org>.

91 'Re-enactment. What's that then?' <www.nares.org.uk>.

historical times, following the path of Chivalry is what ennobles you today, not the circumstances of your birth.'[92] On this point the contrast to Eglinton's joust, where the role of knight was tightly governed by social rank, is stark.

A more difficult issue for today's medieval enthusiasts to grapple with is the fact that the medieval world was fundamentally gendered; accurately re-enacting it entrenches an inequitable division between the sexes, which seems preposterous in our own day. The medieval 'code' governed the behaviour of men; at one level reliving it revolves almost exclusively around the actions of men. After all, the *raison-d'être* of an 'authentic' medieval re-enactment is a martial contest in which women are subordinate. Noble women 'live' in a world where they have no agency; they are weak; their 'honour' is in need of protection. In her online manifesto, Amy Farrell, principal of a well-known organisation, has sought to make a virtue of this vice. Without women, she argues, there would be no chivalry, just brutes

Plate 6 'Dame Amy Staton', Victory at Castle Muskogee, Oklahoma, USA, 2013. Photograph: Richard Andes.

[92] See <http://www.21stcenturychivalry.com>.

with swords.[93] Scott might have agreed; as he noted in his 1819 essay, chivalry could empower women by permitting them to impose 'cold and harsh' tasks on knights.[94] However, there is no escaping the fact that the pursuit of accuracy among re-enactors today creates an inequitable experience: men get to have all the fun. To relive *history*, 'noble' women must be content to be saved. At tournaments they sit and observe the action. Here nothing much has changed since Eglinton and his chums rode through the mud.

Nevertheless, some medieval re-enactment societies are feeling the pressure of the twenty-first century. '[M]ore and more women,' writes Farrell (who herself sports armour and engages in combat), 'want to participate and do the things that primarily men did in the historical time period they are portraying.' This, she claims, has produced a modicum of change: 'Some guilds or organizations have strict rules about this "gender-bending", others are very laid-back in their approach.' This appears to have reached the very top among those interested primarily in martial encounter. Notwithstanding the fact that it was advertised as the ultimate 'sport for real men', the most recent World Championships in Spain, for example, included women's events in polearm, longsword, and sword and shield. The rival World Championship tournament, convened by the Battle of the Nations (with entrants from thirty-two countries), featured women's combat for the first time in 2015.[95]

It is important not to get too carried away by these attempts to negotiate between medieval social conditions and modern values. Most female re-enactors are not knights – and even when they are, liberation often comes at a price. As Farrell admits:

> For the sake of true historical reenactment, it is always best if women participants engaging in these activities adopt a male persona and attempt to closely actuate the appearance of maleness. Appropriate hair length for the period, false beards and mustaches (which, if well-made, can be very convincing) and other methods of creating a male impression are advised.[96]

Similarly, under the rubric 'Frequently Asked Questions', England's Armorial Knights are clear that, while they permit women to fight, 'The only rule is that whilst fighting the woman must portray a man and as soon as the combat is over the woman reverts back to female clothing whilst in camp.'[97] Has defeat been wrenched from the jaws of victory?

Of course, female and male re-enactors alike perform a surfeit of ancillary tasks befitting serfs, but this actually provides little more than an illusion of gender equality. In fact, notwithstanding the fact that women and men can advance through the levels of modern re-enactment societies, the ascending trajectories remain sharply

93 Amy Farrell, 'Women in Chivalry', <http://www.21stcenturychivalry.com>.

94 Scott, 'Essay on Chivalry', pp. 34ff.

95 See <www.usaknights.org>; <www.botn.info>. They lamented the fact that there had been insufficient entrants to do so the previous year.

96 Farrell, 'Women in Chivalry', <http://www.21stcenturychivalry.com>.

97 See <www.armourialknights.co.uk>.

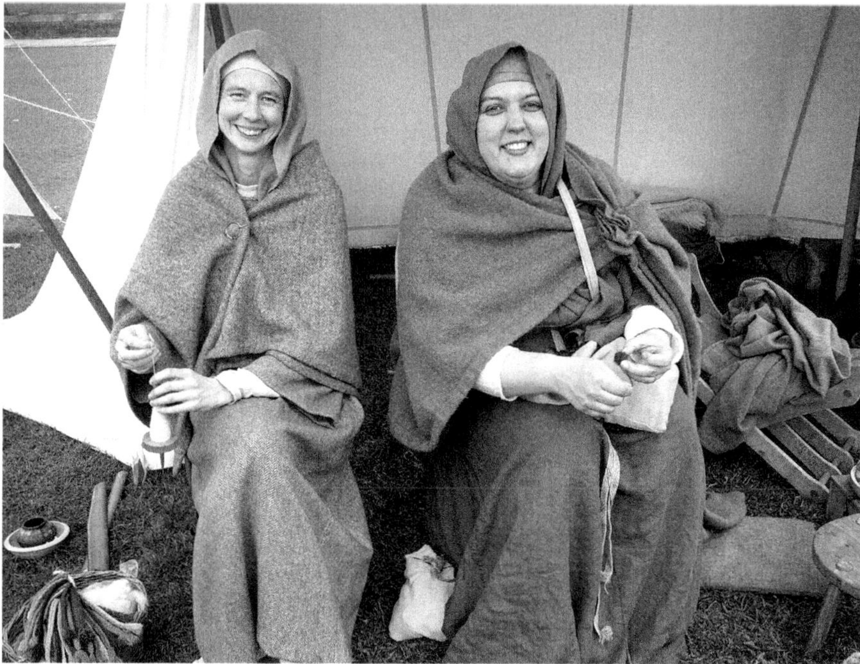

Figure 8.3 Women re-enacting on Palace Green, Durham, England, 2014. Photograph: Veronica Strang.

divided. While men can aspire to progress through the ranks to greatness – to ultimately fight to become the 'champion' at a tourney – the best a female 'peasant' can hope for is a better seat. Entrenching these values (and the divisions that underpin them) is surely problematic, especially if it involves inculcating them into children.

Given the subordination of women, it would not be surprising if the membership of the typical medieval re-enactment society was almost exclusively male. However, there is some evidence to suggest otherwise. Remember that a woman inspired the SCA, and it has not become an overwhelmingly male province. On the contrary: a 2010 survey of SCA-dians showed that fifty-four per cent of the nearly eighteen thousand respondents – nearly half the membership in total – were female.[98] The questionnaire reveals no tensions over the role of women; in fact, the issue that was preoccupying the members at that point was whether to allow same-sex consorts.[99] Irrespective of the exact gender balance, most re-enactment societies number plenty of women apparently content to play 'traditional' subservient roles. Trawl through the countless photo galleries on medieval re-enactment societies' websites and you will see that women feature as often as men, but rarely re-enacting 'male' roles.

A further thorny issue for many modern medievalists is religion. As Scott noted, chivalry was 'blended' with Christianity and knights were animated by 'intemperate

[98] See <http://www.sca.org/scacensus2010>.

[99] See <http://www.sca.org/scacensus2010/samegenderconsort.findings.doc>; thirty per cent of SCA-dians wanted the policy changed to allow same-sex consorts.

zeal for religion'. The oath of chivalry, he continued, was to 'God, the king and the ladies' (in that order).[100] Moreover, in *Ivanhoe* he incorporated a major sub-theme dealing with anti-Semitism, a *leitmotif* given more prominence in the plays that quickly followed the novel's publication. One, *The Hebrew* by George Sloan, even omitted Ivanhoe's name from the title.[101] Remember, too, that the legend of Arthur – translated into our own day most famously by Monty Python – involved the quest for the cup of Christ, the Holy Grail.

Again, however, many modern re-enactors not only recognise the issue as a problem, but also respond to it anachronistically by proclaiming 'codes' that either eschew any mention of God or explicitly proscribe religious content. The SCA, for example, has a clear policy to sacrifice accuracy for tolerance:

> Having no wish to recreate the religious conflicts of the period under study, the Society shall neither establish nor prohibit any system of belief among its members. No one shall perform any religious or magical ceremony at a Society event (or in association with the name of the Society) in such a way as to imply that the ceremony is authorized, sponsored, or promulgated by the Society or to force anyone at a Society event, by direct or indirect pressure, to observe or join the ceremony.[102]

The International Fellowship of Chivalry-Now is equally clear: they welcome people of all faiths, 'along with atheists and agnostics'.[103] On the other hand, some societies, predominantly in the US, openly embrace the historical link between chivalry and Christianity. In practice, this usually becomes simply a qualification for membership. The re-enactors in the Knights Templar of North America, for example, insist that they are not a church, but their ranks are open only to 'baptized Christians'. Similarly, the Sovereign Christian Orthodox United Order of the Red Cross, with chapters in Canada and America, is reserved for 'people of Christian faith'.[104] Phil Sacco, principal of Awaken the Warrior, is a lay preacher and re-enactor of twenty-five years standing. His self-proclaimed mission is to train 'Christian Warriors', particularly among military personnel (he is busily raising funds to send copies of his latest manifesto to Iraq).[105] Others explicitly work religion into their 'code'. Take The Most Noble Order of the Rouse Clan, for example. The Clan's oath – a mish-mash of Trinitarianism, Hebrew nomenclature and the Celtic revival – is advertised on its website (and emblazoned on the back of 'hoodies' selling for just under £40):

> I believe in the Holy Trinity. God, Elohin, The Everlasting Father. God, Jesus Christ, our Resurrected Redeemer and intercessor. God, the Holy Spirit, who

100 Scott, 'Essay on Chivalry', pp. 11, 15, 75.

101 On this point more generally, see Michael Ragussis, *Theatrical Nation: Jews and Other Outlandish Englishmen in Georgian Britain* (Philadelphia, 2010), chapters 3 and 4.

102 See <http://www.sca.org/docs/pdf/govdocs.pdf>.

103 See <www.chivalrynow.net>.

104 See <http://www.knighttemplar.org>; <http://www.medievalfantasiesco.com>.

105 See <www.awakenthewarrior.com>.

> is as both Fire and Water, Ethirial [*sic*] and Concrete. Triqueta. The Eternal Love.[106]

Nevertheless, it is difficult to find any cases where the exclusion of non-Christians from the ranks of medieval re-enactors is accompanied by overt statements that might be considered bigoted.

Plate 7 Re-enactment of the Battle of Grunwald, Poland, 2009.
Photograph: Vova Pomortzeff (Demotix).

The most difficult issue for medieval re-enactors to negotiate is violence. Since Eglinton's enterprise, attempts to revive chivalry by re-enacting it have existed at the uneasy intersection of violence and notions of honourable behaviour. By the time the hapless earl donned his armour (indeed, before the practice first fell out of favour), the chivalric hastilude had come to be regarded as a sporting event involving modified weaponry – blunted lances and rebated swords – but the premise of the trial-by-arms was still blood and guts. Indeed, the role of a knight is defined by combat. Carlyle understood this as an obdurate contradiction. 'Under the living sky,' he wrote with characteristically baroque eloquence in 1843, 'is no uglier spectacle than two men with clenched teeth, and hellfire eyes, hacking one another's flesh; converting precious living bodies, and priceless living souls, into nameless

[106] See <www.orderoftherouseclan.org> and <http://www.zazzle.co.uk/creed_of_the_order_of_the_rouse_clan_hoodie>. The spelling error has been corrected for the garment. The company also sells T-shirts with the slogans, 'The Virile Knight', 'Lancelot Proves His Love' and 'The Sword in the Stone', and Rouse Clan 'tartan' playing cards.

putrescence, useful only for turnip-manure. How did a Chivalry ever come out of that; how anything that was not hideous, scandalous, infernal?'[107]

Modern re-enactors struggle to make a case as to why fighting in period costume with antiquated weapons is not simply an excuse for gratuitous violence – especially when for some it is precisely that. As we have seen, many modern re-enactors are there for what is nothing more a physically testing and violent combat sport. As a consequence, in Britain, re-enactors had to fight a determined political campaign to gain exemption from the Violent Crime Reduction Act in 2006.[108] In the Australian state of Victoria, the relevant legislation contains no formal recognition of re-enactment; the chief commissioner of police can choose – or not – to grant an exemption for the 'genuine reason of performing arts' and 're-enactment activities'.[109] Similar regulations apply in other Australian states, in particular Queensland and New South Wales. In the majority of Australian jurisdictions, those undertaking sword-play of any kind in public are liable to prosecution under the Summary Offences Act. In other words, medievalists re-enact at the pleasure of the local law enforcement officers. As recently as 2013, swords were banned at a large 'Festival of History' in Adelaide, South Australia.[110]

Modern medieval re-enactment is part of a much wider resurgence of interest in the Middle Ages in popular culture, every bit as pervasive as the one that gripped Britain in the first half of the nineteenth century. This is evident firstly in publishing. Diana Paxson's trajectory demonstrates a continuation of the almost symbiotic relationship between fiction and re-enacting that linked Scott and Eglinton. According to her autobiography, as a comparative literature student at Berkeley she was swept away by the Grail legend as told in Chrétien de Troyes' *Perceval: Conte du Graal* (written in the twelfth century) and, at the same time, she was captivated by J. R. R. Tolkien's *Lord of the Rings*, the reading of which she has described as akin to 'joining a secret cult'.[111] The current medieval craze has its own *Ivanhoe* in the *A Song of Ice and Fire* series of fantasy novels that George R. R. Martin (surely a Tolkien-esque affectation) commenced writing in 1991. In 2011, with Martin co-producing, an adaptation of the novels premiered as an HBO television series entitled *Game of Thrones*. The books have consistently topped bestseller lists – one remaining there for eighty-eight weeks – and the television series has already garnered eight Emmy awards. The novels are peppered with the word 'chivalry' and the plot often invokes chivalric tropes amongst encounters with ghouls and dragons and graphic

[107] Thomas Carlyle, *Past and Present* (1843; this edition, London, 1890), p. 218. This was also understood in the colonies. In 1826 one newspaper described chivalry as a 'strange mixture of ferocious cruelty with refined gallantry'. *The Sydney Gazette*, 2 January 1826.

[108] See <www.nares.org.uk>; <http://www.legislation.gov.uk/ukpga/2006/38/part/2>.

[109] Victoria Police, 'Legislative requirements for persons taking part in historical re-enactments', Licensing Services Division, 2008; <http://www.swordforum.com>.

[110] *The Southern Times*, 15 February 2013.

[111] See <http://www.diana-paxson.com/about>; R. H. Thompson, 'Interview with Diana Paxson', The Camelot Project, Robbins Library Digital Projects, <http://d.lib.rochester.edu/camelot/text/interview-with-diana-paxson>. Paxson has gone on to have a career as a fantasy novelist, the best-known of her works being the *Avalon* series.

violence.[112] Readers and watchers are left in no doubt that chivalry is not about opening car doors and giving up a seat on the bus.

Medieval re-enactment has also spawned its own reality television show. First screened on the History Channel in 2012, *Full Metal Jousting* pits sixteen 'amateur' competitors in full-contact action in pursuit of US$100,000. There is no honourable cause here. The 'amateurs' hurtle towards each other at thirty miles per hour. 'Gone is the goofy armor,' runs the publicity screed, 'replaced by Iron-man like suits.' 'Competitors are knocked off horses,' boast the producers, 'often breaking bones.' This is 'Ultimate Fighter for Jousting'.[113] The fact that it appears on the History Channel is a spectacular oxymoron.

Perhaps the *ne plus ultra* of modern medievalism in mass culture has developed in gaming culture. Role-playing computer games (RPGs) generate a highly affective multisensory experience without donning a suit of armour and braving the mud. Would-be medievalists simply press play to be immersed into 'navigable space' (to borrow Lev Monovich's well-known term).[114] There is a plethora of medieval RPGs on the game store shelves. A successful spin-off-cum-rival to the better-known *Dungeons and Dragons* game, for example, is *Chivalry and Sorcery*. First released in 1977 the game has evolved through several iterations, all involving the navigation of complex scenarios replete with monsters and the macabre in pursuit of chivalric quests.[115] According to its promotional literature, *Savage Kingdoms*, a more recent medievalist RPG, has been 'designed with immersion and storytelling at its focus, intended with a scope for the cinematic, the theatrical, and moreover, the awesomely epic'. 'The approach here,' they claim, 'is more story, character development, and campaign emphasis, than an exercise in gadgetry.'[116] Serious gamers develop personas every bit as complex and sophisticated as the SCA-dians. But, like those re-enacting for the fun (or the challenge) of a 'good bash-em-up', the premise of *Savage Kingdoms* (as with other RPGs) is that success is measured according to 'how much damage you deal'.[117] Moreover, there are dozens of simple chivalric games that have an uncomplicated premise with little or no eye to narrative: the gamer pursues an 'honourable' objective – defending the crown or rescuing a damsel in distress – by carving into the flesh of everything in their path. Those 'hankering for some heavily armoured king slaying', writes the reviewer of *Chivalry: Medieval Warfare*, 'now have a superb game that is just what the Knight Templar ordered'. Another reviewer describes the game as 'medieval multi-player blood-letting', and even claims for it the acquisition of affective knowledge similar to that asserted by

112 I am grateful to Julia Crockett for this information.

113 See <www.history.com/full-metal-jousting>.

114 See, for example, Lev Manovich, 'The Practice of Everyday (Media) Life: From Mass Consumption to Mass Cultural Production?', *Critical Inquiry* 35:2 (2009), pp. 319–31.

115 See Michael Tresca, *The Evolution of Fantasy Role-Playing Games* (Jefferson, 2010); Jon Peterson, *Playing at the World* (San Diego, 2013). See also Matthew Churlew, 'The Only Limitation is Your Imagination: Quantifying the Medieval and Other Fantasies in *Dungeons and Dragons*', *Medievalism and the Gothic*, ed. Trigg, pp. 223–40.

116 MikeY, 'Savage Kingdoms: Heroic Sword-and-Sorcery Roleplaying', <https://www.kickstarter.com/projects/115420877/savage-kingdoms-heroic-swords-and-sorcery-roleplay>.

117 Ibid.

some re-enactors: 'playing "Chivalry" is a way to feel like combat could have been'.[118] In one important sense, then, gamers obsessed with simulated visceral carnage are at the front of the line when it comes to those who might claim to be the true children of *Ivanhoe* and Eglinton. Carlyle, at least, would have agreed.

Figure 8.4 A scene from 'Chivalry: Medieval Warfare' computer game. Torn Banner Studios, 2012.

In 1940, nearly a century after Carlyle's florid summation, C. S. Lewis issued a well-known plea for a return to chivalry. Understanding what he meant, by way of conclusion, is helpful when trying to unravel the motivation of those medieval re-enactors today who regard their activity as both honourable and relevant. Like Carlyle, Lewis recognised the paradox: 'The Knight is a man of blood and iron, a man familiar with the sight of smashed faces and the ragged stumps of lopped off limbs.' But, he continued, he is also demure, 'almost maidenlike', 'a gentle unobtrusive man'. Importantly, Lewis wrote, 'he is not a compromise or happy mean between ferocity and meekness; he is fierce to the nth degree and meek to the nth degree'.[119] Lewis saw the world as divided into wolves and sheep eternally locked in a cyclical struggle between barbarianism and civilisation. The attempt to combine both (that is, effectively both halves of a Lancelot's character) in one person, he argued, was a noble experiment, and reviving it offered the only hope of survival at a time when bombs were raining down on London. To join the ranks of the young RAF pilots ('to whom we owe our lives from hour to hour') there was a need to train new Lancelots who would be ferocious and meek at the same time. It may be ungenerous

[118] See <www.ausgamers.com/games>; <www.rockpapershotgun.com>. Medieval RPGs are big business: it is estimated that *Chivalry and Sorcery* sells one thousand copies a month. See <grognardia.blogspot.com>.

[119] C. S. Lewis, 'The Necessity of Chivalry' (1940), *Essay Collection and Other Short Pieces* (London, 2000), pp. 717–20. I am grateful to Suzanne Pickering for this reference.

to suggest that if modern re-enactors know Lewis' writings at all, they probably do so via his multi-volume fantasy series, *The Chronicles of Narnia*. Nevertheless, those who insist on dressing up in 'funny clothes' and swinging swords in fields in an attempt to relive – and perhaps better understand – a nexus of combat and honourable values relevant to fighting the good fight today, instinctively embrace him. The gamers playing *Chivalry: Medieval Warfare* or *Kill Streak* by hacking and slashing in a simulacrum of gore to save damsels in distress probably do so too, as do fantasy novel readers and trashy TV watchers. Historians bent on ignoring modern medievalism seem destined to fall behind those who are doing history for themselves.

Index

Medievalism

I
Anglo-Saxon Culture and the Modern Imagination
edited by David Clark and Nicholas Perkins

II
Medievalist Enlightenment: From Charles Perrault to Jean-Jacques Rousseau
Alicia C. Montoya

III
Memory and Myths of the Norman Conquest
Siobhan Brownlie

IV
Comic Medievalism: Laughing at the Middle Ages
Louise D'Arcens

V
Medievalism: Key Critical Terms
edited by Elizabeth Emery and Richard Utz

VI
Medievalism: A Critical History
David Matthews

VII
Chivalry and the Medieval Past
edited by Katie Stevenson and Barbara Gribling

VIII
Georgian Gothic: Medievalist Architecture, Furniture and Interiors, 1730–1840
Peter N. Lindfield

IX
Petrarch and the Literary Culture of Nineteenth-Century France: Translation, Appropriation, Transformation
Jennifer Rushworth

X
Medievalism, Politics and Mass Media: Appropriating the Middle Ages in the Twenty-First Century
Andrew B.R. Elliott

XI
Translating Early Medieval Poetry: Transformation, Reception, Interpretation
edited by Tom Birkett and Kirsty March-Lyons

XII
Medievalism in A Song of Ice and Fire *and* Game of Thrones
Shiloh Carroll

XIII
William Morris and the Icelandic Sagas
Ian Felce

XIV
Derek Jarman's Medieval Modern
Robert Mills

XV
François Villon in English Poetry: Translation and Influence
Claire Pascolini-Campbell

XVI
Neomedievalism, Popular Culture, and the Academy: From Tolkien to Game of Thrones
KellyAnn Fitzpatrick

XVII
Medievalism in English Canadian Literature: From Richardson to Atwood
edited by M.J. Toswell and Anna Czarnowus

XVIII
Anglo-Saxonism and the Idea of Englishness in Eighteenth-Century Britain
Dustin M. Frazier Wood

XIX
Subaltern Medievalisms: Medievalism 'from below' in Nineteenth-Century Britain
edited by David Matthews and Michael Sanders

XX
Medievalist Traditions in Nineteenth-Century British Culture: Celebrating the Calendar Year
Clare A. Simmons